BLESSINGS
OUT OF BUFFETINGS

BLESSINGS
OUT OF BUFFETINGS

STUDIES IN II CORINTHIANS

BY

ALAN REDPATH

Pickering & Inglis
LONDON · GLASGOW

This book is dedicated
to the three churches
it has been my joy and privilege to serve—
Duke Street, Richmond;
Moody Memorial Church, Chicago;
Charlotte Chapel, Edinburgh—
with my loving appreciation.

Oh tried and tested Christian,
Beset on every hand
By storms of strife, remember
Thy Father holds command!
E'en though the tempest rages,
Thy chastened heart may sing,
For He doth purpose blessing
Through all thy buffeting.

Be strong and of good courage,
Though foes thy soul assail.
No weapon formed against thee
Hath power to prevail;
For thou shalt share the triumph
Of Christ, thy conquering King,
Who purposes a blessing
Through all thy buffeting.

Rejoice to be found worthy
Of suff'ring for His name,
Who on the cross of Calvary
Bore all thy weight of shame.
When He shall come in glory
His ransomed Home to bring,
Thou'lt know in full the blessing
Attained through buffeting!

AVIS B. CHRISTIANSEN,
"Blessings out of Buffetings"

PREFACE

THE contents of this book originally formed the basis of a series of messages delivered from the pulpit of Moody Memorial Church, Chicago, over a period of six months. After further prayer and preparation I was in the course of giving them again at Charlotte Chapel, Edinburgh, when I was taken seriously ill. At first this came as a somewhat shattering blow, but soon it was seen to be another evidence of the mercy of God. The contents of this book began to live in a new way, and truths which I had thought to be well learned became part of my experience.

Blessing out of buffeting suddenly became a truth which lived all over again. " . . . every branch that beareth fruit, he purgeth it, that it may bring forth more fruit" (John 15: 2)—and out of the painful and trying buffeting of the past months I trust that blessing will flow in a new way out of my life, and out of the pages of this book.

I can say out of a full heart, "My grace is sufficient for thee: for my strength is made perfect in weakness" (II Corinthians 12: 9). I trust that the message of this book will bring strength and the blessing of God to some buffeted and bewildered servant of His who, like me, may be knocked down but not knocked out (II Corinthians 4: 9, PHILLIPS).

My special thanks are due to all who have worked so hard on the manuscripts, and to my wife who once again helped in the revision and correction during the preparation of the book.

ALAN REDPATH

Charlotte Chapel, Edinburgh

CONTENTS

Paul, an apostle of Jesus Christ by the will of God, and Timothy our brother, unto the church of God which is at Corinth, with all the saints which are in all Achaia.

Grace be to you and peace from God our Father, and from the Lord Jesus Christ. Blessed be God, even the Father of our Lord Jesus Christ, the Father of mercies, and the God of all comfort; Who comforteth us in all our tribulation, that we may be able to comfort them which are in any trouble, by the comfort wherewith we ourselves are comforted of God. For as the sufferings of Christ abound in us, so our consolation also aboundeth by Christ. And whether we be afflicted, it is for your consolation and salvation, which is effectual in the enduring of the same sufferings which we also suffer: or whether we be comforted, it is for your consolation and salvation. And our hope of you is stedfast, knowing that as ye are partakers of the sufferings, so shall ye be also of the consolation. For we would not, brethren, have you ignorant of our trouble which came to us in Asia, that we were pressed out of measure, above strength, insomuch that we despaired even of life. But we had the sentence of death in ourselves, that we should not trust in ourselves, but in God which raiseth the dead: Who delivered us from so great a death, and doth deliver: in whom we trust that he will yet deliver us; Ye also helping together by prayer for us, that for the gift bestowed upon us by the means of many persons thanks may be given by many on our behalf.

II CORINTHIANS I: I-II

I

BLESSINGS OUT OF BUFFETINGS

In commencing what I trust will be a practical and down-to-earth study of Paul's second letter to the church at Corinth, I might point out that the great difference between the themes of First and Second Corinthians is that in First Corinthians we have the account of a church which is being instructed and corrected, whereas in Second Corinthians we have the account of a man who is being disciplined and matured. Nowhere does Paul open his heart to his readers so completely as he does in this second letter as he relates some of God's dealings with him in his inner life. By revealing something of the price he has paid, his ministry is vindicated and his authority recognized.

News has reached Paul from Titus (II Corinthians 7: 7) of the mixed reception of his first letter. There were those, a majority, who had genuinely repented of sin in the church and dealt with it thoroughly; there were others, a minority, who challenged his authority, suspected his motives, and questioned the validity of his ministry. His answer, as recorded here, is an amazing mixture of tender love and stern rebuke.

Notice the language of verses 3-5 of the opening chapter: "Blessed be God, even the Father of our Lord Jesus Christ, the Father of mercies, and the God of all comfort; Who comforteth us in all our tribulation, that we may be able to comfort them which are in any trouble, by the comfort wherewith we ourselves are comforted of God. For as the sufferings of Christ abound in us, so our consolation also aboundeth by Christ."

These verses open to each of us a ministry which is unique. Not everyone is called upon to preach the Word of God in public; not everyone is called upon to bear testimony to Christ before a crowd. But if any of us know the Lord Jesus Christ in reality then God opens for each of His children a ministry which is unique— a ministry of comfort, which simply means the ability to communicate Holy Spirit life to others. Such a ministry is, as we shall see, intensely costly. It is those who experience the suffering of Christ who in turn experience the comfort of the Holy Spirit; these are they who live richly and therefore are used mightily.

Personally, I would rather have the spiritual gift of bringing life to one broken heart than the ability to preach a thousand sermons. Indeed, any public ministry which has not at its heart something of the tenderness which has come because of the personal experience of what Paul calls "the sufferings of Christ" is lacking in the one thing that really matters. I wonder if there was ever a greater need for a ministry of comfort (using that word in the sense that Paul uses it here).

You do not have to look far to find broken hearts, broken lives, and broken homes. Perhaps in a degree far greater than ever before in my life, I have looked recently into the faces of such. Somehow I felt deep down in my soul the awful plight of men and women without God and without hope in the world. I have seen not one but thousands of people with no homes, people who sleep night by night on the pavements of Indian cities without any covering, adults and children all together. As I felt something of the pang of it in my heart, it was then that God began to show me the true meaning of this text, " . . . the God of all comfort; Who comforteth us in all our tribulation, that we may be able to comfort them which are in any trouble, by the comfort wherewith we ourselves are comforted of God." In other parts of the world the need may be less exposed to the public eye, covered with a veneer of civilization and reserve; yet it is there in all its urgent claim upon every Christian.

You have often heard it said—have you not?—that you cannot bring help and comfort to someone else unless you have been through his trouble. I believe that it is true only in a very limited sense. If it were entirely true, it would put tremendous limitations upon the ministry which Paul had in mind in this letter.

For instance, if you sit by someone who has suffered a deep bereavement and you never have—does that mean you cannot bring any message to his heart? Or you are in touch with someone who has been in desperate physical pain, and you know little of that— does that mean you are excluded from a ministry with such a person?

Surely not. But you see, when Paul speaks about his ministry of comfort, he speaks about it having come out of an experience in his own life which has qualified him for such a ministry. Consider therefore the training for this ministry.

Look at this verse again and you will see something of the training through which Paul has passed for this unique ministry when he says, "Who comforteth us in all our tribulation, that we may be able to comfort them which are in any trouble. . . ." Paul is speaking about something that has happened to him, an experience of affliction. He might have in mind the thorn in the flesh of which he spoke. He does not betray exactly the nature of the affliction, but I am quite sure that it was something far deeper than a mere physical experience. Indeed, in the fifth verse he says, " . . . as *the sufferings of Christ* abound in us, so our consolation also aboundeth by Christ." And then you notice how he opens his heart to us in the following verses concerning the training through which he has passed for a ministry of this kind: " . . . whether we be afflicted, it is for your consolation and salvation . . ." (v. 6); " . . . we would not, brethren, have you ignorant of our trouble which came to us in Asia, that we were pressed out of measure, above strength, insomuch that we despaired even of life" (v. 8); " . . . we had the sentence of death in ourselves, that we should not trust in ourselves, but in God which raiseth the dead" (v. 9).

Clearly Paul is speaking here about some deep experience through which he has passed, for he speaks about the sufferings of Christ abounding in us. And therefore he is making it perfectly clear that if we would ever qualify to bring blessing to one poor needy life, one broken heart, it is going to require a spiritual experience of suffering on a deep level.

I want to try to show you what that means, and I shall introduce it by asking some questions: Have you ever felt the throb in the heart of God over a soul without a Saviour? Have you ever felt in your own soul the pain, the agony of the cross, the concern in the heart of God for a soul without Christ? Have you ever been really caused to take hold of God in prayer for someone who seems so helpless, so hopeless, so lost?—perhaps your next-door neighbor? Does it give you five minutes' concern? If it does, you have just begun to enter, in a little measure, into the fellowship of the suffering of Christ.

You can never bring any blessing to someone in need unless first it has touched your own heart. The moment it begins to grip you, you will be led into a school of suffering about which an unbeliever knows nothing. There is nothing in physical pain which in itself produces holiness, but the sufferings of Christ, which are the outcome of our union with Him, become the source of Holy Spirit consolation, and so maturity of character, and this in turn becomes the secret of sharing blessing with others.

Here Paul is speaking about a training which he has passed through for this ministry that he might bring comfort to others. He has himself been comforted in his own tribulation; and he has found that comfort and that experience of God in his time of affliction, not simply for blessing in his own heart, but that he might be made a channel of blessing to another in need.

So, therefore, we introduce our subject by reminding ourselves that the precious and sacred ministry of bringing heavenly comfort and help to one poor, broken, lonely life is not something that we can do lightly with a mere pat on the shoulder. It is something that is going to cost us deeply. The true character of it we will see in a moment.

Let me ask you to look not only at the training Paul faced, but at the enabling God gave him, that is, his resources. If I were to translate the fourth verse of this chapter accurately, you would notice a distinction between two words: "Who comforteth us in all our afflictions, that we may be able to comfort them which are in any affliction, by the comfort wherewith we ourselves are comforted of God." Notice two words in sharp contrast: *affliction*, *comfort*.

"Affliction" is the word that was used by our Lord when He said, " . . . in me ye might have peace. In the world ye shall have *tribulation* . . ." (John 16: 33). This is far deeper than mere physical suffering; it is something that was to be the portion of His disciples and the experience of all who would follow Him.

The word "comfort" is the word *paraclete*, which is the Bible word for the Holy Spirit. And so you have the two side by side: on the one hand the depths of tribulation which is the portion of God's people, and which is part of the training for the ministry of comfort to another; on the other hand the ensured enablement and reinforcement of the *paraclete*, the Comforter. Look at that precious verse again: "Who comforteth us . . ."—that is to say, "Who sends the Holy Spirit, the *paraclete*, to us in all our affliction"—"that we may be able to comfort them which are in any affliction, by the comfort wherewith we ourselves are comforted of God."

See then this simple principle: if you and I are to be a blessing to someone in need, perhaps just to one person whose heart is broken, who is without God and without hope, and if we would have that sacred, precious ministry, we are assured that this is something absolutely impossible to us by ourselves, by any human talent or ability. This is not a ministry that we will acquire at the university, or at a college, or at any school, but it is something that the Holy Spirit will give to us. It is He who will be our strength and enduement. But He will come to us only in the measure that we have entered into the affliction which the Lord said would be the portion of His people.

You do not go far before you find that the people of God throughout the world are going through times of unprecedented pressures and tensions and problems. It would seem as though God is allowing times of testing to come to His people, not that they might despair, but that as they share in the fellowship of the suffering of Christ they may know in a new measure the enduement of the Holy Spirit. Out from this pressure of affliction, the church will begin to fulfill again this tremendous ministry of comfort and blessing which is her unique and glorious task. I am quite sure that these days of pressure upon the church have a very special significance in the mind of our Lord; and I am quite sure that if any of you know something about this in your own life, it has a very special significance for the ministry the Lord has for you.

Paul is speaking about the enablement which will accompany only a man who has really submitted to and accepted the affliction. In other words, in the spiritual sense of the word it is true that the ability to bring comfort and blessing to one life depends not upon having shared their experience, but upon having submitted to the suffering which God imposes upon His people.

Now, what is that suffering? We are not left in any doubt, for again I say that it is something that is not a physical principle, but a spiritual principle in life. We see therefore the sacredness of this personal ministry, and understand that it is going to mean training in a school through which the Lord puts His people. We see that we are absolutely assured of heavenly enduement for it, provided we are prepared to accept the discipline—and what is that discipline?

Let us look at the price of this ministry as Paul gives it in verses eight and nine. Notice the language Paul uses in these verses: what tremendous words they are! " . . . pressed out of measure, above strength . . . we despaired even of life: . . . we had the sentence of death in ourselves. . . ." As Phillips puts it in *Letters to Young Churches*: " . . . we were completely overwhelmed, the burden was more than we could bear, in fact we told ourselves that this was the end." When we ask why this should be, we have the answer in verse 9: " . . . that we should not trust in ourselves, but in God which raiseth the dead"; or to quote from Phillips again: " . . . we had this experience of coming to the end of our tether that we might learn to trust, not in ourselves, but in God Who can raise the dead."

In other words, God has one great purpose for His people above everything else: it is to destroy in us forever any possible confidence in the flesh; it is to bring us to the place where self-confidence has passed into history and has been exchanged for a confidence in God, who raises the dead. Paul speaks about an experience when he was pressed out of measure, above strength—as a ship that has been too heavily laden with cargo gradually sinks under the pressure of the load until it seems that it is in a fatal condition; or a weary animal that sinks in despair beneath a burden far beyond its strength.

"Now," says Paul in effect, "I have been through this in the spiritual sense. I have had the sentence of death passed upon myself. I have despaired even of life. There has been a moment in my experience when I have been brought to such a place as this. When I came to the place where I knew in myself I was helpless, hopeless, and could do nothing, somehow everything went to pieces. I had the sentence of death in myself, and why? So that I should no longer trust in myself. That basis of confidence was gone, and was replaced by a trust in the Lord who raises the dead."

In other words, here is the price of this ministry to others. Is it not amazing? If you would bring blessing to one heart in trouble, one thing is going to stand in the way and make it absolutely impossible. No matter how you may or may not have entered physically into the sufferings of another, no matter how much you may be able to share something through your own experience of that very thing through which another person has passed—even though you have done all this, yet if in your life there is still that confidence in the flesh, then your ministry is lost. For this ministry is a ministry of the Holy Spirit alone, and He cannot work where there is self-confidence.

Does it not seem to you rather remarkable that Paul speaks about this? Could there be any man who was more delivered from self-confidence than the great Apostle? He had it all shattered when he met the risen Saviour and Master on the road to Damascus, had he not? Yes, but then the Lord knew the perpetual peril of its recurrence! God's ways and methods with His people are always directed along the line of shattering forever any confidence in the flesh. He could not afford to take any risks with a man for whom He purposed such a ministry.

Do you not find in your life that the flesh is very subtle along these lines? For instance, you will say, "I have become so zealous in the service of the Lord!"—and a little voice will whisper, "Yes, you will be able to get through anything because of your zeal." You begin to say to yourself, "My prayer life has progressed so tremendously. I am really growing!"—and self begins to boast of its spirituality: "I have years of Christian experience behind me. I have learned so much!" And so God moves in, for He cannot afford to allow that to go on. By varied ways He will deal with us, as in all sorts of subtle ways there is the whisper within which always makes us want to trust in ourselves.

I wonder if you, like I, have ever walked around the corridor of your own soul. Have you ever examined what goes on there? You can remember the great hopes that you had in yourself—but those hopes have been shattered. Have you ever gone through your life and reminded yourself of imaginations and dreams?—but now it is all a valley of dry bones! Have you ever found yourself with your prayer life gone to pieces, and your Bible become so stale, whereas only recently you had been boasting about how real it was? And all these things seem to be a complete mystery. Why has it turned out like that? I wonder if the Lord is going to bring through these verses new light upon your experience because He wants to turn the mystery of that experience into a ministry.

All along, God has been directing your life until it has come to a place where with the Apostle Paul you may say, " . . . in my flesh . . . dwelleth no good thing . . ." (Romans 7: 18), and you have lost any trace of confidence in anything self can do. You have the sentence of death in yourself; that is the price of bringing blessing to one needy heart.

To use a simple illustration: if ever you are called upon to rescue somebody who is drowning, I think that you would probably wait until that person is going down for the third time. If you were to intervene at any point at which the man or woman were kicking and resisting and fighting for himself, you would be in great danger of being drowned with him. But if you were to go to the rescue when the drowning person were at the end of his strength and had no confidence left in his own deliverance, at that moment he would be weakened and still, and you could be used to bring deliverance.

God's great purpose with His people all over the world today—through all the pressures and tensions which are being brought upon us—is that we might be brought to the end of self-confidence, where we no longer trust in ourselves but in God, who raiseth the dead.

Look again at verses 3 and 4: " . . . the God of all comfort; Who comforteth us [that is, who ministers to us by His Holy Spirit] in all our tribulation [affliction], that we may be able to bring comfort [Holy Spirit life and blessing] to any which are in any trouble [affliction], by the comfort [the strength, the enabling] wherewith we ourselves are comforted of God."

Everyone is brought within its scope, and we should be sent out into this world, in all its darkness and need, conscious that each of us has a ministry, a sphere of testimony—perhaps right next door, perhaps in our own home. But it is a ministry so tender and so delicate that you could easily blunder, and perhaps the second condition of the one to be comforted would be worse than the first unless the Holy Spirit were to show you the principle behind such ministry. He will explain to you some of the things which have happened in your life and which are complete mysteries to you, but which are in fact intended to be a ministry—the ministry of Holy Spirit life to another in need.

For our rejoicing is this, the testimony of our conscience, that in simplicity and godly sincerity, not with fleshly wisdom, but by the grace of God, we have had our conversation in the world, and more abundantly to you-ward. For we write none other things unto you, than what ye read or acknowledge; and I trust ye shall acknowledge even to the end; As also ye have acknowledged us in part, that we are your rejoicing, even as ye also are ours in the day of the Lord Jesus. And in this confidence I was minded to come unto you before, that ye might have a second benefit; And to pass by you into Macedonia, and to come again out of Macedonia unto you, and of you to be brought on my way toward Judaea. When I therefore was thus minded, did I use lightness? or the things that I purpose, do I purpose according to the flesh, that with me there should be yea yea, and nay nay? But as God is true, our word toward you was not yea and nay. For the Son of God, Jesus Christ, who was preached among you by us, even by me and Silvanus and Timotheus, was not yea and nay, but in him was yea. For all the promises of God in him are yea, and in him Amen, unto the glory of God by us. Now he which stablisheth us with you in Christ, and hath anointed us, is God; Who hath also sealed us, and given the earnest of the Spirit in our hearts. Moreover I call God for a record upon my soul, that to spare you I came not as yet unto Corinth. Not for that we have dominion over your faith, but are helpers of your joy: for by faith ye stand.

II CORINTHIANS I: 12-24

2

NOT FICKLE, BUT FAITHFUL

THERE are many different ways and means which the Lord uses and
applies to His people, that through buffeting may come blessing.
One of them is the misunderstanding of our motives, even by our
friends. That is a painful kind of buffeting indeed! But what blessing
lies at the root of it when we learn to do what Paul did: to apply
great spiritual principles to the smallest issues of our everyday life.
And after all, unless you and I learn to do that, we will never know
how to apply spiritual principles to the crises. The peril which
confronts all of us is that of taking even more of life's situations
under our own control so that when the crisis arrives, we find
ourselves incapable of making contact with heaven.

In this chapter it seems that a very trivial thing had happened to
Paul, such as can happen to any of us. He planned to return to
Corinth for a second visit, as he wrote in the fifteenth and sixteenth
verses. He expected to receive a love gift from the Corinthians that
would help him go on in his journey toward Jerusalem. In fact, he
had already written to them to tell them to expect him, for the roots
of this chapter go back to the last chapter of his previous letter:
"Now I will come unto you, when I shall pass through Macedonia:
for I do pass through Macedonia. And it may be that I will abide,
yea, and winter with you, that ye may bring me on my journey
whithersoever I go. For I will not see you now by the way; but I
trust to tarry a while with you, if the Lord permit" (I Corinthians
16: 5).

But the Lord did not permit. And Paul's concern to get to Jerusalem under the guidance of the Spirit was so irresistible that he
by-passed Corinth and left them out. There is always a crowd of
folks looking for the slightest inconsistency in a servant of God, and

for the opportunity to publish it far and wide; and so those at Corinth began immediately to accuse Paul of being inconsistent and fickle, of saying one thing and then actually doing another.

Yes, our message centers around this very simple thing—failing to keep a promise—for out of that the Corinthians built up a case for Paul's unreliability, and condemned it, saying in effect, "After all, if he cannot be trusted to keep his appointments, how can we ever trust the authority of his ministry?"

Notice how strenuously Paul denies it: "When I therefore was thus minded, did I show lightness [fickleness]? or the things that I purpose, do I purpose according to the flesh, that with me there should be yea yea, and nay nay? But as God is true [faithful], our word toward you was not yea and nay" (II Corinthians 1: 17-18). And he goes on to explain in the closing two verses of the chapter why he did not come: "I call God for a record [witness] upon my soul, that to spare you I came not [forbear to come] as yet unto Corinth. Not for that we have dominion [lordship] over your faith, but are helpers of your joy: for in faith ye stand [fast]."

"Now," says Paul in effect, "that was the reason I did not come to you: you must learn to stand on your own feet; you must not depend upon anybody else for your Christian strength and character. The prop must be removed."

I do not wish to digress, but I must interject here a very deep conviction that some of the props that are being taken away now in the withdrawal of missionaries from many parts of the world may be overruled in the sovereignty of God to teach us that national Christians are to stand on their own feet; for that reason Paul by-passed Corinth. But behind it all there is a spiritual principle, a principle upon which he lives his life every day, without any moment of change, and he gives it in verses 20 to 22, in effect: "I live my life in the absolute conviction of the certainty of God's promises. How many soever be the promises of God in Christ, is the yea. And because I am so sure of God's promises in every issue of my life, therefore I have responded to them in the total commitment of my life to God who has promised me everything. Wherefore through Christ is the amen to the glory of God by us."

Because in his life he is sure of God's promises, Paul is saying, and in answer to that conviction he has said "Amen" in his soul to all of them, there has been communicated into his life the very character of God. For he says, in effect, "He that established us with you in Christ and has anointed us is God; who also has sealed us and given us the earnest of the Spirit in our heart."

All of this simply means that a man who has believed God's promises, and has said "Amen" to them in the depths of his soul without any hesitation, is a man to whose life has been communicated the divine character of the Holy Spirit. Therefore the charge of fickleness in such a man is a sheer absurdity. For a man of God to be a double-dealer in his relationships with other people is an utter contradiction of terms.

Let us look at these precious truths a moment, recognizing that here is a man whose life has been so gripped by eternal reality that the faithfulness of God has become part of his character. Because God has proved Himself faithful to him, Paul must be absolutely faithful in his dealings with others. Here is a simple lesson that lies at the very root of the exposition of this portion of Scripture. When God says "Yea" and my heart says "Amen", His character by the Holy Ghost is implanted in my life to make fickleness with other people, even in the smallest detail, a sheer impossibility. Is it not amazing how out of a simple little issue like this comes to us some of the greatest truths in the Word of God?

In the *King James Version* of II Corinthians, you would almost feel that both the "yea" and "amen" are on God's side: " . . . all the promises of God in him are yea, and in him amen . . ."; that is to say, His promises are both given and confirmed by the Lord Jesus. But surely the *Revised Version* throws a different light upon this passage, and another slant upon this verse. True, every promise of God is "yea" in Christ: it is centered in the Lord Jesus; it is made known and made real because of Him. The "yea" is the voice of absolute authority, of absolute assurance. But the "amen" is my voice, your voice—the voice of absolute faith and complete obedience. The one has to do with divine revelation, which is unshakable; the other has to do with personal faith and commitment to it, which should also be unshakable.

Consider some of the things that are "yea" in Jesus Christ, some of God's certainties which are made known to us in the Lord Jesus. How many they are!—but I can only mention one or two. I think about the certainty of God's heart. How would I ever know that God loved me? How would you ever know that God is love, except for a place called Calvary concerning which the Apostle John says, "Herein is love, not that we loved God, but that he loved us, and sent his Son to be the propitiation for our sins" (I John 4: 10). The fact that God is love carries with it the "yea" of Calvary, the absolute certainty that He is love demonstrated at the cross.

What about the certainty of forgiveness? Perhaps some people who read this book have not troubled themselves too much about these things, but I believe that even the most superficial of lives, the most thoughtless and heedless of people, come to recognize their urgent need of a clear message concerning sin and forgiveness. There comes to every life the haunting reality of eternity, of judgment, the memory of a past which has been full of bitterness and shame. And the only message upon which any soul can hang its whole weight with absolute confidence is that "we have redemption through his blood, the forgiveness of sins . . ." (Ephesians 1: 7); " . . . Christ has suffered . . ., the just for the unjust, that he might bring us to God . . ." (I Peter 3: 18). When God does forgive the soul, is there any limit to His forgiveness? Is God not only a God of love, but a God of forgiving mercy? The cross of Calvary where He died, the Just for the unjust, sends down to us through all the centuries the great "yea" of Jesus Christ to the fact of God's forgiveness.

But then I think also about the certainty for my life, for in the Lord Jesus there is One who is the way, the truth, and the life. Not only is He the Way into life, but the Standard for my life. There is a standard set for me and for all who would claim His pardon; for if I would claim His forgiveness and take my place happily and gladly under the blessedness of the "yea" of God's forgiving mercy, then I must also take my place happily under His leadership and under His dominion, and accept His standard for my life, the pattern for every one of His followers, to which all who would rest in the Lord Jesus must conform.

Perhaps one day in Christian living there will be uncertainties about some things; but the great lines of moral character, the great standard of Christian living, the great ethic of what a Christian ought to be is traced for us by the firm hand of the Lord Jesus in, for example, the Sermon on the Mount. That is why we sing:

> Be like Jesus, this my song,
> In the home and in the throng
> Be like Jesus all day long,
> I would be like Jesus.

Has your heart said "amen" to that?

The certainty of life, the absolute, clear, unshakable certainty is that if I am to rest in His pardon, then I must accept His standard unswervingly. Furthermore, in the Lord Jesus there is a certainty for the future. Apart from Christ everything about the future would be so dark. We would not know a thing beyond this brief spell we call life. But there is One who has gone over the gulf and come back again, and who brings us the tremendous assurance from His Word: "I am the resurrection, and the life: he that believeth in me, though he were dead, yet shall he live" (John 11: 25).

You see, "How many soever are the promises of God: in Christ is the yea." They are all in Christ, and in Him is the "yea"; and Paul presents to us, as the reason for his consistency and absence of fickleness in daily living, that in his heart there has been the "amen" to all the promises of God.

Today deep calls unto deep and claims the response of your "amen" and my "amen" to the promises of God which are "yea" in Christ. Let us look therefore at this second thing, the commitment of my life. " . . . wherefore also through him is the Amen unto the glory of God through us." Do you see how this is so important for our daily life? There ought to be some kind of correspondence, some kind of mutual likeness between the "yea" of God in Christ and the "amen" of our hearts. The stability of His promises that are all settled in Jesus ought to be answered by the stability of our "amen" without any hesitancy or reservation. Surely it is a poor compliment to meet the promises that have been sealed in heaven by the blood of Jesus with a faltering "amen" that almost sticks in our throat. Surely it is an insult to the Lord in His great faithfulness and goodness to respond with hesitancy in our hearts to the "yea" that is so sure.

Paul is saying that the charge of inconsistency leveled against him is a sheer impossibility because God's unswerving "yea" in Christ has been met by an unswerving "amen" from his soul. He has looked up into the face of his Lord concerning pardon, concerning God's love, and concerning God's standards for his life, and he has said, "amen, Lord", unreservedly. Therefore, because he is so gripped by that relationship, he cannot be faithless in his relationships to other people. In other words, truth has so gripped this man that the one thing that matters to him is that he should be obedient to it, for that transaction must spread its influence to every part of his life.

Now I would underline something here for your heart. Somehow I think it is just along this line that the church today—that is you and I—is guilty of some measure of failure. What a fantastic contrast there is between the great "yea" of God and the half-hearted "amen" of our hearts! The reason, I believe, is partly moral and partly intellectual. Many of us are so afraid of giving unhesitating conviction in response to spiritual things, in case we are thought dogmatic or narrow. We think it looks like an attempt to boast of advanced education to say, "Well, I think—perhaps—it may be". But the language of the Christian church when it has been living in real victory in relation to the promises of God has never been, "We infer—we calculate—we think." It has always been, "We know." Whatever uncertainties may lie beyond us concerning some of the great issues of life, yet the love of God, the pardon of God, the standards for life that come to us in Jesus Christ—about these things there is no doubt. We know. And therefore our "amen" is to be as sure and as final as is God's "yea" forever.

From that moment when a man says "amen" to the Lord in these matters, his life is to be gripped constantly by the reality of the promises of the Word of God. That is one thing that I believe the Christian church lacks today—a grip of eternal truth upon our souls— so that when God says, "Thou shalt not," something rises in us that says, "Why?" When God forbids a certain course of action, strangely enough Satan can come along and persuade us that a course of action contrary to the teaching of Scripture may be completely right. I grieve in the instance of a Christian who can placate himself (or herself) that it is right to marry a non-Christian, and convince himself that it is right in order that he might satisfy the loneliness of his heart, and convince himself that that kind of thing is permissible to a child of God. Satan does that today to the people of God.

Oh, but when God says "yea" concerning standards of life, my heart has to bow before the throne of all the universe and say "amen". And until it does, eternal truth has never gripped my soul. Until that happens, I shall be constantly fickle, unreliable, and unstable in my relationships with other people.

The church today is lamentably weak in its grip upon eternal reality, and therefore Christian homes are lamentably weak in their testimony because they are permitting things that are contrary to the testimony of the Word of God.

Have you said "amen" to the Lord in your soul? I believe that God waits for every one of His children to have a day when they crash! Have you had your crash? That crash is not something emotional, nor is it a moral breakdown; it is the moment when from the depths of your soul there is an "amen" to all the will of God. And heaven resounds with rejoicing because it has heard the "amen" to His pardon, the "amen" to His standards, no matter how narrow the world may think they are. By the grace of God, His standard is to be our standard, and therefore to Him we say "amen". Has that happened in your heart? If so, observe the inevitable spiritual outcome of that great moment in life: the communication of his character.

Paul's argument is simply this: How can I, with such a message burning in my soul, ever be guilty of fickleness? Surely the message must make the messenger like it. Surely communion with a faithful God whose promises are "yea" must make a man faithful in all other relationships. As I have said, for a man to be a Christian and a double-dealer is an utter impossibility. Why? Because God, whose promises are "yea" in Christ and who hears the "amen" of our hearts, thereupon without delay—at that moment, instantaneously—communicates His character to make us stable.

Notice Paul's precious words in the two closing verses: underline them, and test your Christian life by them: *establish, anoint, seal, earnest.* He establishes us in Christ; that is to say, the fixity with which the Lord Jesus set His face towards Jerusalem, the constant and tenacious purpose of obedience to His Father's will—that becomes a part of my life, too. Days of broken promises and hesitancy of obedience become less frequent, for He establishes us.

How does He do it? He does it by the anointing of the Spirit. John says, " . . . ye have an unction from the Holy One . . ." (I John 2: 20), and the man and the woman who have said "amen" in happy, glad abandonment to the will and Word of God have received this. The anointing of the Holy Ghost which enabled Jesus to obey His Father in heaven unswervingly is the same anointing of the Holy Spirit that has come upon the child of God who has said "amen" to all God's will. It is Christ in us, and only Christ in us by the anointing of His Spirit, who can deal with the fickleness of our nature and the wandering of our hearts, and bind those wandering hearts to Him.

Having anointed us, see what He does: He seals what He anoints.

The seal impresses its likeness upon everything it touches. So a man sealed with the Spirit is made strong with the strength of Christ, wise with the wisdom of Christ, gracious with the gentleness of Christ, holy with the purity of Christ. Sealed! And all these are marks of His divine ownership, the mark of the moment when God raises the flag of heaven over the territory of the soul and seals with the Spirit.

If every inward profession of faith is matched with an outward righteousness of life, then we make it plain that truly we are genuinely His. So we have the earnest of the Spirit, the down payment which guarantees—with evidences that are unmistakable in a man who is living a life that is faithful—that he will one day see His lovely face. And there is no such guarantee in my Bible for any other kind of life.

Thus Paul brings all these great principles to bear in answering a simple charge—"Paul, you broke your promise! Paul, we cannot trust you! Paul, you are completely fickle!" To all of which he tells them that he uses the greatest principles of life to direct his conduct in the smallest detail, and therefore fickleness is impossible.

There may be two kinds of people reading this book. The one kind, like the chaff with no roots, is swept by every wind, unstable. Christian principles are at the mercy of passion and whim, and are forsaken when it seems more convenient. Oh, they would not call themselves unbelievers, because they believe everything most Christians believe. They would not call themselves anything but fundamental, conservative Christians—but in reality they are chaff! Principle is thrown overboard at a moment when it is inconvenient, because their hearts have never said "amen" to the Lord.

Then there are others, and they are like the tree rooted deep and rising high; their roots go as deep underground as their branches spread up into God's sky. They have echoed in their hearts "amen," because they know with me something of the battle of saying "amen" to Jesus. It could be said of them: "I have set the Lord always before me: because he is at my right hand, I shall not be moved" (Psalm 16: 8). There has come into that life such a stability by the unction of the Spirit that it bears the seal of His ownership—all because there was a day. And there is many a day when, sometimes with tears, sometimes with the flesh in rebellion, sometimes when everyone around you says you are narrow, extreme, bigoted, yet nevertheless in your soul alone with God you say, "Lord Jesus,

amen. Amen to Your love, amen to Your pardon, amen to Your
standards, amen to all of Your will, Lord!" Therefore, because you
have said "amen," fickleness and unreliability have gone forever.

So let our lips and lives express
The holy gospel we profess;
So let our works and virtues shine,
To prove the doctrine all divine.

Thus shall we best proclaim abroad
The honors of our Saviour God,
When His salvation reigns within,
And grace subdues the pow'r of sin.

Our flesh and sense must be denied,
Passion and envy, lust and pride;
While justice, temp'rance, truth and love,
Our inward piety approve.

Now thanks be unto God, which always causeth us to triumph in Christ, and maketh manifest the savour of his knowledge by us in every place. For we are unto God a sweet savour of Christ, in them that are saved, and in them that perish: To the one we are the savour of death unto death; and to the other the savour of life unto life. And who is sufficient for these things?

II CORINTHIANS 2: 14-16

3

VICTORY THROUGH CAPTIVITY

MOST expositors of this particular portion of the Word of God seem to be in agreement that, from the twelfth verse of this chapter right through the sixth chapter, Paul digresses in order to open his heart, as he very seldom does (so completely at least) in any other of his letters, concerning what it really means to him to be a minister of the gospel. He reveals something of what it has cost and some of the things that have brought him much joy. As we shall see later, he does not digress completely from what he has just been saying in the previous verses of this chapter; there is a very real relationship between the triumph of which Paul speaks here and the application of it to the situation in the church of which he has been speaking a few verses previously. What then has Paul to say about his ministry?

Whatever the experiences through which he has passed, somehow he would not let us think anything else than that from beginning to end it has been a glorious victory. " . . . thanks be unto God, which always causeth us to triumph in Christ. . . ." One version of the New Testament translates it this way: "Thanks be unto God, who through our union with Christ, leads us in one continual triumph." Paul is going to speak to us in succeeding chapters of the heartaches, the pressures, and the burdens he has borne, but he would underline from the very commencement that all through the story of his life there has been, because of his union with Christ, one continual victory. It is a victory along a particular road—as suggested by our title to this chapter—a victory through captivity, and what Paul says about his life as a Christian should, I am sure, be true about the lives of each one of us today. Amidst the heartaches and disappointments, the burdens and trials, as well as the joys of

31

Christian living and all that is involved, nevertheless because of our union with Christ the story should be one of continual triumph.

" . . . thanks be unto God, which always leadeth us in triumph in Christ" (rv). I think it is important to notice that that is the word —"who always *leadeth* us in triumph"—because it is quite clear that Paul had a very graphic picture in his mind as he used this language. It would be a picture—very familiar to Corinthian Christians—of a victorious Roman general returning from battle in his chariot, indeed with a whole procession of chariots and soldiers. A large crowd would gather to acclaim the victory in the battle, and the most significant thing everyone would notice would be the prisoners chained to the chariot wheels and dragged along the ground to their complete degradation. As the general rode by in his chariot, followed by soldiers in other chariots dragging more prisoners, bound and chained, the crowd would break out in a tumultuous roar as they rejoiced in the victory, and the air was filled with the odor of incense which was being burned and offered in thanksgiving to heathen gods. Such is Paul's picture in these verses. "Thanks be unto God," he says, in effect, "who drags me, not reluctantly but so happily, at the chariot wheel of His victory, and causes the air around me to be filled with the fragrance of His knowledge and His presence because of the victory that He has won by grace in my life."

Bear in mind the background of the man who is triumphing in this situation! Paul was not an immoral man or a degraded man, but a very self-righteous, proud, and arrogant Pharisee. Such a man is sometimes more difficult to face with the claims of the gospel. One day in his life he had a personal interview with the Lord Jesus, and from that day he began to count all his righteousness as but filthy rags in the sight of God. He had exchanged all that for the righteousness which God had offered him through faith in the Lord Jesus; and everything else he counted gladly as refuse, that he might win Christ. Because of this there had been a day when he held out his hands to the Lord and said, "Lord Jesus, today put Your chains upon my heart. You know how my heart is so prone to wander, and how wilful and stubborn and proud it can be. Lord, please, I want You at this moment and for the rest of my life to chain me up to Your chariot wheel. I want to be enchained and enslaved by Your love, because I know that is the road to liberty and freedom. Put Your chains on me, Lord, and never let me away!" What an amazing thing that such a man, so proud, should have such

a complete capitulation as that! That a man who was considered a
paragon of virtue and goodness of life and morality of living should
one day hold out empty hands to the Lord and ask Him to put His
chains upon him! He had found no freedom in his religion, no joy
in his self-righteousness; it was all utter bondage. But one day the
love of Calvary had begun to melt his heart, and just as the warmth
of sunshine begins to melt the ice until it is reduced to water, so as
he gazed and gazed upon the Saviour and came to understand
something in his own soul of the meaning of those nail prints and
of what it cost God to die in his place, Paul said, "Lord Jesus, chain
me to Thyself!"

> Make me a captive, Lord,
>   And then I shall be free;
> Force me to render up my sword,
>   And I shall conqueror be.
>
> I sink in life's alarms
>   When by myself I stand;
> Imprison me within Thine arms,
>   And strong shall be my hand.

Triumph by captivity! Liberty in bondage! Freedom through
slavery! Triumphant living by union with a crucified, living Lord!
A triumphant life meant all that to Paul. It is the only way of triumph
for any of us.

He goes on to say something else, however. Because it has been a
life of triumph, it has been a life of testimony.

" . . . [God] maketh manifest the savour of his knowledge by us in
every place" (v. 14). Just for a moment, go back in your mind to the
picture which Paul put before the Corinthian Christians, and see
the prisoners of war being dragged along the ground. That which
was their degradation was to Paul, in terms of spiritual experience,
his greatest honor: that he could be a slave of the Master. As you
see these prisoners being drawn by their chains and listen to the
roar of applause, you might ask yourself, "Why the cheering?" The
cheering was not for them but for the honor of the general who had
captured them. Every chain that was put around them and tied to
his chariot wheels was the symbol of his power. No doubt, as they
were dragged along the road, they carried with them broken spears
and shattered arrows. Every weapon they had once used in their

defense was shattered and drawn along with them, symbolizing the general's total area of authority.

So Paul says, "Thanks be unto God! In Jesus Christ He has chained me to His chariot wheel, and for the rest of my life, I am His slave and, because of this, inevitably—not by sermons I preach or by words I use, but by my life—in my daily routine there is made manifest and clear the savor, the scent, the fragrance of His knowledge by me in every place." Or as the *Revised Version* puts it: " . . . thanks be unto God, which always leadeth us in triumph in Christ, and maketh manifest through us the savour of his knowledge in every place." "I am so happy," says Paul, in effect, "since the chains were put on me and since the Lord manacled my hands and took hold of my life and made me His slave. I am so thankful that, as I am taken along the journey of life, inevitably other people will see the weapons I once used to trust in are now destroyed and shattered. Whereas I once trusted in my self-righteousness and my ability, in my sheer determination and will power, now I gaze upon my lovely Lord, and these others are all lying shattered around me. Because I have been put in chains by the Master, therefore wherever I go I carry the savor of His knowledge in every place." This is a witnessing life! When the Christian has really stretched out his empty hands, recognizing the futility of his own life, and he has been chained with his whole life to the Lord Jesus, other things in which he once trusted for life, for salvation, for death, and for eternity, lie shattered and ruined around him. He has seen the emptiness of everything that he is—except for grace and the cleansing of the precious blood—and the self-life lies in ruins. He has come to the point of no return and has crashed before God. He has seen the things in which he once trusted lying as utterly useless, but because he is chained with chains that no man can see and is bound by cords of love to the altar, wherever he goes there is something about him that brings the savor of the knowledge of the Lord, and the people do not become conscious of the human channel but of Him. So Paul witnesses to the fact that this life, no matter what it has meant in terms of testing and affliction, is a triumphant life, a testifying life. But he also says that it is a fragrant life.

"For we are unto God a sweet savour of Christ, in them that are saved, and in them that perish" (v. 15). In the paraphrase of Phillips' *Letters to Young Churches* the meaning is conveyed dramatically: "Thanks be to God Who leads us, wherever we are, on His own triumphant way and makes our knowledge of Him to spread throughout the world like a lovely perfume! We Christians have the unmistakable 'scent' of Christ, discernible alike to those who are being saved and to those who are heading for death. To the latter it seems like the very smell of doom, to the former it has the fresh fragrance of life itself." Paul is saying that since he has been made a captive of his wonderful Lord, he leaves a scent wherever he goes. The real Christian, the genuine believer who has passed through this very same thing, also has a scent about him. Paul is careful to say that the scent is breathed in heaven; but not only there, for it is breathed down here on earth. He says, "For we are unto God a sweet savour of Christ." One day the Father looked down upon the Son and said, "This is my beloved Son, in whom I am well pleased; hear ye him" (Matthew 17: 5). He said it at the moment of His obedience and submission to all the will of God, and He said, "This is my beloved Son." The scent, the savor, the obedience of His life and the surrender of His will went up to heaven. Your life carries with it a scent, and the aroma of it is going up to glory. I wonder if it is pungent; I wonder if it is pleasant, I wonder if it is something which reminds the angels and the Father in heaven of the day when Jesus was down here; and as He could look down upon this little planet which was in rebellion against Him, and say, "This is my beloved Son," I wonder if in some measure heaven can look down upon your life and mine and say that very thing. Since you and I have been captive for the Lord and bound in chains to His chariot, God the Father looks down and sees you in Christ, and Christ in you, and says, "There is my beloved Son!" This is the scent of a life that is triumphant by captivity; but it is not only mounting to heaven, it is going out into the world. " . . . we are unto God," says Paul, "a sweet savour of Christ, in them that are saved, and in them that perish: To the one we are the savour of death unto death; and to the other the savour of life unto life." What a responsibility this is for the child of God! No wonder Paul exclaims, " . . . who is sufficient for these things?" Wherever he goes (as Phillips puts it) to some people he carries the very smell of doom. To those who have no use for the things of God, to the unconverted and the ungodly (not necessarily the immoral, though any man who is ungodly is immoral just for that reason), a Christian who has been made a captive of the Lord Jesus, his self-weapons lying in shattered ruins around him, carries with him the smell of doom. At least that man who is not born again, and who has not cared for the things of God, will be brought abruptly to a halt in his life as he meets a man who is a captive to the Lord. A captive is triumphant, fragrant, attractive, and the ungodly man will either have to get right with God or get rid of the Christian altogether. The smell of doom reveals to him the fact that unless he gets converted, the judgment of God is upon him.

Moreover, not only is the captive a savor of death unto death as a Christian, but he is a savor of life unto life. What fragrance, comfort, and joy come to us when, from time to time, God gives us the privilege of fellowship with captive Christians! Theirs is the scent of life! I put the question in its spiritual sense: "What sort of aroma goes up to heaven and around on earth from your life? Is it the savor of Christ, or will He have to say, as He did to Simon Peter, " . . . thou savourest not the things that be of God, but those that be of men" (Matthew 16: 23)?

Let us return to what is perhaps the most significant thrust of this portion, and its most challenging application. It is, as I have said, a digression from the main theme of Paul's letter, and is the beginning of his great statement about what it means to be a Christian. That is evident from this whole passage, yet somehow I cannot think that we get to the real heart of our text if we consider it apart from the earlier verses of this chapter.

Why has Paul written the second time to the church at Corinth? Not simply to explain the reason why he had not come to see them again. He has written to them once more in order that they might fulfill their spiritual duty concerning a brother who had been excommunicated from the church. I do not need to go into this passage in great detail, but you will recall that while the church at Corinth was arguing and protesting about denominationalism and a thousand and one other things that caused them to be full of strife and division, they were blind to one dreadful sin that was going on in the life of at least one of their membership, the sin of immorality.

Paul had already spoken about this sinning brother: " . . . deliver such an one unto Satan for the destruction of the flesh, that the spirit may be saved in the day of the Lord Jesus" (I Corinthians 5: 5). In other words, Paul had already written to them concerning the absolute necessity of discipline concerning the brother who had sinned. Sin cannot be tolerated within the fellowship of the church, and the offender must be dealt with and delivered to Satan for the destruction of the flesh (but ultimately, remember, for the saving of the soul).

Now Paul writes to them again as he has something else to say to them about this. He writes from the experience of a Christian life that has been made captive to Christ and therefore is witnessing and, above all, is fragrant. (There is an area today which, I admit, is very dangerous, very delicate ground, but it is an area which desperately needs the fragrance of a Christian.) Paul says to them, concerning a brother, "Sufficient to such a man is this punishment, which was inflicted of many" (v. 6). In other words, "I am grateful to you, Corinthian Christians, for doing what I asked. I am glad that you faced the necessity of discipline of the man who is excommunicated, but this punishment has gone far enough." " . . . contrariwise," he goes on to say, "you ought rather to forgive him, and comfort him, lest perhaps such a one should be swallowed up with overmuch sorrow. Wherefore I beseech you that you would confirm your love toward him. . . . Lest Satan should get an advantage of us: for we are not ignorant of his devices" (II Corinthians 2: 7-11).

Do you realize what Paul is saying? "I want something of the fragrance of your Christian life to penetrate into this area. Here is a man who has been excommunicated because of his sin. This was dealt with immediately; but now remember that God's last sentence upon a man who is repentant is never judgment but always grace. Therefore we need to be careful lest our brother be overcome with much sorrow. We are not ignorant of the devices of the devil; we must be careful that having disciplined the man we do not slay his soul. We did it for the salvation of his soul; now let us be careful, having completed one side of the treatment, that we adopt the other, lest Satan get an advantage of us. There is nothing that the devil would like to do more than, having exposed the man's sin, to keep on reminding him of it and telling him that he is of no use and never will be of any use, that he is finished for the rest of his life and quite possibly will end in hell. Now, I want you to go to that man and confirm your love to him by forgiving him and by comforting him." Do you see what we are getting at here? May the Lord help us to see that whereas—and let us confess it before God—we certainly are very neglectful these days of church discipline—afraid perhaps because of embarrassment—we are far more neglectful concerning the exercise of forgiveness of the brother who is in the wrong. Of course there must be discipline. Of course there can be no excusing sin in the name of a false kind of sentiment. Love which simply goes out in sentiment to the man who has been tripped up by the enemy is not the love of God. Love will never be shown at the expense of holiness. *But,* holiness must never be shown at the expense of slaying love.

I wonder if this is not an area into which many of us need to move. Paul says, "Forgive him and comfort him." There is a kind of forgiveness which is worth literally nothing, in which perhaps the church might welcome the man back into fellowship and then put him on probation for five years or so. His reinstatement is a sort of legalistic welcome which will always remind him that he is a failure, and which will always point a finger of accusation at him, reminding him of what he used to be. There is a kind of forgiveness which is almost like that which David offered Absalom, and because of which Absalom never saw the king's face for two years. But Paul says to this church, in effect, "I want you to forgive him and comfort him," and when forgiveness gets into the realm of comfort, I tell you that forgiveness forgets.

I am so thankful that I am a man whom God has forgiven and, praise God, whose sin has been forgotten. That is the only kind of forgiveness that would give my heart a moment's peace. When God forgave, for Jesus' sake, He buried my sins in the depth of the sea to remember them no more against me, as if they had never happened. What kind of forgiveness am I offering to others who offend? What kind of mercy do I show to the man whom Satan has tripped? Do you not see that when Paul says, in effect, "Thanks be unto God, who always leadeth us in one continual triumph in Christ, and maketh manifest the savor of His knowledge in every place, we are a savor of life unto life or of death unto death," the fragrance of the Christian life is needed most in the area I have just discussed? That is the area it seldom reaches, because at that point all that the man who has stumbled may feel, at least from many of us, is the sentence of condemnation.

I pray God that as you conclude this chapter, it may be indeed as men and women who have held out their hands and their wills to be chained up by the living Christ, to live in that perfect liberty which is the outcome of bondage; and that, as the fruit of this, in your life there might be poured out the inevitable fragrance, the scent that will remind people of the Lord; and that it may be evident most of all in our forgiving mercy to those with whom, for one reason or another, we are out of fellowship. That will only be possible as we recognize that our sufficiency is of God and it is He who

always leads us in triumph in every place (especially in this place of
forgiveness) in Christ and so makes our knowledge of Him spread
like a lovely perfume.

> Fill me with gladness from above,
>   Hold me by strength divine;
> Lord let the glow of Thy great love
>   Through my whole being shine.
>
> Make this poor self grow less and less,
>   Be Thou my life and aim.
> Oh, make me daily through Thy grace
>   More meet to bear Thy name.

Do we begin again to commend ourselves? or need we, as some others, epistles of commendation to you, or letters of commendation from you? Ye are our epistle written in our hearts, known and read of all men: Forasmuch as ye are manifestly declared to be the epistle of Christ ministered by us, written not with ink, but with the Spirit of the living God; not in tables of stone, but in fleshly tables of the heart. And such trust have we through Christ to God-ward: Not that we are sufficient of ourselves to think any thing as of ourselves; but our sufficiency is of God; Who also hath made us able ministers of the new testament; not of the letter, but of the spirit: for the letter killeth, but the spirit giveth life. But if the ministration of death, written and engraven in stones, was glorious, so that the children of Israel could not stedfastly behold the face of Moses for the glory of his countenance; which glory was to be done away; How shall not the ministration of the spirit be rather glorious? For if the ministration of condemnation be glory, much more doth the ministration of righteousness exceed in glory. For even that which was made glorious had no glory in this respect, by reason of the glory that excelleth. For if that which is done away was glorious, much more that which remaineth is glorious. Seeing then that we have much hope, we use great plainness of speech. And not as Moses, which put a veil over his face, that the children of Israel could not stedfastly look to the end of that which is abolished: But their minds were blinded: for until this day remaineth the same veil untaken away in the reading of the old testament; which veil is done away in Christ. But even unto this day, when Moses is read, the veil is upon their heart. Nevertheless when it shall turn to the Lord, the veil shall be taken away. Now the Lord is that Spirit: and where the Spirit of the Lord is, there is liberty. But we all, with open face beholding as in a glass the glory of the Lord, are changed into the same image from glory to glory, even as by the Spirit of the Lord.

II CORINTHIANS 3

4

THE TRANSFORMED LIFE

"BUT we all, with open face beholding as in a glass the glory of the Lord, are changed into the same image from glory to glory, even as by the Spirit of the Lord" (II Corinthians 3: 18). In the succeeding chapter Paul begins to open his heart concerning some of the buffetings that he has taken because he is a Christian. But before he does so, he has something to say about the resources he has found in Jesus Christ in order that he can stand the test when the buffeting comes. That is why he is able to say (4: 8-9) that although he is troubled, he has not been distressed, although he is perplexed, he has never been in despair, although he has been persecuted, he has never been forsaken, and although, as Phillips put it, he has been knocked down, he has never been knocked out! Paul has been able to take the buffetings because he has made a great discovery and received a great ministry, described in the words of our text, where we too can find spiritual resources adequate for any buffeting.

This is a very practical subject, because any of us who would be followers of the Lord Jesus Christ must expect the buffetings: from within and from without; from our foes and from our friends; from Satan, who would seek to attack on every possible quarter the man who is set upon being the best for God. I am sure that none of us escapes something of the buffeting. Life is full of it, and the question that arises when the buffeting comes is, "Have I really got what it takes to stand them, or have I to become a spiritual casualty?"

As Paul opens up this subject, he contrasts what the Jew had and what the Christian had—a contrast of the revelation of the Old Testament with the revelation of the New. This is the theme of the third chapter. Notice some of the contrasts between the Old and the New, contrasts which led Paul to say that in this new covenant he had discovered resources adequate for every pressure of life.

Verse 3: " . . . the epistle of Christ ministered by us, written not with ink, but with the Spirit of the living God; not in tables of stone, but in fleshy tables of the heart"; in other words, the revelation of God is not something which is legal or external or outside of Paul, but something that has come into the very depths of his soul, that has touched the hardness of his heart and melted it. Verse 5: "Not that we are sufficient of ourselves to think anything as of ourselves; but our sufficiency is of God"; not something that causes Paul to boast in himself, but rather something that has caused him to renounce all self-confidence and put his confidence in the Lord. Verse 6: " . . . not of the letter, but of the spirit: for the letter killeth, but the spirit giveth life"; not a ministry which has brought him under a sense of condemnation and guilt, but a ministry of grace which has set him free from all of that and given him life and righteousness, purity and victory.

Finally, verses 13 and 18: "And not as Moses, which put a veil over his face, that the children of Israel could not stedfastly look to the end of that which is abolished. . . . But we all, with open face beholding as in a glass the glory of the Lord. . . ." Notice the contrast: not the one but the other; not the condemnation but the deliverance; not the letter but the spirit; not an external God but an internal reality; not death but life; not a veil of uncertainty concerning the things of glory and heaven, but an open face beholding the glory of the Lord.

"Now," Paul is saying, "I can take any buffeting in the reality of that experience!"

To make this simple and practical I would take three words to sum it all up as we ask, What are the resources which are adequate for any buffeting and which enable us to say, as Paul says in chapter 4: 1: " . . . seeing we have this ministry, as we have received mercy, we faint not"? Seeing that I have this ministry—this about which he speaks in the third chapter—that is such a glorious reality to him, and has made religion not just an external obligation but an indwelling life, that has brought me out from death into liberty and joy, that has taken away the veil from his face and enabled him to see God—seeing I have received this ministry, I faint not. I have something which enables me to take it in the face of all the buffeting that comes my way, for I can always find resources that are adequate to take the knocks.

The first word is "contemplation": " . . . we all, with open face beholding as in a glass the glory of the Lord. . . ." I do not think that the *King James Version* quite conveys what Paul had in mind. " . . . beholding as in a glass . . ."—if that is all I can see of the glory of the Lord (as it were, in the dimness or possibly even the distortion of a glass), this is not superior to the Old Testament, because Moses saw God face to face. Therefore I go to another translation of the New Testament to help me to get at the root of this. Actually there is one word in the Greek New Testament which is translated in all these words, "beholding as in a glass," and it is suggested that a better rendering would be "reflecting, as a glass does, the glory of God." Or again, "All of us, as with unveiled faces, we mirror the glory of the Lord" (WEYMOUTH). Ah, that helps me! If I look into the mirror, it will only reflect that which it sees. It receives something upon its surface and then reflects that out into the world around it. We all, with unveiled faces, beholding as in a mirror, catch the light and reflect the glory of the Lord. We reflect, as a glass does, and we do it with unveiled faces.

"This," says Paul, in effect, "is my first and dynamic secret which enables me to take all the buffeting that comes my way. I have a clear view of my Saviour, with open face." But, you say to me, this is impossible! What about the veils of sense and of sin? What about the things that would hide our Saviour from our eyes? Surely no man could look with an open face upon God?

Wait a moment—who is the one we see? It is not the great luster of that mighty throne of all heaven—one day we will see that; one day Jesus our Lord, who has washed us in His blood and indwelt us by His Spirit, will present us faultless before the throne of glory with exceeding joy; one day we will be so transformed that we will be able to see God face to face and not shrink from the vision; but not now in this human body. Well, then, how is it Paul says he sees the glory of God? Is it not what the Apostle John says to us in the opening verses of his first Epistle and in his gospel: "That which was from the beginning, which we have heard, which we have seen with our eyes, which we have looked upon, and our hands have handled, of the Word of life . . .; That which we have seen and heard declare we unto you . . ." (I John 1: 1-3); "And the Word was made flesh, and dwelt among us (and we beheld his glory, the glory as of

44 BLESSINGS OUT OF BUFFETINGS

the only begotten of the Father), full of grace and truth" (John
1: 14).

This, claims Paul, is the One he has seen, the One who said,
" . . . he that hath seen me hath seen the Father . . ." (John 14: 9).
He is saying, "I have had a clear view of God as He has revealed
Himself to my heart in Jesus Christ, and what have I seen? I saw
in Him the glory of a life lived in total abandonment to the sovereign
will of His Father in heaven. I saw a life lived in utter poverty yet
in absolute contentment. I saw a life triumph over every temptation
that ever tempted me, and I saw Him victorious at every point where
I have failed. I have seen Him come so near to the poor, to those
who are sick, and to those who are in need. I have seen Him holy,
separate, harmless, and undefiled; so close to the sinner yet never
contaminated. Ah, but most of all I have seen His tears, I have heard
His crying, and I have listened to the cry which said, 'O my Father,
if it be possible, let this cup pass from me: nevertheless not as I will,
but as thou wilt' (Matthew 26: 39). I have seen the nail prints, the
marks in His hands and His side; I have seen the thorns on His
brow. And yet, I have heard the cry, 'My God, my God, why hast
thou forsaken me?' (Matthew 27: 46). I have seen Him made sin
on my behalf, God in Christ, reconciling the world to Himself.
I have seen the glory of God in the face of Jesus Christ and, bless
His holy name, I have seen an empty tomb, an ascended Saviour,
and I have met Him face to face when He said to me, 'Saul, why
persecutest thou me? . . . it is hard for thee to kick against the pricks'
(Acts 9: 4-5).

"I have had a clear view of Jesus. I have seen Him, felt Him, and
I have known Him in a far deeper way than simply by the outward
physical appearance; I have felt the reality of His life begin to burn
in my heart. I have seen in Christ the glory of a life that is totally
submitted to the sovereignty of God. That glory has begun to take
hold of me, and I have begun to see that this is the one life that God
expects of any man He made in His own image. I have seen the marks
of the cross upon Him, and by His grace the marks of the cross
have been put upon me and I am no longer my own; I am bought
with a price, redeemed by His precious blood. Yes, I have seen Him
—not in the outward physical sense only, but in the inward sense of
a deep spiritual reality. I have had a clear view of Jesus and my life
will never be the same again."

But who has seen Him? Is it only the giants, like Paul? " . . . we

all, with open face beholding as in a glass the glory of the Lord. . . ."
We all—not merely the Moses, the Elijahs, the spiritual aristocracy
of the Old Testament times and the whole multitude afraid at a
distance in the valley; not only Paul on his face on the Damascus
road, blinded by the vision—*we all*, the weakest, the poorest, the
most sinful, the most defiled. The spiritual aristocracy of the church
of Jesus Christ is not the preacher or the prophet, but the sinner
saved by grace. It is the soul who has come like the publican of old
and said, "God be merciful to me a sinner" (Luke 18: 13), and it is
the soul bowed before Calvary and seeing (as Paul saw) the glory of
God in the face of Jesus Christ. As the Epistle to the Hebrews says,
"Having therefore, brethren, boldness to enter into the holiest by
the blood of Jesus, By a new and living way, which he hath consecrated for us, through the veil, that is to say, his flesh . . .; Let us
draw near with a true heart in full assurance of faith . . ." (10: 19-22).
Paul's resources are dug deep in the fact that he had a clear view of
his wonderful Lord.

Let me pause to ask you solemnly in the presence of God—you
are taking the buffetings, aren't you? The buffetings of the devil in
your soul? The buffetings in the home life which is perhaps so
utterly and hopelessly confused and divided? The buffetings of
lack of understanding from your friends who couldn't care less,
and perhaps from your parents too? You are taking the buffetings?
Beloved, have you got what it takes? Have you now a clear view of
Jesus? You see, we all, with open face—the veil removed, rent in two
by His cross—draw near in full assurance of faith, and we see Him.
Have you looked into His lovely face in contemplation? Oh, not
just a moment's glance while upon your knees with your Scripture
portion and then a dash out into the world. Not just a long time
spent in preparing the fashion of the body to come to the house
of God, or to meet the onslaught of the day—but a long time in
preparing the heart as you have gazed upon your lovely Lord.
Have you met Him like that today? A clear view of Jesus Christ is
that which is needed to take all that comes across our path.

My second word is "reflection" and, as I have said to you before,
what a mirror sees it reflects, and it can reflect only what it sees and
what it receives. We, all of us, with unveiled faces, mirror the
glory of the Lord. You see, in the life of a man who has seen Christ
—the glory of God in the life, death, and resurrection of our Lord,
the glory of God in a life submitted to the sovereignty of His Father

—inevitably truth begins to dominate character, and the life of
Jesus Christ begins to be reproduced in and through him. Don't
you think it is a very lovely thing? Have you watched it through
life? When a husband and wife live together for many years and
they are devoted to each other, finding the center of their affection
in the living Lord Jesus, don't you think it is a wonderful thing that,
as they live and pray together, walk and talk together, they become
not only like Him, but like each other? Put an iron within range of
a magnet and the iron becomes magnetized.

> Turn your eyes upon Jesus,
> Look full in His wonderful face;
> And the things of earth will grow strangely dim
> In the light of His glory and grace.

Turn your eyes upon Jesus not with the quick look but the gaze, and
believe me, that which you see becomes a very part of your life and
character—" . . . reflecting as does a mirror."

You see, the whole argument and force of this is simply, as Paul
says, "In whom the god of this world hath blinded the minds of
them which believe not, lest the light of the glorious gospel of Christ,
who is the image of God, should shine unto them" (II Corinthians
4: 4) That is the fate of a man who is unsaved.

My friend, you don't blame people for living as they do. You
cannot hold up, as it were, holy hands in horror as you see the world
live. What do you expect? That is the way the natural man does live
—you don't expect him to live on any higher level! It may be
expressed in different ways, but the root of it is that the god of this
present world has blinded the eyes, the minds, of them that believe
not; and I ask you, who in the name of heaven has the power to
take the veil from ungodly faces, to take the blindness out of an
ungodly man's mind? Do you think that a university education will
do it? It will not. Do you think that brilliance of intellect will do it?
Never. Do you think that an outstanding grasp of theology will do
it? No. I will tell you what will: "For God, who commanded the
light to shine out of darkness, hath shined in our hearts, to give
the light of the knowledge of the glory of God in the face of Jesus
Christ" (II Corinthians 4: 6). That is what will do it.

The man who gazes upon and contemplates day by day the face
of the Lord Jesus Christ, and who has caught the glow of the

reality that the Lord is not a theory but an indwelling power and force in his life, is as a mirror reflecting the glory of the Lord. Wherever he goes, people begin to ask questions as to why he triumphs when others fail; why it is when at business everything is at sixes and sevens and all is upset and confused, he maintains a sense of poise; how it is, when facing buffeting of one kind or another, he reacts with such patience; how it is, when the general level of conversation is so impure he is never dragged down, and how he stands above it, not in a sense of rebuke to others but in a sense of testimony to the fact that, because he belongs to God, he cannot descend to another level. He has caught the glow and is reflecting it. *We all* reflect as in a mirror. Has anything been getting through to your life?—any light, any reflection, any glow?

It was over thirty years ago that the Lord Jesus met me when I was far away from Him, and I came to Christ through the testimony of an office colleague, who did not preach at me but lived Christ before me, and by whose life I was condemned. I met him recently at Keswick, and again it was my privilege to be alongside my spiritual father and listen to some of the things he had to say. He rose to the top of the tree in business, becoming very successful, but as we talked together, I was reminded of some words he had spoken years previously: "I have found in my life that as far as business success is concerned, with all its pressures, the price in terms of eternity is too great to pay."

Is there any light getting through? Is any of the glory of God getting through to others through your life? If not, perhaps it is because the pressures upon you are so great. In your home, in the care of that precious little family, in your responsibilities in business life, in the pressure of study—be careful that the price in terms of eternity is not too great. Be careful to recognize that if the light is not getting through, it is because you are not looking at Him long enough.

Our third word is "transformation": "But all of us as with unveiled faces we mirror the glory of the Lord are transformed into the same likeness, from glory to glory, even as derived from the Lord, the Spirit" (WEYMOUTH). Here Paul is saying that the secret of his ability to stand in the power of the Lord against all of the buffetings of life is not simply that he has beheld Him in Jesus Christ and therefore reflects Him to others, but that as he beholds Him he is being transformed into His own likeness. " . . . ye shall know the truth, and the truth shall make you free" (John 8: 32), said our precious Lord, and that word "set you free" is the same one as is used here for the word "liberty"—" . . . where the Spirit of the Lord is, there is liberty" (II Corinthians 3: 17)—freedom, deliverance. Paul tells us that our ability to take things and to stand against all that Satan flings at us means we are learning the secret as we behold Jesus. He lifts us up above it all, and by His power we stand where once we used to fall; and so we are transformed.

Maybe the great concern in your heart today is that this life might be your life, that this ability to take things might be yours. I wonder if that statement which I have just made comes to you as good news? Are you battling with yourself, defeated in life, going down under the buffeting? You face so many battles! None of us stands above you in this, because we know it all in our own hearts, but we would gladly tell you the good news that you overcome not by battle but by faith. You overcome not by inward struggle but by upward look. Any battle for victory, power, and deliverance—from ourselves and from sin—which is not based constantly upon the gazing and the beholding of the Lord Jesus, with the heart and life lifted up to Him, is doomed to failure.

If I could just get across to you the word that the Holy Spirit would quietly speak to you, it would be: "Give up the struggle and the fight; relax in the omnipotence of the Lord Jesus; look up into His lovely face and as you behold Him, He will transform you into His likeness. You do the beholding—He does the transforming. There is no short-cut to holiness."

" . . . changed into the same image from glory to glory . . ." (v. 18) —this is a lifelong, glorious experience, and it will be perfected one day in heaven. Paul tells us (Philippians 3: 21) that He "shall change our vile body [this body of sin in which dwells no good thing], that it may be fashioned like unto his glorious body. . . ." Yes, He will do that!

It will all be perfected one day. In the language of Ephesians 4: 13: "Till we all come in the unity of the faith, and of the knowledge of the Son of God, unto a perfect man . . ."—not unto multitudes of perfect people but unto a perfect man. It takes all of the church through every generation every color, every race, all living in contemplation of the Lord Jesus, reflecting His glory and being transformed into His likeness; it takes every one of us, redeemed by blood, the whole temple of the Spirit, the whole body of Christ, one day to be made a perfect man like Him. It is going to be perfected one day.

Meanwhile, day by day, through this life in which you live amid all the pressures of circumstances, are you able to say with the Apostle Paul, in effect, "Therefore having received this ministry, I faint not" (II Corinthians 4: 1)? Buffeted, knocked down but never knocked out, cast down but never in despair, persecuted but never forsaken, because—praise the Lord!—you have found the answer to what it takes to stand in the ministry you have received: a clear view of Jesus, in contemplation; in reflection of His glory in the midst of the battle; and then being made like unto Him as day by day your heart is lifted up to the Lord Jesus and He imparts to your life the sweetness and loveliness of His character. Oh, may that be your portion this day as you are able to say, "Thank God, by grace, I have got what it takes!" I have received a ministry: contemplation, reflection, transformation.

Therefore seeing we have this ministry, as we have received mercy, we faint not; But have renounced the hidden things of dishonesty, not walking in craftiness, nor handling the word of God deceitfully; but by manifestation of the truth commending ourselves to every man's conscience in the sight of God. But if our gospel be hid, it is hid to them that are lost: In whom the god of this world hath blinded the minds of them which believe not, lest the light of the glorious gospel of Christ, who is the image of God, should shine unto them. For we preach not ourselves, but Christ Jesus the Lord; and ourselves your servants for Jesus' sake. For God, who commanded the light to shine out of darkness, hath shined in our hearts, to give the light of the knowledge of the glory of God in the face of Jesus Christ. But we have this treasure in earthen vessels, that the excellency of the power may be of God, and not of us. We are troubled on every side, yet not distressed; we are perplexed, but not in despair; Persecuted, but not forsaken; cast down, but not destroyed; Always bearing about in the body the dying of the Lord Jesus, that the life also of Jesus might be made manifest in our body. For we which live are alway delivered unto death for Jesus' sake, that the life also of Jesus might be made manifest in our mortal flesh. So then death worketh in us, but life in you.

II CORINTHIANS 4: 1-12

5

THE PRICE OF FRUITFULNESS

"For God, who commanded the light to shine out of darkness, hath shined in our hearts, to give the light of the knowledge of the glory of God in the face of Jesus Christ" (II Corinthians 4: 6). Phillips puts it like this: "God, Who first ordered Light to shine in darkness has flooded our hearts with His Light. We now can enlighten men only because we can give them knowledge of the glory of God, as we see it in the face of Jesus Christ."

In this chapter Paul has some tremendous things to say concerning the ministry. It is here that he opens his heart and speaks to us regarding what it means to him to be a minister of the gospel. This chapter is a tremendous challenge, a great comfort, and a great revelation of God's purposes for each one of us as His servants.

Paul speaks first about the character of the ministry in the words of our text. What is this ministry? "The ministry which I have received," he calls it, and this, in effect, is what he received: "God hath shined in our hearts to give the light of the glory of God in the face of Jesus Christ."

But this ministry which has been received must be communicated, and I notice that in the fifth verse he says: " . . . we preach not ourselves, but Christ Jesus the Lord; and ourselves your servants for Jesus' sake." And then Paul explains that we can only communicate this truth and this ministry at great personal cost: "So then death worketh in us, but life in you" (v. 12).

Our subject, therefore, is this whole matter of Christian ministry, and I would remind you that this is something which involves every one of us. You often hear it said of a particular individual that he has had a call to the ministry, and of course we know what is meant by that: such a person has given his life for training and preparation for preaching the gospel. But the truth is that from the moment the Holy Spirit reveals to us Jesus Christ and comes to live in our hearts and we are born again, life becomes a ministry. It is no longer a self-seeking, aimless, purposeless existence, but it is a ministry. Just as a rug is laid on a floor, so a man who has met God in the face of Jesus Christ begins to lay down his life in the service of Christ and of others. "For even the Son of man came not to be ministered unto, but to minister, and to give his life a ransom for many" (Mark 10: 45). This is the principle which must grip not only those who may be called into the ministry in the first and primary sense, but all who have been redeemed by the blood of Christ and who share the life of His indwelling Spirit. To all such, life becomes a ministry. As we think about this ministry, we must ask ourselves if we really are in the ministry. Is God using it and blessing it for His honor and for His glory?

First of all, let us consider the character of this ministry: What is it that we have received? " . . . God, who commanded the light to shine out of darkness, hath shined in our hearts, to give the light of the knowledge of the glory of God in the face of Jesus Christ." As in the creation, God's first words were, "Let there be light," so in that tremendous moment when we were born of the Spirit of God, the light dawned and shone into our hearts. It shone not merely as an influence, not only as a doctrine or creed, but it shone in the revelation to our hearts by His Spirit in the person and in the face of Jesus Christ. As Paul says (Galatians 1: 15-16), " . . . it pleased God . . . To reveal his Son in me. . . ."

Think now about the face of Jesus Christ. Have you ever looked into His face? This is a theme that would baffle any preacher, and even an angel in heaven would seem to be inadequate to proclaim it, but I would try to talk to you about the face of Jesus Christ. For it is only those who have gazed into His face and understood something of that revelation who know anything of life as a ministry.

As you look into the face of Jesus Christ you can see it from so many different angles and viewpoints. For instance, I look into the face of Jesus Christ when God became a Baby, and I think of Him in a manger, and I see Him there as One who has turned aside completely from all self-seeking and all the things that fill our minds and dominate our lives. It could have happened in a palace, it could have taken place in a mansion, but surely there is a tremendous glimpse of the glory of God in the face of Jesus Christ as in poverty He came to Bethlehem.

Again, I think of Him as a child of twelve as He sat and taught in the Temple, and with a Spirit-instructed mind He baffled all the learned professors of His day. They "were astonished at his understanding and answers" (Luke 2: 47). I see the glory of God in the face of Jesus Christ as He taught there.

I see Him in a carpenter's shop in Nazareth, standing among the shavings. I see something of the glory of God in the face of Jesus Christ, in the divine leisureliness in the heart of our Lord as He was content to await God's time there, knowing that His hour had not yet come. In quietness and confidence in all those surroundings He worked in that carpenter's shop. He became the Carpenter (not *a*, as one of many, but *the* carpenter of Nazareth). Nothing imperfect ever came from His shop.

I think of Him too in His ministry as He fed five thousand people with a few loaves and fishes, and met every need. I hear the word of authority as it comes from His lips, and I see the devils begin to tremble and acknowledge His absolute sovereignty. I see the glory of God in the face of Jesus Christ as He rebukes the powers of sin. As He ministers, every tone of His voice and every look on His face, and every word He speaks—whether it be a word of tenderness and gentleness or a stern rebuke—reveals the glory of God in the face of Jesus Christ.

But I see Him most wonderfully on the cross, for surely there is no place that the glory of God in the face of Jesus Christ is revealed more clearly as at Calvary, where He laid down His life for us. I see the glory of the love of God that stooped so far in order to save us from our sin; and I see the glory of the justice of God in the face of Jesus Christ who allowed Himself to be made sin for us rather than that sin should go unpunished or that the Lord God should be dishonored. To those who have eyes to see, the glory of God in the face of Jesus Christ is revealed, as nowhere else, at the cross of Calvary.

But I think of Him too on the third day when He arose again triumphant over the grave and over all the powers of evil. As He ascended into heaven, all heaven's host fell down to worship the Lamb of God who had been slain, and who had risen again. Here is the glory of God in the face of our ascended Lord! And in my mind I see it even more glorious on that day when He shall come as

King of kings and Lord of lords, and before Him every knee shall bow and every tongue confess that He is Lord; and I can see that same Lord Jesus and the glory of God shining through.

"Now," says Paul, in effect, "this is what I have seen, this is the revelation that has come to my heart, this is the ministry that I have received. As the sum and substance of it, there is a person, there is a life, there is God manifest in Jesus Christ. The light of the knowledge of the glory of God in the face of Jesus Christ has shined into my heart and I have looked into His face. I have seen His lowliness, His leisureliness, His authority over the powers of sin, His release of life from the empty tomb, His ascension into heaven—and one day I will see Him come back. Yes, I have seen the glory of God in the face of Jesus Christ, and I have received this ministry, for because of Calvary there has been a Pentecost, and the ascended Lord has brought me in repentance to His feet, and now it is Christ *in* me."

Such is the character of our ministry: the glory of God in the face of Jesus Christ. Have you seen God in Jesus? All that you could ever know of God you will find in the Lord Jesus Christ. Have you gazed into His face and recognized His grace and love, His tenderness and authority, His atonement, His resurrection, His ascension, and His reign in glory? One day He is coming back. All the sum and substance of what God has to say to this world is said when He has spoken in these last days in His Son. Have you looked into the face of Jesus Christ like that, and has that look brought you in submission to His feet to receive His spirit into your heart, or the life of an indwelling Lord? We have nothing to say or to give to a poor world today except as we have received that ministry in the person of our Lord. I think that if we gazed into His face, we would be a lot more reverent in our living; we would be more careful in our speech and more dignified in our bearing as Christian people. There would be about us the marks of men who have met God in the glory and in the face of Jesus Christ in all His greatness, and this would take the lightness and the superficiality out of our living. The church which broke the Saviour's heart was full of hard work, sacrificial service, patience, and sound doctrine, *but* it had lost its first love, its paramount love. Has something happened to cool *your* ardor? All affection dies if it is not nourished. The beginning of breakdown occurs when we take each other for granted. Love withers if it is not fed, for then it cannot stand up to the strains imposed upon it. That is true spiritually. Your ministry can go to seed or to externals. You may have all the mechanisms, but if the white flame of love has gone, you have fallen. You can be a fallen Christian without a stain on your moral character if the fire has gone out.

If you have seen the glory of God in the face of Jesus Christ, you will never be the same again. But this is not something to enjoy selfishly, for Paul speaks about the communication of this ministry: "For we preach not ourselves, but Christ Jesus the Lord; and ourselves your servants for Jesus' sake" (v. 5). This is Paul's concern constantly, for he adds, " . . . that the life also of Jesus might be made manifest in our body . . . that the life also of Jesus might be made manifest in our mortal flesh" (v. 10-11).

Paul has received this ministry—and so have you—not for selfish enjoyment but for its communication through you to others. And it is the unique responsibility (I say "unique" because nobody else is capable of doing it) of the man redeemed and indwelt by Christ to communicate Him to others. That which lies at the root of all suffering and unhappiness, that which is at the bottom of so much tension in personal living and church life, is not so much some things outside ourselves, but it is ourselves, individually. It is the self which is always seeking to be exalted, praised, vindicated, with the result that Christ Himself is put into the background. This is the principle of life upon which the world lives, in which it exalts self and dethrones God. Now, when you become a Christian, you are redeemed in order that this new principle of life—in which you no longer proclaim yourself but proclaim Christ Jesus the Lord—becomes that which is communicated to others.

Let me ask you lovingly and earnestly, Whom are you proclaiming, not only by speech but by living? Let us remind ourselves of the glory of God in the face of Jesus Christ; this glory must shine through the Christian, this ministry must be communicated so that we may make manifest in these mortal bodies of ours the life of the Lord Jesus. In other words, there is a life to be revealed—not just a system of theology, but a life, a character, a principle of action—through the Christian church which is the only hope amid the darkness, immorality, and spiritual bankruptcy of the world today.

We have seen a little glimpse of the glory of God in the face of Jesus Christ as He lay in a manger, as He despised things that we hold so important in life, and as He went right through in His great stoop down to poverty. I wonder if we have anything of that in us today—of that character which despises things that the world holds very close, which enables us to hold lightly all that people hold so tightly to themselves? I wonder if the spirit of the manger, the lowliness and self-humiliation that took our precious Lord right down to such depths, has gripped our hearts and lives as Christian people?

Consider the glory of God in the face of Jesus Christ as He taught and confounded the so-called intellectualism of His day. The Spirit-taught mind is the portion of the person who, through waiting upon God, has been taught by the Spirit of God, and in whose life it is equally true that the foolishness of God is wiser than men, and who has within him the light and enlightenment of soul that can never be obtained from any university anywhere. It has come because it has been imparted by the Holy Spirit into the heart from heaven, "For he shall take of the things of Christ and reveal them unto you. . . . He shall guide you into all truth," in effect, said our Master. He it is who will take of the things of Christ and reveal them to you. He imparts truth to you as no other ever could. Is yours a Spirit-taught mind, a life with the ability in the Holy Spirit to teach what only He can impart?

Again, is there about our lives, as there was about the Lord Jesus (and how this hits home in these days of haste and feverish rush!), a leisureliness of spirit, a quietness of heart, a readiness day by day to wait upon Him for His guidance and direction? Or are we just blustering our way through at our own pace and in our own time, far outmatching the pace of God and leaving behind altogether the guiding of His Spirit? Is yours a leisurely heart today? Spiritual leisureliness and human pressures are not necessarily antagonistic to each other. If there was anybody who knew pressure upon Him, it was the Master, but in the midst of it all there was a divine leisureliness of soul. And this is what a feverish world needs to see and to have revealed to it: that quietness of spirit, that absence of strain and tension, that sense of release in the Spirit of Christ.

> Drop Thy still dews of quietness,
> Till all our strivings cease. . . .
> . . .
> And let our ordered lives confess
> The beauty of Thy peace.

Is there in your heart, as there was in the life of the Lord Jesus, that same sense of authority and power to say "no" to the devil and "yes" to the Lord? Is there that same absolute authority that can keep the flesh in subjection when Satan tempts with all his fiery darts, and that ability to say "yes" to the will of God? As Jesus rebuked the powers of evil, is He by His Spirit rebuking them in your life? Because He has come to dwell in your heart, is there that word of deliverance, that word of power so that when you are faced with all the pressures imaginable, you can stand in the power of God and say "no" to the thing you know is wrong, and "yes" to the Lord?

Is Christ by His life being made manifest through you? Is there any communication of His character through you today? This is why we have had the revelation, and this is why God has shined into our hearts in the light of His knowledge in the glory of the face of Christ. Are you communicating? Whom are we preaching? "We preach not ourselves," says Paul, "but Christ Jesus our Lord." This life is manifest in our mortal flesh so that every child of God, wherever he goes, is a living replica, in some measure at least, of the life of Jesus. This is the great means of communication for which the church exists, and for which you and I are to live day by day.

If there is to be any communication, however, it will prove to be a costly business, and Paul takes the rest of this passage of Scripture to speak to us about the cost of such a life.

J. B. Phillips puts it so graphically: "This priceless treasure we hold, so to speak, in a common earthenware jar—to show that the splendid power of it belongs to God and not to us. We are handicapped on all sides but we are never frustrated: we are puzzled, but never in despair; We are persecuted, but we never have to stand it alone: we may be knocked down but we are never knocked out! Every day we experience something of the death of the Lord Jesus, so that we may also know the power of the life of Jesus in these bodies of ours. We are always facing death, but this means that you know more and more of life."

Here we have brought to us the cost of communication. If we would communicate the character of Jesus (and this is the purpose of our salvation), there is a price we must pay: "So then death worketh in us, but life in you" (v. 12). See it again in the opening part of verses 10 and 11: "Always bearing about in the body the dying of the Lord Jesus, . . . we which live are always delivered unto death for Jesus' sake. . . ."

So Paul tells us a little bit about what it meant to him in order that the character of Christ may get through him and be communicated to others. Why should this be so costly? Because the whole principle of Christian living is totally contrary to the principle on which everyone else lives. The principle of the world is "self-glorification," and the principle of the Christian is "self-crucifixion." The principle of the world is "exalt yourself," and the principle of the Christian is "crucify yourself." The principle of men is greatness, bigness, pomp, and show; the principle of the cross is death. Therefore, whenever a man has seen the glory of God in the face of Jesus Christ and recognizes that this is for communication, at once he comes right into a head-on collision within his own personal living, with all of his principles and motives upon which he has lived until this moment. For, you see—and I hope that every one of us will get this in our souls and that it will burn there like a fire from the Word of God—if there is to be a continual manifestation of Holy Spirit life, there must be a constant submission to the crucifixion of the flesh, not simply sometimes, but *always*.

There is the cost. And the cost in the Christian life does not mean that of necessity the Christian has to give up things which he once enjoyed. You may never go near a motion picture theater; you may be very selective in your use of the television; you may have put a taboo on tobacco and alcohol—but none of these things touches this issue of the price to be paid to communicate the life of Christ to others. It is far deeper than that, for deep down in the Christian's life, always and all the time, there is to be a "no" to every demand that the flesh may make for recognition, and every demand that the flesh may make for approval, and every demand that the flesh may make for vindication. Always the Christian must bear about in his body the marks of the Lord Jesus. There is never a breaking through of communication of His life in your heart and through you to others in heavenly conviction and authority which will challenge or bless them unless at that point there has been a personal Calvary.

Remember the tremendous statement our Lord Jesus made on the last day of the feast: "If any man thirst, let him come unto me, and drink. He that believeth on me, . . . out of his belly shall flow rivers of living water" (John 7: 37-38). And then later, by explanation, John said, " . . . this spake he of the Spirit which they that believe on him should receive: for the Holy Ghost was not yet given; because that Jesus was not yet glorified" (John 7. 39).

Do not let ourselves be involved in a dispensational argument at this point; this is not what is at stake. The issue is whether the life of Jesus Christ is being communicated. Is the Holy Spirit getting through? Is the life of Christ manifest in you day by day in your contact with others? If it is not, it is because Jesus is not yet glorified.

He received of the Father the promise of the Holy Spirit *after* Calvary, and there is no Pentecost without a Calvary. It is of no use crying to God for the unction and power of God the Holy Ghost, because He will constantly point you back again to the cross, and say to you, "If you are prepared to face this principle of always bearing about in your body the death of Jesus Christ, then inevitably the Spirit will get through." That is a heavenly principle.

But somebody may ask, "What do I mean by 'bearing about in the body the dying of the Lord Jesus'?" I could not possibly quote this in terms of personal example to any of you in the situation of your life, but I can give you a simple principle, and I believe you can relate it to your own personal context. Whereas in a given situation of circumstances up to this point, there would naturally and normally be an immediate reaction which reveals self, there is now a reaction which reveals the character of Jesus Christ. Where once you showed resentment, now you are long-suffering. Where once you were angry, now you are gentle. Where once you demanded vindication of your position, now you are happy to leave it all in His hands.

I heard a Christian saying to another Christian, "You know, when so-and-so spoke about me like that, it was only natural for me to react as I did." Exactly—only natural! And that is the level upon which so many professing Christians live. The result is that the Holy Spirit never gets through, and there is no communication or manifestation of the life of Jesus.

Now I complete the circle of the message by going back to the point at which I began. I spoke of the ministry of the Christian life being like the laying down of a rug upon which other people walk and receive comfort and are helped. The whole principle of Christian living as a ministry is a life which reacts like that. In all situations and in every circumstance, there is death to my likes and wishes, to my ideas and ambitions and my rights, for a Christian's only right is to do the will of God. And immediately there is the communication of the life of Jesus Christ!

When Satan comes in like a flood, as he did in attacking our Lord, what is your reaction? Do you reveal self and lose the battle? Or do you reveal Christ and so gain a victory? There is always victory through the simple principle of accepting death and saying, "Lord, in this thing I am helpless, and I die to every effort to overcome. I look up into Thy face and I expect the communication of Holy Spirit life upon the altar of self-crucifixion."

It all comes to this: I see the glory of God in the face of Jesus Christ, in the measure in which I am prepared to die. Upon a crucified life there comes the authority of the Holy Ghost and the communication of the life of Jesus Christ in blessing to others. Why is it that so many Christians behave like kindergarten children? Because they have not seen His face! That is the only hope for the church today. That is basically the only answer—the life of Jesus manifest in this mortal body.

May the Lord give you a ministry that sees the glory of God in the face of Jesus Christ. Then the Lord will enable you to communicate that life as you yourself face the price of it in death.

> And all through life I see a cross—
> Where sons of God yield up their breath;
> There is no gain except by loss;
> There is no life except by death;
> There is no vision but by faith,
> No glory but in bearing shame,
> No justice but in taking blame.
> And that Eternal Saviour saith,
> Be emptied now of right and name.

In an art gallery there is a portrait of the great General Booth, with radiant, glowing face, bent in prayer over an open Bible. One evening, as the janitor was closing that room for the day, and all the crowd had gone, he found an old man gazing at the picture with tears streaming down his face and saying over and over again, "Lord, do it again, do it again." Would you say that to Him now?

For our light affliction, which is but for a moment, worketh for us a far more exceeding and eternal weight of glory; While we look not at the things which are seen, but at the things which are not seen: for the things which are seen are temporal; but the things which are not seen are eternal.

II CORINTHIANS 4: 17-18

6

STRENGTH FOR THE BATTLE

In our previous chapter we underlined the fact that the Christian ministry is not a question for the man in the pulpit only, but because from the moment we receive Christ into our lives as Saviour and Lord, life becomes a ministry. No longer is it an aimless existence to satisfy ourselves; it becomes a ministry for the blessing of other people. The church is the only organization in the world which exists entirely for the sake of those who are not members of it.

Naturally, then, in the sequence of his thought, Paul, having exposed to us the real nature of the ministry and what is involved in it, now tells us how he receives strength for the battle; and that is what we all need to know. If the ministry means that Jesus Christ is to be communicated by the power of His Spirit, and if it is to involve us day by day in the principle of the cross and death to ourselves, how do we receive strength for the battle? What is the secret of motivation? May the Lord make the answer very real and personal to us.

It is fascinating to notice how Paul describes this battle. Let us look at his *description* in verse 17: "For our light affliction, which is but for a moment, worketh for us a far more exceeding and eternal weight of glory." This is what he says the ministry is to him. It involves affliction, and the trouble with so many people is that the affliction has seemed so great and the battle so strong that they have fallen by the wayside. There have been casualties—on the mission field, in home ministry, and in Christian testimony. The battle has been too hot; the enemy fire has been too heavy.

But Paul speaks of the struggle as only a trivial affliction. We are tempted to say that if it was only a light affliction to him, he could not possibly have known our suffering. He could not have known how you have suffered from pain for years, could he? He could not know anything about what you've been through! Light affliction? He's no man to tell us about this if he has known only light affliction. Look at what we've faced!

Oh, but wait! Was this the kind of thing about which Paul was speaking? Not at all. If you want to spell out affliction, you can spell it out over Paul's life in these words: "Are they ministers of Christ? (I speak as a fool) I am more; in labours more abundant, in stripes above measure, in prisons more frequent, in deaths oft. Of the Jews five times received I forty stripes save one. Thrice was I beaten with rods, once was I stoned, thrice I suffered shipwreck, a night and a day I have been in the deep; In journeyings often, in perils of waters, in perils of robbers, in perils by mine own countrymen, in perils by the heathen, in perils in the city, in perils in the wilderness, in perils in the sea, in perils among false brethren; In weariness and painfulness, in watchings often, in hunger and thirst, in fastings often, in cold and nakedness. Beside those things that are without, that which cometh upon me daily, the care of all the churches" (II Corinthians 11: 23-28).

Light affliction? Do you notice that nothing on that list is the kind of thing about which we talk and complain that we have to endure. Remember, though, that Paul was not free from such things. He could speak about "a thorn in the flesh," but this light affliction, as he calls it, is a realm of suffering that came to him simply because he was a Christian. It is the kind of thing that is inevitable the moment a man takes his stand in his life for the thing that is right; the moment his life and character begin to be governed in the light of eternity—from that moment there is affliction, multiplied affliction. This is the kind of thing Paul is talking about. And yet, all that he went through was not really necessary! He could have avoided and escaped every bit of it. So can you; so can I; but if he was to be true to his Master, if he was to be real in his Christian profession, inevitably and constantly this must come to him. And he calls it "light affliction"!

It comes to you when in a godless home you bow your head at a meal and ask a blessing; when for the first moment in a home where people do not understand, you give a word of testimony; when those who love you most begin to laugh at you. It happens in a business when you stand clear of the thing that is disreputable. It happens on the mission field when you refuse to allow yourself to descend

STRENGTH FOR THE BATTLE

to the level of the average Christian life. It happens in daily life, constantly, when a man recognizes that because he belongs to the Lord he must live according to a new principle. From the moment he begins by grace to live Christ, there comes upon him what Paul calls "light affliction."

Because we know that some of this is inevitable, some of us have flinched from it at one time or another. What Paul calls "light affliction" perhaps has been too heavy for us. There have been moments when the affliction and the pressure of it all has been so great that we have given in. We feared the loss of prestige, or the loss of popularity, and because of that some are no longer in the fight as Paul was. They have no heart for battle any more. But this light affliction is purely trivial, that is all. Not only is it trivial; Paul says it is temporary: " . . . light affliction, which is but for a moment . . ." (v. 17).

"Well, Paul, when do you expect to be free from it?"

"At the moment when I see Jesus face to face; not until then. I have in the name of the Lord declared myself on His side. That has meant for me the renouncing of sin, the renouncing of a self-seeking existence, and the beginning of life as a ministry. And because of this I am expecting all through my life to know this light affliction. There will be no escape, but it is only for a moment. In the light of the truth, as I see it, in the light of eternity, it is not going to last long—perhaps a decade, perhaps two decades, I do not know. But how short a time in comparison with eternity! It is only temporary."

Not only that, but it is a transforming affliction, for Paul says it "worketh *for* us a far more exceeding and eternal weight of glory" (v. 17). Notice the contrast: affliction, glory; light affliction, weight of glory; light affliction that is but for a moment, weight of glory that is eternal. This affliction, this thing that happens inevitably because I am a Christian, this constant sense of attack from without and within because I am true to the Lord, is working for me—as it were, hammering out for me—an eternal weight of glory. That is Paul's description of the affliction. That is how he describes the battle: trivial, temporary, transforming. Oh, that heaven could be so real to us that we could live in that sense of liberty and power!

But if this is how he describes the battle, I want to look more closely at the context to learn how Paul finds the secret of deliverance in it. From where does he get his strength? What is it that makes him feel it is so worthwhile to be on the Lord's side even though it brings affliction upon him every day? The kind of suffering about which the unbeliever knows not a thing is happening to the Christian constantly. And Paul says it is working *for* him. It is worth every minute of it, and he is thankful for it. How do you get strength like that for a battle?

Paul would tell us he found it because he looked somewhere. He has looked at the things that are unseen, eternal, not at the things that are seen because they are merely temporal. The word used for "look" in this verse does not mean a casual glance; it is the word you would use if you were to pick up a telescope and try to bring something far away into view and into focus. It is a word that suggests an intense examination, a constant scrutiny, a steady gaze.

Now, Paul says, because I have looked and understood, because I have taken the time not to glance casually at spiritual things, but sat down and thought them through and examined them with my mind and my heart until they came into clear focus, something tremendous has happened in my life. Because I looked so intensely, that look brought conviction. What sort of conviction? "We having the same spirit of faith, according as it is written, I believed, and therefore have I spoken; we also believe, and therefore speak; Knowing that he which raised up the Lord Jesus shall raise up us also by Jesus, and shall present us with you" (vv. 13-14).

"I have looked long into the face of my Lord," says Paul, in effect, "I have looked beyond this earthly life. As I have gazed, I have thought about heaven, and because of this I have a faith like they had in Old Testament times. As they believed, so I believe, and therefore I speak. I have been gripped by this same spirit of faith because this has become a conviction that the God who raised Jesus from the dead is going to raise me also together with you. And one day we are going to meet again in heaven, and stand beside each other as we have ministered to each other here upon earth. We are going to stand together before the judgment seat of Christ to give an account of the things done in our bodies. Because I believe this, I can never be the same man again. No longer can I hold truth as a mere theory; no longer can I simply discuss the correctness of doctrine. I have been gripped by the reality that one day I am going to meet God face to face. I am going to stand before the judgment seat of Christ, and you will stand there too."

But somebody says, "That is not a place to be afraid of—that is the believers' prize day! I shall never be afraid at the great white throne of judgment!" No, bless God, if you are saved by grace and redeemed by blood and your name is written in the Book of Life, you will not be. But surely, then, this place is a place to look forward to, this judgment seat of Christ, where I receive my reward and I am given a position of privilege in heaven.

It is not only that. I ask you to observe what Paul said of it in the following chapter: "Knowing therefore the terror of the Lord . . ." (5: 11). This is the thing that grips the heart of the Apostle. One day he and the Corinthian Christians are going to stand together before the judgment seat of Christ. He has said some things to them and said them very plainly. He talked to them about a brother who had to be excommunicated from the church, and pleaded with them about carnal Christian living, that they might recognize that it is spirituality and not carnality that is going to count. He has done this, and they have misunderstood his apostleship and his message. One day he is going to give an account for his ministry before the judgment seat of Christ, and they are going to give an account concerning their response to it. Because he believes, this eternity has gripped his soul, and the things of time do not matter except that one day when he stands before Christ he shall by His grace be without blame.

" . . . we look not at the things which are seen, but at the things which are not seen. . . ." (4: 18). My friend, it may only be one decade, it may be two—I do not know. But this much I do know— one day pastor and people will stand together before the judgment seat of Christ. That is a very solemn thought to me as I look back over twenty-five years of pastoral ministry. How have I acted? Have I been kind, have I been loving, have I been gracious, have I been Christ-like? Have I lived in a way that is worthy of a servant of God? Have I prayed behind my ministry as I ought to have done? Would there have been far more blessing in London, Chicago, and in Edinburgh than there has been if I had been the man I ought to have been? These things I have been asking myself as my soul has been gripped with this verse.

Lovingly let me ask—How have you reacted and what has been your response to the message through the many years that you may have sat under the ministry of some servant of God? What has been your conversation outside the church concerning the preacher and the leadership? How have you received the ministry? Has it been kind, has it been Christ-like, has it been gracious? God who

raised up Jesus shall also raise me up together with you, and we
shall stand and look into His face. Will I have cause then to hide
my head in shame for my failure to pray, my failure to speak as God
would have me speak, my failure to love as God would have had
me love, my failure to respond in terms of a crucified life? Will you
have cause to be ashamed because you have failed to respond, failed
to love, and failed to pray? You never attend a prayer meeting; you
never stand with others at an open-air meeting. You have not really
been behind your pastor. Have you thought about it in relation to
eternity and the judgment seat of Christ? I think I can truly say I
have taken a look in some measure as Paul did, and I have gazed
long into the face of Jesus, so that the greatest reality is not the
things of time, but the judgment seat of Jesus Christ. Somehow
your life and mine must be regulated by that conviction.

A conviction, yes, but not only as he looked did Paul become
possessed of a conviction; he came to know a compassion in his
heart: "For all things are for your sakes, that the abundant grace
might through the thanksgiving of many redound to the glory of
God" (4: 15).

Paul's light affliction! But he does not want any self-pity, or the
pity of people who come and say, "Paul, I feel sorry for you because
you are going through all this, and you are doing so only because
you are so out-and-out as a man of God. If only you would lower
the standards a little, you would take the heat off." "No," says Paul,
"it is only a light affliction, and I must go right through—and you
see, it is all for your sake."

"Why?"

"So that as you watch me going through it you will see that as I
face it every day of my life an abundance of grace is sent down to
me from heaven. And because that is so, it will result in thanksgiving
on your part, thanksgiving for one who has faced it and gone through
with it, and so it will all redound to the glory of God. Ah, yes, I
have taken a long look as I have thought about the judgment
seat of Christ, and eternity has come very near. Because of that
I have started loving in a new way, and all things are for your
sakes."

Not only is he possessed of this deep conviction that has fashioned
all his life, not only has it resulted in a wonderful compassion as he
recognizes that it is all part of the ministry for their sakes, but he
is possessed of a new courage: "For which cause we faint not; but

though our outward man perish, yet the inward man is renewed day by day" (v. 16).

Yes, the outward man is perishing, and we can all say the same! It is so hard sometimes to keep going and maintain the pace while the outward shell in which we live is decaying.

But something else is also happening: the inner man is being renewed every day. I am receiving strength for the battle, strength to bear the affliction. For this cause I never faint because day by day I am finding an abundance of grace to meet my every need. And therefore, though the outward man is perishing, it is so wonderful to have day by day that fresh touch from the Lord, that fresh supply of manna from heaven, that fresh strength for daily duties so that I know I shall never faint: " . . . as thy days, so shall thy strength be" (Deuteronomy 33: 25); " . . . they that wait upon the Lord shall renew their strength . . ." (Isaiah 40: 31). So Paul would speak to us as he describes the secret of how he finds his strength.

Let me recapitulate. This light affliction which is going to last all our lives has come to us because we have accepted the cross, we have received Christ and crowned Him as our Lord. From henceforth we are living for Him and Him alone, and for His glory. And we know that the gospel of the grace of God makes even greater demands upon us than the law of the Old Testament ever could. The grace that we have received ensures further grace so that we might obey, and this calls for the incessant affliction which comes to a man who, in a world that is all out of gear, is standing for the right, and who in his soul is fighting a battle.

Are you in the battle? Or are you so foolish that you have only looked at the things that are seen? Are you completely given over to the things that are temporal, to the making of money, and to the prosperity of business? Once things were different; you did stand true, but you thought the price was too much to pay, and look at you now—no testimony, never at a prayer meeting, no zeal for God! Yet one day you will lay all aside and leave everything behind, and you do not know when. Have you given yourself to the temporal? Are you in the fight or have you given up? I wonder if there was a point where the heat was turned on in your soul and it proved too great; and you did not listen to the Word which says, "Ye have not yet resisted unto blood, striving against sin" (Hebrews 12: 4). When Satan put the pressure upon your life—perhaps in a moral issue or perhaps in a personal one—and the temptation came at you, you gave in and took your eyes off the Lord Jesus. You settled with the enemy, and gave in to the flesh. So, I repeat, are you in the fight today, or have you given up?

It did not begin at the moment when the heat was really on, or at the moment of some great temptation. Do you know when it began? It began when you preferred the temporal to the eternal. It began when you robbed God of His tithe (Malachi 3: 10). So many give to Him a few spare coins, but how many give what He demands? But I would not speculate. You know and God knows the moment when you turned away from the principle of the cross. You ceased to look at the things that are unseen. Oh, how you have suffered, and how others have suffered! How many have never heard the truth from your lips and will spend eternity in hell because you have failed to speak? You could not speak because your heart was cold. How many men of God (including the preacher) have suffered because you have opposed them at every turn simply because of the stand they take for truth?

It began with a look, as it did with Eve, but it did not end there. And alas! O tragedy of tragedies!—you may be a child of God, redeemed by the Spirit, one who looked to Jesus! But now you have taken your eyes away and you are no longer in the fight. Do you want to get into the fight again? "Turn your eyes upon Jesus, look full in His wonderful face!" And from that moment life takes on a new meaning. Suffering?—yes, but only trivial, merely temporary, and wonderfully transforming. For with that look comes conviction —and life is lived in the light of a judgment day; compassion— and life is lived for Jesus' sake; courage—you faint not, for the inner man is renewed day after day.

For we know that if our earthly house of this tabernacle were dissolved, we have a building of God, an house not made with hands, eternal in the heavens. For in this we groan, earnestly desiring to be clothed upon with our house which is from heaven: If so be that being clothed we shall not be found naked. For we that are in this tabernacle do groan, being burdened: not for that we would be unclothed, but clothed upon, that mortality might be swallowed up of life. Now he that hath wrought us for the selfsame thing is God, who also hath given unto us the earnest of the Spirit. Therefore we are always confident, knowing that, whilst we are at home in the body, we are absent from the Lord: (For we walk by faith, not by sight:) We are confident, I say, and willing rather to be absent from the body, and to be present with the Lord. Wherefore we labour, that, whether present or absent, we may be accepted of him. For we must all appear before the judgment seat of Christ; that every one may receive the things done in his body, according to that he hath done, whether it be good or bad.

II CORINTHIANS 5: 1-10

7

CONFIDENCE AT THE END
OF THE ROAD

WE have seen some of the things which are involved in the commitment of our lives to Christ as revealed by Paul. Nobody—or certainly very few—has ever been buffeted so severely as the Apostle, and similarly very few have had such blessing and have been so triumphant in the midst of their buffeting. The reason was that Paul had learned to look away from things that are temporal to things that are eternal. And this deep gaze brought conviction, enabling him to see that the light affliction is but trivial and temporary, and that it has a transforming power about it because it is working together for the glory of God.

One day, however, buffetings will come to an end, and so will blessings, at least as they are experienced on this earth. Life has a terminus to it, sooner or later. This is the great certainty of the future amidst so much that is uncertain. Therefore I am so glad that Paul, in logical sequence to what he has been saying, now opens his heart to us concerning his attitude toward what lies at the end of the journey. Because of this we find him living in absolute confidence. For instance, we read: "Therefore we are always confident, knowing that, whilst we are at home in the body, we are absent from the Lord" (v. 6); "We are confident, I say, and willing rather to be absent from the body, and to be present with the Lord" (v. 8). For him, life down here meant being present in the body, but absent from his Lord and exiled from heaven. He anticipated a day when that situation would be reversed, when he would be absent from the body and present with the Lord, and concerning this event he had absolute confidence.

As we look at the testimony of this man, we are constrained to ask whether we share the same confidence concerning the end of the

73

journey. And if we do, how has this affected our daily life? Does it make any difference as to how we live and our sense of responsibility toward others and toward the Lord?

Observe first, therefore, that Paul introduces into the picture the possibility of catastrophe. He says, "For we know that if our earthly house of this tabernacle were dissolved . . ." (v. 1). Notice the language he uses to describe his body: this earthly house, this tabernacle —this tent in which he lives.

There are two important things about that statement. In the first place, " . . . if"—he is not quite sure about something. In other words, it is just possible that he may never die at all because he is a believer in the Lord Jesus Christ; and He may come before that day. Therefore, says Paul, he really does not know whether he will go through the valley of the shadow at all.

In the second place, he does not say, " . . . if *I* be dissolved"; he says, " . . . if the earthly house of this tabernacle be dissolved. . . ." In other words, he is out of harm's way altogether. " . . . if our earthly house of this tabernacle were dissolved, we have a building of God, an house not made with hands . . ."—the essential man is going right through the experience without harm, unscathed. This is how Paul regards the possibility of catastrophe, the future, the thing that we call death. " . . . if our earthly house of this tabernacle be *dissolved* . . ."—I pause a minute at this word. It is the strongest word he could use. It is the same word that was used, for example, by our Lord Jesus when He referred to the destruction of the Temple. In Matthew 24: 2 He said, in effect, "Not one stone left but that would be *thrown down*." This is the word Paul is using as he envisages the worst possible thing that could ever happen to him, the possibility that he would suffer a violent death. Remember, it was very possible that such a thing might happen to him. Paul never pampered his body, he did not care for it unduly, he did not bother with it except to buffet it and keep it in subjection lest he should fail in self-discipline. In fact, he used his body simply to blaze out his life as a missionary, that was all. It was a vehicle through which the life of Jesus was being made manifest to others.

As we have already acknowledged, the outer man was perishing. Every day brought a sense of weakness and fatigue, tiredness and exhaustion. Paul knew what it was to be lonely, to experience shipwreck, to be hungry, to be desolate and downtrodden, to be beaten, and to suffer constantly. And his body was being buffeted as very few others ever have been, and always for the cause of Christ.

Therefore he envisages this tremendous thing that might happen: one day his body might be completely destroyed, one day it might be hurled to the ground, one day he might be stoned to death. It is a very good thing, is it not, to bring to your mind the worst possible thing that could ever happen to you and look it in the face? That is the way to deal with your fears. And that is what Paul is doing at this point.

Notice that Paul immediately switches from catastrophe to what I have called the preciousness of a very wonderful contrast.

What does he say? " . . . we have a building of God, an house not made with hands, eternal in the heavens" (v. 1). He does not fear that he is going to roast in purgatory for two thousand years. He does not alarm himself about the possibility of any intermediate stage between this life and heaven. He just contemplates the moving out of one department of life into another—out of a tent into a home; out of a temporary building into a permanent one; out of one that was quite suited for earthly use into one that will be admirably suited for use through all the ages in glory. You ask what it will be like? I dare not embark on that theme except to say that in it you will never be weary, never have pain, never be thirsty or hungry; you will never sin, *and* you will see God face to face and yet be unafraid (Revelation 7: 14-17).

During one of London's air raids in 1944, a lovely house was reduced to a heap of rubble. Buried beneath it was a fine Christian family. The next day a poster was found on a tree in the garden; it said: "He that dwelleth in the secret place of the most High shall abide under the shadow of the Almighty" (Psalm 91: 1).

In the face of the possibility of what could happen to us, here is the contrast. We have a building, one of those mansions about which Jesus spoke: "In my Father's house are many mansions: if it were not so, I would have told you" (John 14: 2). "And I know, says Paul, in effect, "that this is what awaits me. This is that which has been promised to me, and therefore if the worst possible thing happens, I will just go straight out of this tent, leaving it on one side, into a building in which I will live for all eternity—not a building of bricks and mortar, but a body that is gloriously indestructible because it is fashioned like unto His glorious body."

That is a tremendous confidence to have for the last moment of life, is it not? I wonder if you and I have that same confidence concerning death? If we can look it full in the face, if we can consider the worst possible thing that could happen, and yet face it without fear, without any sense of trembling, then we must have absolute confidence that if Jesus does not come first, death—no matter how violent or painful—will simply be the moment when we lay aside this tent in which we live and enter a building which God has prepared for us.

If a man can speak like this, the question that comes to mind immediately is twofold: What is the basis of his confidence? Is he on solid ground? If he *is* so sure of himself, what difference is it going to make for the rest of his life down here? Let me answer the first question first, as Paul tells us about the pledge of his confidence.

Look for instance at verse 5: "Now he that hath wrought us for the selfsame thing is God, who also hath given unto us the earnest of the Spirit." As Paul thinks about the tremendous possibility that confronts him, the experience of leaving a tabernacle and entering into an eternal building, he has absolute confidence about that experience because he knows that God has made us for that purpose. We are not made for this world. This is just a temporary experience, a training ground; this is the place where eternity is decided for all of us; this is the place where decisions are made and characters are formed which affect eternal destinies. But it is only a temporary situation, and God has not made us for this earth. He has made us for heaven. He has made us for Himself. He has wrought us for this selfsame thing. He has formed us for this very purpose. And in order to prove it, He has done a very wonderful thing. He has deigned, in His condescending love, to come to be with us in the tabernacle in which we now live. Therefore, Paul says, he has the earnest of the Spirit. He has the assurance in his heart because within him he had the indwelling of the Spirit of God, the foretaste of glory—" . . . Christ in you, the hope of glory" (Colossians 1: 27). Therefore he never ceased to be confident because in his heart there dwells the living Christ. One day the Comforter whom He has sent to be with him and in him—well, He and Paul will leave this earthly tabernacle together! The Comforter will never leave Paul, for Christ said so: " . . . lo, I am with you alway, even unto the end of the world" (Matthew 28: 20). There is coming a day, Paul says, when the two of them will leave this tabernacle behind, and will go straight into the presence of the Father.

Because of this, says Paul, we groan while we are in the body: "For in this we groan, earnestly desiring to be clothed upon with our house which is from heaven: If so be that being clothed we shall not be found naked" (vv. 2-3). To explain that, he says, "For we that are in this tabernacle do groan, being burdened: not for that we would be unclothed, but clothed upon, that mortality might be swallowed up of life" (v. 4).

Do you see the argument? Paul says that he has the earnest of the Holy Spirit, and because of this he groans—not that one day he will be stripped of everything and left spiritually naked, but that everything that is mortal within shall be swallowed up in life. He has that life now, and the Spirit of Christ within him is battling in his heart for truth and righteousness. There is a constant warfare going on in the soul between good and evil, between right and wrong. But there is coming a day when the Spirit and Paul will leave this body of sin and enter the presence of the Father. Then mortality will be swallowed up in life. There will be no more battle and struggle against temptation, no more crying out to God for deliverance, no more confession of failure and breakdown and sin. That will all be past history, for everything that is mortal within him, says Paul, will be swallowed up in life.

So he has the earnest of the Spirit and His presence is expressed with a sigh that goes up to the throne in heaven from Paul's heart day by day—"Oh, Lord, for that day when this mortal shall be laid aside, when this corruptible shall have put on incorruption, and everything that is mortal in me will be swallowed up! Then there will be no more enemy, no more battle and warfare, no more struggle and temptation!"

Does that sigh ever go up from your heart to heaven? If a man is content with life as it is—content with his earthly surroundings and with temporal things—what evidence is there in such a life that there is the Spirit of God? Is there within your heart that longing to be delivered forever from the conflict and from that which Paul describes as he writes, " . . . the flesh, lusteth against the Spirit, and the Spirit against the flesh . . . so that ye cannot do the things that you would" (Galatians 5: 17)? It will all be over on that day.

Paul says that one basis of assurance is the Spirit within him, the cry that makes him know that this earth is not his home, and he longs for the day when he will meet his Saviour face to face. But that was not the only basis of his assurance. He had met Jesus

Christ face to face, and the assurance that one day the tabernacle would be changed for a home was contained in the promise of the Lord when He said, in effect, "I go to prepare a place for you, that where I am there you may be also. And I will come again and receive you unto myself" (John 14: 2-3). This was the promise vindicated by the fact that on the first Easter morning Christ rose from the tomb. Some little while after He spoke personally to Paul: "Saul, Saul, why persecutest thou me? . . . I am Jesus whom thou persecutest" (Acts 9: 4-5). And from that day on, Paul belonged completely to Christ. He had met the risen Saviour. He had been assured that one day the tabernacle would become a home because he had the earnest of the Spirit within him, he had the promise of Christ, and because he had met the Lord Jesus personally.

As you face the end of an earthly journey, do you have that same pledge of confidence? Have you met the risen Lord? Has there been a moment in your life when you have seen that He indeed has vindicated all His claims to be the Saviour of the world, and that He is alive from the dead? That resurrection demands God's future judgment, and unless you clothe yourself with God's offer of salvation through faith in a crucified, risen Saviour, you become part of that judgment and will be condemned. Have you met the risen Saviour and turned to Him, receiving and trusting Him? Have you that same basis of confidence?

Furthermore, Paul was absolutely confident because of a family relationship: he had received the Spirit of adoption whereby he cried, "Abba, Father!" He knew God so intimately, not as a stranger but as a Father, because he believed in Christ. He was a member of God's great family, and he knew that the Father would one day welcome him home. You see, this man was sure, and he had grounds for his confidence because Father, Son, and Holy Spirit witnessed to him of the absolute assurance that one day he would be with Jesus.

I imagine that most of us—indeed all who read this book, I trust— have that same assurance. You can say, "Yes, I have met Jesus Christ personally in life's journey. He has cleansed me from sin and I have received Him into my life and heart. He is my Saviour. I have the earnest of the Spirit within my heart, and in some measure I know the groaning and discontent with this earthly life—the loneliness, the frustrations, and the longing to be with Christ and with those whom I have loved and who have gone before me. I know all these things, and life becomes more and more restless in my desire to be with Him. I am one of His family and call Him 'Abba, Father.' I have these evidences."

Very well. Let me come to the thing that presses upon my mind and heart most of all. If we have such absolute confidence, then we are able to say, " . . . for I know whom I have believed, and am persuaded that he is able to keep that which I have committed unto him against that day" (II Timothy 1 : 12). If we can face death not as an enemy but as an angel, that will take us out from a life of frustration into a life that is full and complete in the presence of the Lord. If that is so, what difference does it make to us right now?

I want you to notice the priority claims that came to Paul's life. In the face of the tremendous possibility that confronted him, and with the absolute confidence that it would simply usher him into the presence of God, what has he got to say? "Wherefore we labour, that, whether present or absent, we may be accepted of him" (v. 9). Let me clarify one thing lest you misunderstand from the translation of that verse in the *King James Version*. Paul is not suggesting that he is working as a Christian now in order that one day he might be accepted before God. That is what you might think he says, but certainly that is not what he says. The matter of his acceptance before God was settled when he met Jesus Christ and he was "accepted in the beloved." The basis of your acceptance before God is not on the basis of your work or service, but on the basis of His precious blood, of His work for you on which by faith you rely. This is settled.

But what is Paul actually saying? Weymouth's translation is very helpful: "Wherefore we labour, that whether we be present or absent we may be pleasing to Him."

In other words, Paul is saying, "I am sure of heaven, because of what Christ has done for me. I have within me the earnest of the Spirit; I know that God is my Father. But this has not sent me to sleep; it does not carry me to heaven on flowery beds of ease. It has put into my life one master ambition, and I care for nothing else; wherefore I labor that whether I be present in the body or absent, I may be well pleasing to Him."

This is the Christian's concern now. Every other relationship and every other interest of life is motivated by this one: "Will it please my Lord? Is this something that I may do because it pleases Him, or is it something that I just cannot do because it would displease Him?" That is the test.

I wonder how many of us apply this principle in our daily lives—especially, may I venture to say, young people? For instance, what about entertainment, recreation, the motion pictures? People will recommend that you see a film because it has a religious emphasis, and therefore you cannot afford to miss it. Are you quite sure about that? I am not going to spend one penny of the money that God entrusts to me in supporting an industry which is basically rotten, even though occasionally it may produce a film with a religious flavor to satisfy its own conscience. I know perfectly well the kind of thing that the film industry uses as bait to get people inside the theater, and that is no place for a child of God. Can I afford to miss it? Rather, can I afford to go? Does it please Jesus? These are the basic questions.

A man, especially a Christian man in leadership, has to pay the price of leadership and there are some things he cannot afford to do at all. If he is not prepared to pay the price of leadership and walk with God and seek in every decision to please Him, and if he is in any doubt whatsoever to avoid it, the sooner he resigns from the Christian leadership the better. The example is going to count more than anything else.

These are days when a Christian has to watch his every step. With all solemnity I ask you, Does the same tremendous motivating passion grip your life? Do you say that, whether you are present or absent, you labor constantly, and from this you have no vacation? Are you laboring so that one day you may be acceptable to Him, and that every day you may please Him and have His smile upon you? Is the ambition of your life narrowed down to that one thing? And therefore, in every decision you make, every place you go, and everything you think about—your dress, your books, your money, your circumstances—first of all do you ask yourself whether it is pleasing to the Lord? This is not restrictive; rather it is the only way in which Holy Spirit power is released in your life. Fail there and you may have many "things" while lacking the supreme thing—the mark of a man of God.

As I prepared this chapter I asked, "Lord, what have I done this week that has been pleasing to You?" And that question went like a stab into my heart. Has there been a friend who has been in need, and have I spoken to him or her about Christ? Has there been somebody sick or lonely, and have I visited him? Has there been a single thing done this week that would please the Lord? Has there been a word spoken for Jesus in situations which demanded a testimony? Or have I been silent?

Does this motivating passion really grip our hearts because we are sure of the end of the road? If this motive does not grip your life, if there are not accumulating evidences of grace and the life that lives to please the Lord Jesus, if these things are not to be observed at all, then you may talk about faith and you may boast of your spiritual experiences, but you have very serious reasons to question whether you have any life at all. If faith is your assurance concerning death and glory, if your experience of the Spirit of God dwelling within you has not created a flame that burns in your heart until you live for one thing alone—to please Jesus your Lord—then what business do you have to claim to be His child?

Paul was sure about heaven, but he had a great fear, even a terror in his heart. Look at one verse beyond that which we read: "Knowing therefore the terror of the Lord . . ." (v. 11).

Why? Because we must all appear before the judgment seat of Christ, and do you know what that word "appear" means? It means that our motives will be exposed; the things that have lain behind our actions will be revealed; the things that have really governed our lives will be demonstrated. We must all have our lives laid bare before the tribunal of Christ (NEB). And on that day the verdict of Jesus Christ concerning His people will meet with a unanimous "Amen" from the whole universe.

When God promotes or demotes on that day, when He exalts or humbles, when He clothes or strips us of everything we have by profession, the whole creation will acknowledge His justice. "Knowing, therefore," says Paul, "the terror of the Lord, we persuade men. . . ." Is it not strange? A man with confidence, a man with absolute assurance, a man to whom death was simply an entering into a home from a tabernacle, was gripped in his soul by one great ambition—to please God—and yet gripped in his soul by the fear of that day when every motive would be revealed.

God grant that your assurance may be precious to you, that your confidence may be absolutely basic and soundly grounded upon the Word of God, and above all, that there may be evidences in your life which justify your confidence that your one ambition is not to please other people, not to do the thing that is popular, but to please Him who is your Saviour and Lord.

For we must all appear before the judgment seat of Christ; that every one may receive the things done in his body, according to that he hath done, whether it be good or bad. Knowing therefore the terror of the Lord, we persuade men; but we are made manifest unto God; and I trust also are made manifest in your consciences.

II CORINTHIANS 5: 10-11

8

THE JUDGMENT SEAT OF CHRIST

BEFORE studying the verses in II Corinthians 5, I wish to direct your thoughts to other passages which throw some light upon our subject.

First, Romans 14: 10-13: "But why dost thou judge thy brother? or why dost thou set at nought thy brother? for we shall all stand before the judgment seat of Christ. For it is written, As I live, saith the Lord, every knee shall bow to me, and every tongue shall confess to God. So then every one of us shall give account of himself to God. Let us not therefore judge one another any more. . . ."

I Corinthians 3: 12-15: "Now if any man build upon this foundation [Jesus Christ] gold, silver, precious stones, wood, hay, stubble; Every man's work shall be made manifest: for the day shall declare it, because it shall be revealed by fire; and the fire shall try every man's work of what sort it is. If any man's work abide which he hath built thereupon, he shall receive a reward. If any man's work shall be burned, he shall suffer loss: but he himself shall be saved; yet so as by fire."

Now, our text in II Corinthians 5: 10-11: "For we must all appear before the judgment seat of Christ; that every one may receive the things done in his body, according to that he hath done, whether it be good or bad. Knowing therefore the terror of the Lord, we persuade men. . . ." I wonder if there is any other verse in the New Testament which at once comforts and challenges the believer as this one does. Certainly when the Holy Spirit begins to apply the truth of this verse to a man's life, it begins to burn and scorch in his conscience until he begins to see that there is not a day, seven days a week, fifty-two weeks a year, when he lives but that it must be related to that day of which this verse speaks—"For we must all appear before the judgment seat of Christ. . . ."

Of course it is well that we should understand (and I am sure that most of you do) that the judgment seat of Christ referred to in II Corinthians 5 and in the other portions has to do with Christian people. The judgment which awaits the unbeliever (which, for example, is dealt with in Revelation 20) is something very different. Here the issue at stake is our response to the love of God revealed to us in Jesus Christ; in the judgment of the unbelievers, the issue is the ultimate rejection of that love. In the judgment of the believers, God is dealing with people who have established a relationship with Christ; unbelievers have never established that relationship.

That this is so is confirmed, I believe, by the word used in connection with this reference to the judgment seat. The word is different from that which is used in connection with the judgment of the unbeliever. In the case of the unbeliever (Revelation 20) it has to do with punishment and penalty; in the case of the believer the primary meaning has to do with awards, or loss of them, in heaven. But at the same time, having said that, let it also be said that any conception of the judgment seat of Christ which gives us the idea that it is going to be—what shall I say?—a happy prize-day for the Christian when everything else about his life is completely overlooked and forgotten, is far from the truth.

Put the main thoughts together from the opening verses: " . . . every one of us shall give an account of *himself* to God" (Romans 14); " . . . the fire shall try a man's *work* of what sort it is" (I Corinthians 3); " . . . we must all appear before the judgment seat of Christ; that every one may receive the things done in his *body* . . ." (II Corinthians 5). Our body, our work, ourselves—this is an inclusive situation in which the whole redeemed personality of a man indwelt by the Spirit of God is brought personally before the judgment seat of Christ.

The Scriptural emphasis on this subject presents it to us as solemn, indeed, and yet one (if it is rightly understood) which puts passion into our prayers, sacrifice into our service, and a real dedication into our daily living. Are not these qualities—passion, sacrifice, dedication—conspicuous by their absence today? Is that not why our witness is so ineffective? Why are they lacking? Surely because we do not really live in the light of the great day of which we are now thinking. As we seriously consider this appointment with God which awaits every one of us, you will notice some *facts* about it in our text and in the following verse. Just because these facts have gripped Paul's heart, there has come into his soul a holy *fear*: "Knowing therefore the terror of the Lord. . . ." And because of the fear his whole life has been gripped with a new *fervency*: " . . . we persuade men. . . ." To Paul the greatest reality of life is that he is going to account for himself before God. He speaks therefore, about the certainty of this day. He says we *must* appear before the judgment seat of Christ. This is not a possibility, but a certainty; not even a probability, but a definite appointment on the calendar with God.

If we ask why this should be so, we do not have to go very far for the answer. The absolute injustices of life on earth demand that there shall be a day when right is vindicated and wrong is condemned. How many Christian people—and maybe you are among them—have suffered because of motives that were misjudged and actions that were completely misconstrued! How many Christians have lived a whole life of suffering simply because of the damage that has been done to them by somebody else! Many have gone through life with a wound in the soul from which there seems to be no deliverance, no recovery, no forgetfulness! How many have served faithfully and yet have had no recognition, but rather a great deal of abuse! Yes, there is a wonderful comfort in knowing that we *must* appear before the judgment seat of Christ. And many who have spent a lifetime with a sore heart and a sense of utter frustration may find wonderful solace in the assurance that, among the great things that will happen on that day, right will be vindicated and wrong condemned.

But wait a moment—how readily do we pass final judgment upon somebody else when we have very little knowledge of the facts? It is this with which Paul challenges us when he says, " . . . why dost thou judge thy brother? or why dost thou set at nought thy brother? for we shall all stand [together] before the judgment seat of Christ. . . . Every one of us shall give an account of himself to God. Let us not therefore judge one another any more . . ." (Romans 14: 10-13).

In other words, Paul would say to us, "Silence that critical tongue, for we must appear before the judgment seat of Christ. Stop that hobby of judging another, which has become the practice of so many lives, because Christ Himself is at the door. And remember, the one we are judging is our brother. Let the world condemn him if it will, but simply because we are intimately related in Christ let us get alongside him and love him, or at least overlook his failures without seeking to condemn him for his faults. Let no man judge another because one day, in the light of the judgment we have passed on others, every one of us must stand before the judgment seat of Christ. Silence then the censorious tongue. Cast the burdens of the misjudged motive and the misunderstood action at the feet of the Lord and leave them until that day when He shall vindicate, for vengeance is His and He will repay. Such is the certainty of the fact that we must appear before the judgment seat of Christ."

Notice in this verse the universality of it. We must *all* appear. Romans 14: 11 says: "As I live, saith the Lord, every knee shall bow to me, and every tongue shall confess to God." The strong Christian and the weak Christian will stand, for no imagined progress in piety or holiness will exempt us from this personal interview at the judgment seat of Christ, and no weakness will excuse us from it.

The man who has been entrusted with only one talent will appear before the judgment seat of Christ along with the man who has been entrusted with ten. And the leaders, the teachers, the ministers, the elders, the deacons, as well as the more obscure church members (and perhaps the Christian who never had the courage to join any church) must all appear before the judgment seat of Christ to give an account of their stewardship. Not one shall escape, nor will there ever be the possibility of the omission of one from this date on the calendar. We must *all* appear—without exemption or excuse.

You will also note the authority of this day. It is the judgment seat of *Christ*. He will make no mistake, because He discerns the heart. He will impute no wrong where it is not due, and He will give no credit for something that appears to be right while the motive has been sinful. He will search to the very core of every matter, and there will be a standard of perfect justice as the Lord examines the motives for every action of every one of us on that day. "For God shall bring every work into judgment, with every secret thing, whether it be good; or whether it be evil' (Ecclesiastes 12: 14).

Think of the absolute authority of that judgment from which there is no court of appeal—a judgment that is final, and just, and absolutely true; a judgment based not upon appearances, but upon the infinite knowledge of our God and Saviour. Oh, the dreadful, awful, solemn authority of the judgment seat of our Lord!

Further see the individuality of it. " . . . that *everyone* may receive the things done in his body, . . . whether it be good or bad." There is nothing indiscriminate about that. It is not a question of God calling people before Him in terms of a church fellowship or even a Christian family. It is a man and a woman being separated even from the context of their family and standing alone to give an account of himself and herself before God. This is husband and wife, parent and child, separated from each other.

The account is to be given not of a group, but of an individual, and the account is to be given not only of the individual's deeds and thoughts and intentions, but of *himself*: " . . . every one . . . shall give account of himself to God" (Romans 14: 12); " . . . as he thinketh in his heart, so is he" (Proverbs 23: 7); "Thou hast set our iniquities before thee, our secret sins in the light of thy countenance" (Psalm 90: 8). The issue on that day is not the amount of work I have done or the quantity of service I have rendered, but what kind of person I have been as a believer and a Christian.

It is then that we will also have to give an account of our judgment of other people because, the Lord Jesus told us, when we judge another, we lay down His standard of judgment upon us. You remember that He said (Matthew 7: 1-2): "Judge not, that ye be not judged. For with what judgment ye judge, ye shall be judged: and with what measure ye mete, it shall be measured to you again." Very often those who are most censorious in their judgment of other Christians are the very people who need the greatest mercy from God, but their very censoriousness invites God to deal with them in the very same measure that they have dealt with others.

The final fact here is the impartiality of God's judgment—the deeds done in the body, whether they be good or bad.

Do you really feel, as you read the language of these verses and put the teaching together that you can exempt a Christian from the judgment of his sin in that day? Can you possibly escape the conclusion that at the judgment seat of Christ it is the sins of a Christian that will come before His throne for judgment? Of course, I know that our eternal destiny and the eternal punishment of sin was settled when we met God in Jesus Christ at the cross. If that was a real and genuine experience of a new birth, then the sin question in terms of eternal banishment from the presence of God was settled for ever. But as to eternal loss in heaven—that is not settled. The issue is before us. How can you possibly separate sin from works? For the Holy Spirit says that everyone shall give an account of himself, that man's works shall be tried by fire to prove what sort it is, and that every man shall give an account of the deeds done in his body.

You cannot separate sin from works and deeds done in the body, for here is the total judgment of a redeemed soul at the judgment seat of Christ. It is this that confronts every child of God: the things done in the body, whether they be good—gold, silver, and precious stones—or whether they be bad—wood, hay, and stubble.

I like a little comment by Dr. Harry Ironside on this subject. In his study of Paul's First Letter to the Corinthians he said, "Just look at that little word s-o-r-t, sort. It is not how much we have done that is going to count, but it is the quality of what we have done that is going to matter." Every man's work, of what *sort* it is: that which has been for the glory of God—gold, silver, and precious stones, that which has been in the power of self and for the glory of man—wood, hay, and stubble.

We sum up, therefore, what the Bible teaches concerning the judgment seat of Christ which every Christian must face. On that day, the Lord will go over the Christian's life from the moment when His grace met him and saved him from the bondage of sin into salvation in Christ. And the whole of his Christian life will be brought before him as one great panoramic picture. Furthermore, the character of Christ's judgment will be based on a man's judgment of others. When he has been merciful, Christ will be merciful with him. When he has been severe, Christ will be severe with him. When he has forgiven others, Christ will forgive him. When he has not forgiven others, neither will Christ forgive him (Matthew 6: 14-15).

Everything which has been done in dependence upon the Holy Spirit and for the glory of God will merit the "Well done" and receive the reward. Everything which has been done in the energy of the flesh and for the glory of self will be burnt up and destroyed to one's eternal loss. Only that which is of the new life and of the new nature, and which is the outcome of redemption, will get through the fire of that day to the very presence of the King of kings where it will stand forever. But that which has been done in the body, that which has been sinful, that which has been of an unworthy motive, that which has been for the glorification of the flesh shall be on that day destroyed like wood, hay, and stubble.

Do you say, "I am conscious in my life that there has been so much of selfishness and carnality and sin, so much of sheer un-Christ-like behavior. What can I do about it if I am going to face this tremendous day of which you speak?" There is one thing you can do, and you can do it today, right now. You can go into the presence of God in the name of the Lord Jesus and you can judge yourself on every one of those things known to be contrary to His will. Do you remember what Paul says in I Corinthians 11: 31? " . . . if we would judge ourselves, we should not be judged."

In the face of that great day which will come to all, there is one thing that will take the fear out of it, and leave only hope and confidence. If you are prepared today to judge unquestionably in the presence of God that which you know in your life to be out of His will, and that which is sinful and contrary to His purpose for you, then you can trust Him for the cleansing by the precious blood of Christ.

I would say lovingly but firmly that if you are not prepared to do that, you need to question yourself very seriously concerning the genuineness of your conversion. The Apostle John says that he who is born of God does not continue in the practice of sin (I John 3: 9). It would be a sheer contradiction, an impossibility, in the light of the teaching of the Word of God.

If in the course of your Christian life Satan trips you up and causes you to fall and to be ashamed, what must you do? At that moment, in the presence of God, you must judge it as sin; do not ally yourself with it, but judge it and condemn it. Look up into God's face and trust Him for forgiveness and cleansing, pardon and restoration, and power to overcome. But if you refuse to do that, and continue to allow yourself to be the victim of habit and sinfulness, then you will face a dreadful day when you come to meet with God. The time lag between the moment of sinning and the moment of forsaking and confessing is a sure indication of the true nature of a man's walk with God. No one who has enjoyed the intimacy of His presence and the power of His Spirit can endure His absence for long!

Yes, it is a tremendous moment about which Paul speaks and which brings fear into his heart! So, in the light of these facts, let us see the fear that came upon him. It is a fear which is the outcome of recognizing the facts of the great judgment day.

What was the fear that gripped Paul's heart? Well, he has just been speaking of absolute confidence concerning victory over death, so it could not be that. No, Paul's fear is not of hell; it is a fear of heaven. It is a fear of being ashamed at the coming of the Lord. It is a fear of those eyes which are like fire piercing him through and

through, of finding himself in the presence of God with sin in his
life which has never been judged and put away, and which has
never been destroyed in the name of the Lord. It is the fear of
meeting the scorching gaze of a pure and holy God who died and
who lives to keep him. It is the fear of meeting such a God, and
(as he says in I Corinthians 9: 27) finding that, having preached to
others, he himself might become a castaway. It is not a fear of
eternal judgment or of eternal punishment, but the fear of an
eternity in heaven reflecting upon a life that has failed to deal
adequately, in the power that God gives, with the sin which has
constantly beset.

"I fear, therefore I buffet my body and keep it in subjection," says
the Apostle, in effect, "lest having preached to others, I myself might
be disqualified at that great day. I fear; therefore I hasten to forgive
others lest He will not forgive me. I fear; therefore I hasten to judge
all He shows me to be sin in my life and to cease to judge others."
This is a fear of getting into the very presence of God when the
opportunities of confession and repentance are gone, of knowing
that in your heart there has been sin unjudged, and that you have
not been willing to face up to it. I repeat, any man who can face that
happily, and go through life knowing that he is bound by habits
which he has never brought out to be judged, has every right to
question his conversion. Sin, if it is to be forgiven, must be forsaken.
Any other doctrine of forgiveness is a fallacy.

With Paul's fears there came a new fervency: "Therefore, knowing
the fear of the Lord, we persuade men . . ." (II Corinthians 5: 11,
RSV); " . . . every knee shall bow to me, and every tongue shall
confess to God" (Romans 14: 11)—and there is the whole purpose
of the judgment which confronts us all: it is always with the view
toward the total submission of our hearts to His sovereignty and
the confession of His authority. Before Him every knee shall bow,
and every life in the process of time must either bend or break.
It must either bend before the throne or be broken before the justice
of an almighty God.

I am reminded of the language of the Apostle Peter when he says
that the time has come that judgment must begin at the house of
God. If it first begins with us, what shall be the end of those who
obey not the gospel of God? And if the righteous scarcely be saved,
where shall the ungodly and the sinner appear (I Peter 4: 17-18)?

"Therefore, knowing the fear of the Lord, we persuade men, . . ."

says Paul. And the greatest power in his ability to persuade others is that "we are made manifest unto God; and I trust . . . in your consciences." In other words, it is plain to the Lord—and we trust it is also plain to you—that this fact of the judgment seat of Christ has so gripped our hearts that we could not go on living as we have been. The fear of God has brought us to a judgment of sin in our own lives, to a confession and a forsaking of it. We are therefore manifest to God, and we trust that we are manifest also to your own conscience.

This is a solemn subject, and yet it is one that brings great comfort to our hearts if we are prepared to do what Paul did. Are you ready for that accounting day? It could be today, and this may be your last opportunity to confess, to break, to judge yourself, to get right with God, to purify yourself as He is pure, to show mercy and forgiveness to others, that you may qualify to receive all these things from Him. When the opportunity is gone and suddenly (for these things happen unexpectedly) you are ushered into the presence of God, will you go into His presence with sin that is unconfessed and unjudged? With resentment unbroken, with wrong unforgiven, with broken fellowship unrestored? Dare you face that judgment seat with a life that is not right with God? This may be—God only knows—your last opportunity to judge yourself so that you will not be judged.

I am persuaded that if you are prepared to do this, knowing the fear of the Lord, then your power of persuasiveness with others will be tremendous. Remember that the power of your persuasion in other people depends upon your self-judgment in the light of the judgment seat of Christ. Have you ever tried to give testimony to others and to speak to them about Jesus, and found your tongue tied? You have been helpless to speak a word and you have known why, because as you have tried to talk you knew that there was a sin in your life that was unconfessed and unjudged. At that moment you lost all your authority and ability to persuade others.

It is out of the heart that the mouth speaketh. I trust that if this is the last moment any of us might have here on earth, before we stand before the judgment seat of Christ, that in our hearts we have judged ourselves, condemned our sins, refused to live with them, and trust in the blood of Christ to cleanse us, that we might walk with God. So we shall look forward to that judgment seat not as a place of fear, but a place of comfort, where we will look into His face and hear, "Well done!"

For we commend not ourselves again unto you, but give you occasion to glory on our behalf, that ye may have somewhat to answer them which glory in appearance, and not in heart. For whether we be beside ourselves, it is to God: or whether we be sober, it is for your cause. For the love of Christ constraineth us; because we thus judge, that if one died for all, then were all dead: And that he died for all, that they which live should not henceforth live unto themselves, but unto him which died for them, and rose again. Wherefore henceforth know we no man after the flesh: yea, though we have known Christ after the flesh, yet now henceforth know we him no more. Therefore if any man be in Christ, he is a new creature: old things are passed away; behold, all things are become new.

II CORINTHIANS 5: 12-17

9

WHAT KIND OF PEOPLE ARE WE?

PAUL'S definition of a Christian is one of the most dynamic and revealing to be found anywhere in the New Testament: "If any man [not a few people, some of whom would live on one standard and some on another; but—*if any man*] be in Christ [in whose life the great miracle of the new birth has taken place and who has been born from above; like the branch is in the vine and the tree is in the soil, he is in Christ], he is a new creature. . . ." "New," is not used to convey the sense of something recent, as you would buy a new coat to replace an old one; it is used in the sense of becoming a totally different kind of person. At the moment of his new birth there has come to live within him a new life; and because of this he is now governed by a new principle, arrested by a new motive, moving in new company, surrendered to new objectives. This is not a question of a man having reformed his life, nor of some new things that have been added to old things. He has not merely changed a few practices or habits; Paul says that if any man be in Christ, he is a totally different kind of person: " . . . old things are passed away; behold, all things are become new." Notice the contrast: *if any man—all things have become new.*

Here then is the New Testament definition of a Christian. It prompts the question, "What kind of people are we?" In the light of some things that confront us, I believe it is the most significant question of the hour. We, who claim to be in direct succession of the church—in this line of inheritance in which we are also in Christ—and therefore have this same experience, what kind of people are we?

You will notice the sixth verse begins with the word *therefore*, and which obviously implies the outcome of reasoning and argument.

Paul has come to this inevitable conclusion and summation of his argument: if any man is in Christ, then he is a totally different kind of person; and because of it he has certain evidences and characteristics about him. Going back to the context, Paul says in verse 11: " . . . we are made manifest unto God; and I trust also are made manifest in your consciences." In other words, there are some things about us which are so self-evident that we do not have to argue for them; they are manifest to God, and we trust they are manifest to others. But remember, as Paul goes on in his argument, that we are not commending ourselves to others; we are not boasting, but we are giving others some reason to glory on our behalf, and we are answering those who simply judge by outward experiences and profession instead of inward reality.

What are these evidences? First, in Paul's life there is a fervor which was revealed constantly: " . . . the love of Christ constraineth us . . ." (v. 14). In the previous verse he said that some people thought him mad, beside himself (I doubt if that upset him one little bit!). Festus said he was mad when he gave his testimony before the court on one occasion; but Paul no doubt reminded himself that the Lord Jesus was said to be beside Himself. But he gives the reason for this fervor that is revealed in his life; the love of Christ, not Paul's love for Christ. The love of Christ is the love eternal, having no beginning or ending. The love of Christ was long before the foundation of this world. The love of Christ was so utterly selfless, for He had nothing to gain by stooping from the throne to the manger. The love of Christ—why, the highest place that heaven affords was His by sovereign right, but He forsook it all and humbled Himself, and made Himself of no reputation. The love of Christ was so patient; it went on loving even though He came to His own and His own received Him not; yet He loved them to the end. The love of Christ took Him right to the cross, and bared His heart to a spear and the sword of the justice of God that was buried in the body of our Lord Jesus. The love of Christ took Him through all the shame, the reviling, the despisings; and, as Paul sums it up in the last verse of this chapter, this is the love of Christ who was made sin for us.

The Holy Spirit has shown this to Paul; it was no theory to him. He had seen something of the glory of God's love and he knew it was this love that constrains us. The word *constrains* is difficult to translate from the original into the English language as it has many meanings. It could be used to mean, "the love of Christ restrains"—as the reins upon a horse hold him back, hold him in check, keep him on the right path, guide him round the bend. Paul says, in effect, "His power has so got hold of me that the love of Christ keeps me back from doing the thing that otherwise I would do, a thing that would be so shameful as to bring disgrace upon His name."

Another meaning of *constrains* in this verse could be translated, "the love of Christ coerces me." Jamieson, Fawcett, and Brown's commentary upon this verse says that "there is an irresistible object which has so controlled the life of a Christian that he lives with one objective in view to the elimination of any other possible consideration." Just as a river in flood is dammed up and restrained in order to be constrained, taking all its power in increasing flow until it bursts into the ocean, so the love of Christ constrains the man of God.

Something has gripped the Christian and possessed him till the world says he is a fanatic. But someone may be saying, "That is not so; it is faith that saves." Faith does it by love, faith worketh by love, and if your faith has not so got hold of you that in some measure you are gripped like this by the love of Christ, then I say your faith is not saving faith, no matter how orthodox it is. Love always blooms on the plant where faith has taken root in the soil of redemption; and where faith takes root, love springs up and bursts out. This is the fervor that is revealed in Paul's life.

Any man who counts for anything in the world, whether good or bad, is a man controlled by one principle. People who are something for a little while, then something else for a little while longer, and nothing for very long, are just like the jet stream which follows a jet plane and disappears in a moment; it does not count for anything. But there are men who are gripped by one principle—your Caesars, your Alexanders, your Napoleons, your Stalins, your Mussolinis, your Hitlers, your Khrushchevs, and others like them. True, they have been bad men, but they are men of one passion, one principle, one concern. And you also have your Wesleys, your Whitefields, your Judsons, your Finneys, your Moodys, your Studds, your Taylors, your Bonars—men of one passion, but good men.

Paul had looked with Spirit-enlightened eyes into the heart of God, and Christ's love for him gripped him, propelled him, impelled him along one line of life to the exclusion of any other attraction. If any would say that this is awful bondage for the Christian, Paul would answer that he found that which he loved to do was the will of God. That which consumed his whole life and governed all his principles of living, seven days a week, was so tremendous that he had no room for any secondary consideration. There were no rivals in his life; therefore he was the happiest man in the world! Some would say that this kind of religion is too emotional; but wait, for another evidence of this man in whose life there is a total and complete transformation is not only a fervor that reveals, but facts that are recognized. This fervor springs from facts. " . . . because we thus judge [with the Spirit-enlightened minds and eyes], that if one died for all, then were all dead" (v. 14). Paul rejoiced in his constraint; that which gripped his life was not emotion, because it was based upon two dynamic facts, substitution and identification.

> Bearing shame and scoffing rude,
> In my place condemned He stood.
> Sealed my pardon with His blood,
> Hallelujah! What a Saviour.

He died for all! " . . . he was wounded for our transgressions, he was bruised for our iniquities: the chastisement of our peace was upon him . . ." (Isaiah 53: 5). The great fact of the substitutionary death of our Lord Jesus is basic; it puts fire in the heart.

The Christian's fervor also springs from the fact of his identification: " . . . if one [Christ] died for all, then were all dead." Paul explains, in effect: I see in the cross that just as by my first nature I was involved in condemnation, guilt, sin, and judgment, so by my second birth in the Lord Jesus I am involved in a new nature, a new life which has died and risen. I died in Him, I was buried with Him, I rose with Him and ascended with Him; though my feet are on the ground, my heart is in heaven, and the spirit of the risen Christ governs my personality. I am identified with Him. Therefore His victory is my victory; His triumph over temptation is my triumph; His resources are my resources; His grace is my grace; His patience is my patience; His meekness is my meekness; His strength in adversity is mine; His power to overcome is mine. I was one with Adam by my first birth, but I am one with Christ by my second birth.

To illustrate, as Paul was saying, here is a slave who escaped from prison. A search is organized to find him, but when the news is received that the slave is dead, immediately the search is called off. Because of the fact of the slave's death, the law has no more hold on him. It has no more power to enforce its condemnation or its judgment. The man died and therefore he is free. When I was a slave of sin, I had no power, no ability to overcome. Once the things that I would I did not, and the things that I hated I did. Once I was poor, wretched, and vile; and by myself, in the flesh, I am no different now from what I was then. But hallelujah! in Jesus one day I died, and from that moment the law had no more encroachment, no more power—it could not touch me. I was free from it, and in Jesus Christ I was set free not only from its penalty but, praise the Lord! indwelt by a new and mightier power that could overcome all the power of sin in my heart. Do you think I can keep quiet about that?

The thrill of our redemption in Christ is like the constraining force in Paul's life. It burns in us because we have been set free by the blood of Jesus. These are facts, not emotions, that are recognized; and because of them the love of Christ has pressurized our lives along one channel.

In the third place, there is a fellowship that is recognized by the Christian in daily life: " . . . he died for all, that they which live should not henceforth live unto themselves, but unto him which died for them, and rose again. Wherefore henceforth know we no man after the flesh: yea, though we have known Christ after the flesh, yet now henceforth know we him no more" (vv. 15-16). Perhaps you have never noticed the significance of these two verses. Here is a fellowship that is recognized in the life of a man who is a new creation: a fellowship God-ward and a fellowship earthward; it is vertical and horizontal.

The love *of* Christ for me has been answered in the heart in which He has come to dwell by the love *for* Christ burning like a fire through me. Love begets love. The love of Christ shed abroad by the Holy Spirit brings a response from the regenerate heart. "Love knows no limit to its endurance, no end to its trust, no fading of its hope. It can outlast anything. It is, in fact, the one thing that still stands when all else has fallen" (I Corinthians 13, PHILLIPS). That is the love the Spirit of God has begotten in us because we have been born again with a new nature capable of reloving and sending back to heaven the flame of consecration,

devotion and love to Him. It is expressed so beautifully by F. W.
Faber:

> O Jesus, Jesus, dearest Lord, forgive me if I say,
> For very love, Thy sacred name, a thousand times a day,
> I love Thee so, I know not how my transport to control,
> Thy love is like a burning fire within my very soul.
>
> Burn, burn, O love within my heart, burn fiercely night and day,
> Till all the dross of earthly cares is burned and burned away.
> O Jesus, Jesus, sweetest Lord, Who art Thou not to me?
> Each hour brings joy before unknown, each day new liberty.

Is there in your heart such a fellowship? Love has answered love,
deep has called unto deep, and in a life which was so barren, cold,
and dead the Holy Spirit has come and kindled a flame of sacred
love upon the heart. Not that our old nature loves God—it is
incapable of doing so; but the new nature by the Holy Ghost has
put the old in subjection, and love is going up to the throne. We
say to Him:

> My Jesus, I love Thee,
> I know Thou art mine,
> For Thee all the follies
> Of sin I resign.

That fellowship is revealed earthward, too; " . . . henceforth
know we no man after the flesh: yea, though we have known Christ
after the flesh, yet now henceforth know we him no more" (v. 16).
If only the church could get hold of this today! What does it mean?
The old things that marked our friendships and dislikes in our
unconverted days put barriers upon our love, and made forbidden
territories of certain areas: distinction of color, distinction of race
and nationality. And Paul says that we used to know Jesus that way
—but not any more. There was a day when our wonderful Lord,
referring to His crucifixion, looked into the faces of His disciples
and said, in effect, "Now it is better for you that I should go away"
(John 16: 7). I can imagine them saying, "Lord Jesus, that takes
some believing. We talked and walked with You, we have been to
Your college for three years; and is it better for You to go away?"
And Jesus answered, in effect, "If I do not depart, the Comforter

will not come. But if I depart, I will send Him to you, and in that day you shall know that I am in my Father, and you are in Me, and I in you." Henceforth we know not Christ after the flesh. Now we know Him in terms of a spiritual union and oneness which is far greater, far richer. Therefore, because there is a fellowship recognized in heaven, there is a fellowship recognized here. I am not going to know men and love them simply because one is white and another is black. I am going to love them regardless of the color of their skin; I will care for them regardless of their background and race, because this flame has burned through background, tradition, prejudice, and everything until I love my fellow men in Jesus' name as He loves me.

As we ask this question, "What kind of people are we?" I say most earnestly that the future of mankind is in grave peril unless there is to be a revival of Protestant religion. I want to be kind, but I want to express what I believe is the Word of God for this hour when I say that in the last several years Satan has had a wonderful millennium in so-called Christian lands. People have forgotten their spiritual obligations in their enjoyment of material luxury, and they think that they can do anything they please as long as they set aside their quiet time. They can plan any program for young people, or play the fool in any way, as long as they gather around the Word at the end of it. Oh, if ever the devil has done something to the church, he has done it today! The mark of distinction of the child of God (apart, of course, from his attendance at church and membership in Christian organizations) is completely eliminated in our daily living. I say, therefore, that there is a desperate need at this moment for a revival of the kind of Christian faith that brought Luther and others like him to be the men they were.

In the book *Come Wind, Come Weather*, written by Leslie T. Lyall of the China Inland Mission, there is the story of a decade under Communism in China. It tells of the day when Communists came in as angels of light and proposed self-government, self-propagation, self-support for the church. They also promised religious freedom. Communism worked for a while, and then the pressure began and it was discovered that Communism meant total allegiance to the régime and its outlook on life. It meant, too, that Christians who were true to the Word of God lived in fear of imprisonment or banishment to some climate that would probably kill them. In that little group of men and women who have been brainwashed until they have nearly gone mad, there have been those who even today stand for their faith and are true to the Lord. When they meet each other on the street, they say, "Goodbye, we will see you inside next time"—"inside" meaning prison. One girl (whose story is told in the book) was arrested because of her fearless testimony, and when the police came to put the handcuffs on her she held out her arms, her wrists close together, and said, "I am not worthy."

What kind of people are we? I never believe in frightening people, but no one needs to be reminded that the Communist power is an ever-present threat. If they do not attack because they fear retaliation by force, they try to do it by corruption from within. There are deadly forces at work in this world, forces that would squeeze the vitals out of our Christian living. It is time some of us stopped playing at Christianity.

What kind of people are we? Is there a power, something that has you in its grip, something that will push you through without any possible alternative? It is the love of Christ! That is the quality the church of Jesus Christ needs now, for survival, in this hour of human history. The one thing that is going to cripple a nation beyond hope of recovery is the failure of Protestant Christians to be constrained by the love of Christ.

Would you hold out your hands to Jesus today, and let Him put the handcuffs on your wrists, and say, "Lord, I am not worthy, but for Thy sake today I am Thine altogether, driven by one master passion with no rival claim outside the will of God"? I beg of you to consider your daily life in the light of this. I beg of you to consider the rival claims that put you out of God's will and enable you to live a lighthearted, happy-go-lucky Christian life with no burden for living in the center of the will of God. I beg of you, for Jesus' sake and for the sake of your testimony, that you will review these things before it is too late, and that you will bear the mark of a man who is constrained by one mighty principle, the love of Christ. Are you that kind of person?

Therefore if any man be in Christ, he is a new creature: old things are passed away; behold, all things are become new. And all things are of God, who hath reconciled us to himself by Jesus Christ, and hath given to us the ministry of reconciliation; To wit, that God was in Christ, reconciling the world unto himself, not imputing their trespasses unto them; and hath committed unto us the word of reconciliation. Now then we are ambassadors for Christ, as though God did beseech you by us: we pray you in Christ's stead, be ye reconciled to God. For he hath made him to be sin for us, who knew no sin; that we might be made the righteousness of God in him.

II CORINTHIANS 5: 17-21

IO

GET RIGHT WITH GOD

WHAT wonderful words these are! I believe it is upon the reception of such words spoken with authority from the throne of God in heaven that our future in this generation and for all time depends. Indeed, without them, any promise of man—whoever he may be— is merely a straw in the wind. They are wonderful, not only because of what they reveal to us of the servants who are described as His ambassadors, but because of what they reveal of God Himself: " . . . as though God did beseech you by us. . . ." Here is God pleading; and with whom is He pleading? You notice in this verse that the word *you* is set in italics in both instances, and the verse would really read this way: "Now then we are ambassadors for Christ, as though God did beseech by us: we pray in Christ's stead, be ye reconciled to God."

Paul was speaking in verse 19 of a world that was already reconciled to God. Notice therefore that the plea here is not to a few people; it is as world-wide as God's tremendous power to reconcile the human race at the cross. The Corinthian church had already been reconciled; that is the whole implication of the message. They had experienced something of the buffeting as well as the blessings of the Christian life, which is what Paul has been talking about and what we have been considering. They have known something of the affliction which is but for a moment—a lifetime on earth—the affliction that comes from being a Christian, from standing for God against sin. They face the judgment seat of Christ to give an account of the deeds done in their bodies. Consequently, it is the whole ransomed, redeemed church—reconciled, pardoned, Spirit-filled—that is now committed to the ministry of reconciliation. In other words, the "all things" that are new (because we now belong to the Lord Jesus) combine together with this one supreme purpose to extend to the whole world and are committed to this ministry of reconciliation. This word is to be proclaimed by the church of Jesus Christ, by every redeemed man and woman in whose life all things have become new, and therefore all things are committed to this ministry. From the lips of every child of God there is going out to the millions in the world, "Be ye reconciled to God!" for the pleading of the heart of God is only made known through the lips of ransomed men and women.

Here then is the voice that I pray all may hear at this moment. It is the voice of God, greater and mightier than any man's voice could ever be. Here is the voice that comes from the throne, and it is the pleading voice of the Lord Jesus, because when God pleads, Christ pleads, and when Christ pleads, God pleads. The two are one, as revealed in the language of verse 20: " . . .ambassadors for Christ, . . . we pray you in Christ's stead, be ye reconciled to God." Notice how Paul interchanges *Christ* and *God*; the two are absolutely one. Here is the deity of our Lord revealed; and the great voice that comes from the trinity in heaven declares, "Be ye reconciled to God."

I would stand in a sense of awe and worship, and in reverent amazement. Here is God the omnipotent, pleading Almighty God, our fortress, our deliverer, our strength, to whom the nations are but drops in the bucket, who has all power in heaven and in earth committed to Him—pleading! Surely this plea for the love of another, this begging that an enemy would put away his enmity, is the part of the one who is inferior, the one who has offended, the offender rather than the offended. It is the place of the rebel, not the King, to plead. But here is deity in the person of God in Jesus Christ breaking through all the patterns of human relationships and human precedents; here is God omnipotent in heaven bending down to this little planet in which there has been a total rebellion against His rule, and saying to the rebel race who lie helpless at His feet, "I beg you to be reconciled to God."

Why should God do that? Because the rebel, though he be helpless, chained, and absolutely powerless, is unconquered by heaven until his heart lies broken before God. Can you imagine it? Would to God I had the lips of a Martin Luther, or a John Wesley, or a Dwight Moody, to bring into focus this picture of deity bending down at the feet of rebellious humanity.

Can you imagine the President of the United States taking a

trip across to Cuba and paying a visit to Dr. Castro, and saying, "It was very wrong of you to steal all our property; but now, let us be friends, I beg of you"? Can you imagine the Prime Minister of England going to Egypt and saying to Mr. Nasser, "It was extremely bad of you to take all our property at the Suez Canal; but come, let us be reconciled"? Of course, these are impossibilities. They could not happen because both sides distrust each other, and would have motives that were not perfectly selfless.

Here, however, is God lowering Himself to plead with rebels that they might accept His pardon. Did I say "lowering Himself"? I ought to have said "exalting Himself," because the greatest thing about the love of God is that He stoops down from the throne to where I am today, and He pleads that I be reconciled to God. This represents, if it represents anything, that in the heart of God there is a great longing that the creature He has made might be reconciled to Him.

" . . . we are ambassadors on Christ's behalf . . ." (v. 20, RV), or "we pray on Christ's account," suggests that it means so much to God if the rebel is reconciled. God, who is absolutely self-sufficient and complete in Himself, yet could see only the travail of His soul and could be satisfied only when one man allowed the love of God in Jesus Christ to subdue his heart and silence the rebellion of his will. God is ready to stoop to any humiliation to achieve the reconciliation of the human heart, not for His sake, but for our sake. So intent is His desire for our love—because when we give it to Him and yield it to Him, it means our salvation—that He stoops to any depths in order to sue for our hearts rather than to lose us eternally.

This may raise an objection in the minds of some, and they may say, "I do not know what you are talking about. God is completely silent to me. The thing that baffles me is that He says nothing, He seems indifferent to all our problems and troubles." But wait a moment; if you think that, you are wrong. The message God speaks at this time is, "Be ye reconciled to God," for only in such a reconciliation can there be your deliverance.

But how does God do this? Observe the method He uses. I would remind you of the tears the Lord shed as He looked upon Jerusalem and said, "O Jerusalem, . . . how often would I have gathered thy children together, even as a hen gathereth her chickens under her wings, but ye would not!" (Matthew 23: 37); and it was He who said, "Come unto me, all ye that labour and are heavy laden, and I will give you rest" (Matthew 11 : 28). Oh, the intensity of the desire in the heart of our Lord, and the pain of disappointment as He wept over the city that refused Him!

Consider also the travail that God has experienced. One thing, more than anything else, shows us what God is, what sin is, and what I am—the cross. Paul concludes the great argument of this portion of his letter by saying, " . . . he hath made him to be sin for us, who knew no sin; that we might be made the righteousness of God in him" (v. 21). Is not that the most earnest entreaty of all, the voice that would seek to pierce the darkness of these days? Christ was made sin for us to make reconciliation possible, to banish our rebellion, to put sin out of the sight of God forever. I do not understand it—and I do not expect that any of us will until we get to heaven—but I do know that whereas the offence of one man could involve the whole human race in rebellion, sin, total corruption, and failure, so the obedience of one Man, even obedience unto the death of the cross, can involve the whole human race in a glorious deliverance from the effects of our sin. His obedience can bring us back as reconciled to God, for the whole ugly load of it has been heaped upon His head as He cried, "My God, my God, why hast thou forsaken me?" (Matthew 27: 46). Oh, the travail God experienced to welcome us back!

You may say, "That is all history; it does not work today. I do not think God is speaking now, in spite of what you say." Is He not? Do you mean to tell me that God has not spoken to this nation in the past two decades? How often a very fond and loving mother would seek to draw her little child's heart away from its faults and its sin by redoubling her kindness and love! How eager she is to overlook the faults, if not to excuse them, and to shower love and affection from her mother-heart, so that the little one may respond to her love and despise the things that are spoiling that little life. Is not that what God has done?

We have all deserved His anger, but He has showered upon us in the past quarter of a century providential blessings that are unprecedented in the life of men anywhere in the world. In so many parts of the world you will see poverty, a lack of many of the things that we possess, and you cannot help but come to the conclusion that our merciful Creator has given us good measure, pressed down and running over. He has been doing for us that which He tells us to do: " . . . if thine enemy hunger, feed him; if he thirsts, give him drink; for in so doing thou shalt heap coals of fire upon his head" (Romans 12: 20). In the providential mercy of a loving Creator-God, coals of fire have been heaped upon the heads of many millions of people in this part of the world during recent years. Do you mean to tell me that God has been saying nothing?

You say, God is silent; He has not spoken. Think of the tears God has shed; think of His travail. Then think of the providence God has given; think of the pricks of conscience He has sent to every one of us. How many an inward prick of conscience has accompanied these outward tokens of God's blessings? Do you mean to tell me that you could stand up and deny this? Has there never been a moment in your life when perhaps in time of loneliness, failure, disillusionment, disappointment, sadness, or bereavement there has not been a voice saying, "My son, give Me thine heart"? I am sure that every individual who is loved (and all of us are loved by a loving God) has known moments when God has supported the overwhelming outward evidence of His care by the inward stab of conscience.

How many a strange longing has swept across your soul in the course of your brief life—a longing for companionship, for love, for friendship, for assurance, for someone to whom you could take every care? Have you known a longing to find the strength to get you through, to pick you up and send you on the road again when you are conscious of so much failure and disappointment? Do you mean to tell me that you have never known such a thing? Of course, you have—we all have! How our hearts have echoed the words, "Jesus, Lover of my soul"! We have known it, and have heard His voice and His pleadings, but we have recoiled from it, misunderstood it, because we have not recognized it. We have silenced it and turned away from Him, resisting the spirit of conviction. Yet, while there is yet time, the word is "Be ye reconciled to God!"

What a mystery that a poor little speck of humanity like you or me has the power to lift its puny little self up before the throne of God and say "no" to all His beseeching love! God beseeches because He has no settled relationships between Himself and creatures like us, and He wants to win our love. He cannot force us, He cannot pry open the human heart and force an entrance; the door opens from the inside. "Behold, I stand at the door, and knock: if . . . (Revelation 3: 20). Ask a theologian to explain that *if* and he cannot; none of us could. The living God, who pleads and beseeches, stands at the door and the rest is left with the man on the inside. A mysterious prerogative, an awful responsibility is placed upon every one of us, and the act of refusal is so simple—just do nothing about it and you have done everything.

There are millions of people today, in and out of churches, who, all of their lives, have unconsciously been refusing the pleading of God. They are indifferent and passive; they hear it all often, but it does not produce any effect. This is the sort of thing they expect a preacher to say—he has been taught to say it, and they wonder why he gets so excited and concerned about it. Then, after church, they discuss the weather or some other subject. Once more, not recognizing it as the pleading of God, they recoil against it and refuse it simply by doing nothing. That is the climax of all folly, for refusing His highest and best is choosing certain ruin.

Why is God so persistent? Why is He so patient, so passionate in His entreaties? Why must Jesus Christ die? Why was it worth His while to bear the punishment of our sins? Why does He let us go through this and that? Why does He speak to our hearts, time and time again, in spite of our refusals? I will tell you why. Because He says, " . . . they that hate me love death" (Proverbs 8: 36).

There is no alternative. "Be ye reconciled to God," for enmity is ruin and destruction. There can be no stronger proof of the sinfulness of the human heart than that God should plead and I should steel my heart and deafen my ear to His voice. The crown of all sin, the disclosure of what we really are by nature, the secret of all true character is that light has come into the world, but men have preferred darkness to light because their deeds are evil. " . . . choose you this day whom ye will serve . . ." (Joshua 24: 15). I beg you, in Christ's stead, be ye reconciled to God!

We then, as workers together with him, beseech you also that ye receive not the grace of God in vain. (For he saith, I have heard thee in a time accepted, and in the day of salvation have I succoured thee: behold, now is the accepted time; behold, now is the day of salvation.) Giving no offence in any thing, that the ministry be not blamed: but in all things approving ourselves as the ministers of God, in much patience, in afflictions, in necessities, in distresses, In stripes, in imprisonments, in tumults, in labours, in watchings, in fastings; By pureness, by knowledge, by longsuffering, by kindness, by the Holy Ghost, by love unfeigned, By the word of truth, by the power of God, by the armour of righteousness on the right hand and on the left, By honour and dishonour, by evil report and good report: as deceivers, and yet true; As unknown, and yet well known; as dying, and, behold, we live; as chastened, and not killed; As sorrowful, yet always rejoicing; as poor, yet making many rich; as having nothing, and yet possessing all things.

II CORINTHIANS 6: 1-10

II

A CALL TO CONSISTENCY

PAUL'S first letter to the church at Corinth had as its great concern the discipline of the church. His second letter has as its chief burden the discipline of a Christian, and the first five chapters, which we have already studied, have had to do with this great theme of discipleship.

In II Corinthians, chapter 1 is the price of discipleship: " . . . we had the sentence of death in ourselves, that we should not trust in ourselves, but in God which raiseth the dead." The theme of the second chapter is that of the privilege of discipleship: " . . . we are unto God a sweet savour of Christ, in them that are saved, and in them that perish." What a privilege!

Then in the third chapter there is what I call the practice of discipleship: " . . . we all, with open face beholding as in a glass the glory of the Lord, are changed into the same image from glory to glory. . . ."

In the fourth chapter we have the power of discipleship, "For our light affliction, which is but for a moment, worketh for us a far more exceeding and eternal weight of glory," and we recalled in that chapter that what Paul called *light* we would call almost overwhelming. But such was Christ's power in Paul's life as a Christian that it was to him a light affliction which lasted but for a moment and worked for him a far more exceeding and eternal weight of glory.

The fifth chapter has as its theme the purpose of discipleship. In order that every Christian who has been trained in this school, who has been facing the implication of the Christian life in the day in which he lives, that from each one there may go out to a world that is rejecting the Lord Jesus and upon which the judgment of God is surely coming imminently, the great appeal, " . . . we pray you in Christ's stead, be ye reconciled to God."

Now Paul turns in chapter six to the church with another great appeal: "We then, as workers together with him, beseech you also that ye receive not the grace of God in vain"—receive not in vain the grace of this privilege of discipleship, and all that has been made known to us in Jesus Christ. In this chapter his appeal is centered in the first ten verses upon the call to consistency in the Christian life, and then, in the closing part of the chapter, to an appeal for consecration in the Christian life.

As we consider these opening verses, the first thrust to our hearts is introduced to us by the very suggestiveness of our text. It is a peril that lies in the path of every believer, that of dissipating the grace of God: I beseech you . . . that you receive not the grace of God in vain." All His fullness of blessing, all that is ours in Christ that Paul has been describing, this wonderful life with its ministry of reconciliation, with its price of discipleship and its privilege, its practice, its power—take heed that you receive not these things in vain. I repeat, there is a tremendous peril to the Christian that he may dissipate the grace of God.

I suggest that Paul brings to us here two ways in which this dissipation occurs, and by which we fling away God's grace until it becomes utterly irrelevant and meaningless to us. The first way is suggested to us in the second verse of this chapter, enclosed in brackets, when he is quoting from Isaiah 49: 8, " . . . I have heard thee in a time accepted, and in the day of salvation have I succoured thee: behold, now is the accepted time; behold, now is the day of salvation." While that verse may say many things to many people, it has been saying one thing to me that I know it will say to anyone who is not a believer in Christ, that God's time for reconciliation is now. God's time for receiving life in Jesus Christ is today. If you shall hear His voice, harden not your hearts. The devil's time is always tomorrow; God's time is always today.

Yes, the verse says that. But the Spirit of God has been saying more to me: it is saying that God's grace is always coming to my heart and life in a very wonderful and blessed experience of now. Yesterday's grace is totally inadequate for the burden of today, and if I do not learn to lay hold of heavenly resources every day of my life for the little things as well as the big things, as a Christian I soon become stale, barren, and fruitless in the service of the Lord.

Now is the day of salvation. This is the moment in which God's grace is available to me, in any emergency and in any situation. Thank heaven that whatever the surprises, disappointments, and problems that may come to me at any moment of any day, I do not have to look back and say, "What did the preacher say last Sunday that I should do at this moment? What was it that I did when I faced that situation last week?" No, for any situation, at any moment, as I live day by day in His will, now is the day of salvation.

Charles Inwood has described this in a lovely way: "It is a constant appropriation of a constant supply from Jesus Christ Himself. As I believe, I receive; and as I go on believing, I go on receiving." Speedily I will dissipate the grace of God, its supply will become stale and ineffective in my life, and I will become totally barren if I am always looking back upon the past, drawing upon past experiences and old deliverances, . . . if I am not proving that the God of Jacob and the God of Elijah and the God of Moody and Taylor is my God today, with grace sufficient at every moment to meet every need. Beware that you do not dissipate the grace of God by failing moment by moment to lay hold of a heavenly supply.

There is another way that the grace of God can be dissipated suggested to us by the third verse. It occurs when we make the grace of God the ground for continuation in sin, "Giving no offence in any thing, that the ministry be not blamed." When he uses the word *ministry*, Paul is not speaking specially of a few people who are called ministers. I reminded you previously that when a man is born again he enters into a life of ministry and service. " . . . as the Son of man came not to be ministered unto, but to minister, and to give his life a ransom for many," so every Christian is called upon to live sacramentally, as broken bread and poured-out wine, in the service of the King of kings and for the blessing of his fellowmen. Now, says Paul, let this ministry of yours never be blamed and held in low repute: "give offence in nothing." You will speedily dissipate the grace of God if you imagine that all His fullness of supply is being given to you to excuse you and to allow you to continue living in sin and failure.

I know full well that God's grace comes to us as a free gift and His salvation is His precious gift through the blood of Jesus in response to our repentance—I am fully aware of this—but I am also aware that my Bible tells me that though the law of God may make heavy demands upon an individual, the grace of God makes bigger demands. If a man would live day by day by grace for the glory of God, the demands made upon him are of a deeper and a more complete and fuller level than the law could ever make. We will see in a moment the wonderful fact that when the grace of God makes the demand, grace meets the demand with heavenly supply. Therefore I must be careful that I do not dissipate the grace of God by making His grace an excuse to continue living in sin.

So Paul, in his appeal for consistency, begins by disclosing the peril of dissipating the grace of God. Let us learn, moment by moment, to lay hold upon heavenly supply; let us learn to regard the grace of God as a great lever that gets underneath and lifts us up constantly to a deeper, higher, fuller life in Jesus Christ that enables us to say, " . . . in all these things [by His grace] we are more than conquerors. . . ."

If Paul makes this appeal for consistency, warning us of the peril of dissipating the grace of God, I find myself asking a question: "Where would I expect that in normal situations the grace of God would be revealed in my life?" The answer to that question is found in verses 4-10, which provide a platform for the display of God's grace in your life. To be quite honest with you, I have to admit that Paul leaves me right behind! As I listen to him opening his heart about what it means to be a Christian, somehow he is far ahead and I have to stand back and admire it all, and recognize that this is an experience through which I have never yet passed and to which I have never yet come. Nevertheless it is an ideal my heart would long to attain. I am sure that I am in the same school and that I understand the principle, therefore I am careful to say, not as though I had already attained, or were already perfect, but this one thing I do, I press toward the mark.

What is the platform upon which the grace of God is displayed in a man's life? What are the areas in which one might expect to see grace working itself out in that life? Is it in some time of great crisis? Is it in the ministry of a pulpit? Is it in some great public work, through some business career or public situation? No, for I find that Paul opens his heart and draws aside the veil to show us some things that are the platform upon which grace is being displayed, things that lie right behind the scenes, that tell us about the reactions of the man, not when he is in the public arena, but when he is alone with God.

In the first place, there are conditions in our lives which have to be borne patiently, conditions which are the theme of verses 4 and 5. As by grace we learn to bear such conditions patiently, so too there are characteristics in our lives that are going to be revealed (vv. 6, 7). As these characteristics are expressed in our lives, there will be contrasts which will be accepted gladly (vv. 8-10). I want you to notice this very carefully: the first of these conditions has to do with what happens to a man in his body. The second of these conditions is what happens to a man in his mind. The third of these conditions is what happens to the man in his spirit.

Here is the whole platform upon which grace is going to be displayed, upon which all the fullness of God—of which I may lay hold every day so that I will not dissipate His grace—is revealed in power to lift me up and enable me to triumph in every area. Here is the platform, and here is a man, as it were, exposed to the gaze of people, and, most of all, exposed to the scrutiny of heaven. Such is the picture of what grace can do for us today, if we receive it not in vain.

What about the conditions that we must bear patiently? There is a group of nine such conditions; note them carefully: affliction, which means physical suffering; necessities, which means that physically you are put on a spot where there is a desperate need and you do not know how to meet it; distresses, which implies that physically you are in such a place that you do not know where to turn; stripes, which means taking punishments. Do you remember that the Apostle says on one occasion that he took forty stripes five times save one for the gospel's sake, one hundred and ninety-five lashes altogether? One hundred and ninety-five strokes of the whip because he was a Christian. You say that is unknown today. No, it is not. The church in China is going through it all the time, and probably the church in Russia too. This is not history but present-day experience in some places. We may just regard them from a distance in this land, but God only knows what the future holds for the people who are true to Him. Here, however, Paul continues with the conditions to be borne patiently: imprisonments, tumults raised by both Jew and Gentile against him; labors, which means the traveling and work in the spreading and preaching of the gospel; watchings, which means his prayer-life as he watched and waited; fastings, which means his personal life of self-denial, as he denied himself the legitimate for the sake of the Lord Jesus.

Do you see why I say that Paul leaves me behind? I suppose he has left you behind too! Yet there are principles here, which must be learned in daily living, which we must be ready to take, conditions that we must face patiently. If I learn to face them, there are characteristics that are to be exhibited daily. They are given in another cluster of nine conditions. Pureness: let us remember there is no piety without purity; no pious phraseology, no evangelical language however good it may sound, is adequate or has any meaning at all unless it is supported by purity. "Blessed are the pure in heart: for they shall see God." A man who is pure is one who is unspotted from the world. Knowledge: zeal without knowledge is a dangerous thing, and therefore Paul says these characteristics are to be exhibited if the grace of God is not received in vain. Long-suffering means tenderheartedness, bearing hard treatment kindly. Kindness: the word is love, charity. By the Holy Ghost, this is the power and fruit of grace, its very character. Love unfeigned, in which I love not for any wrong motive but simply for the blessing of the other. The word of truth and the power of God, that is the best attack against sin. The armor of righteousness on the right hand and on the left, here is the best defense against temptation that I know. Here then are characteristics that are going to be exhibited on this platform on which a man is living his life.

Paul finally moves on to speak of contrasts that are going to be suffered gladly, and there is another cluster of nine such contrasts. Honor and dishonor: evil report and good report; deceiving and yet true; unknown yet well known; dying and behold we live; chastened but not killed; sorrowful but always rejoicing; poor but making many rich; having nothing but possessing all things—the contrasts.

Put yourself in the place of the man on the platform in the arena of his life as he is observed both from heaven and from earth. From the standpoint of this world the man is dishonorable, deceiving, nobody knows a thing about him (he never gets his name in the headlines!), living a perpetual death, constantly suffering, sorrowful, and so poor he does not possess a single thing. That is the aspect from the standpoint and judgment of the world upon the man who is a disciple and who is receiving not the grace of God in vain. He is not held in a great deal of repute by the world, but heaven looks down upon him and observes not only that he is bearing conditions patiently and revealing certain characteristics, but that he is suffering some contrasts gladly for the gospel's sake. Heaven holds him in high honor, and says that he is true, and though he is being chastened, it is bringing forth fruitfulness in character; though he is dying, the inner man is being renewed day by day; though he is being persecuted he is not being killed; though he is sorrowful, inwardly there is a joy that perhaps the world does not detect. Also he is poor, yes very poor, not merely materially but in so many other ways—but I will tell you something that the Lord sees though the world does not: each night when he goes to bed he is so poor that he has not one little drop of grace left! All the grace of God for that day has gone, he is exhausted and without any reserve for tomorrow. But he just goes to sleep for he knows " . . . as thy days, so shall thy strength be," and he waits until the next morning to be filled up again with God's daily grace. But in the process of being poor, he is making many rich: and though he possesses apparently nothing, yet he has access to the treasure in heaven, and nothing can ever touch that or ever take it away.

Here then is the platform upon which grace is being displayed, the platform of a man's life as he is being surveyed by an unfriendly world. As he is not receiving the grace of God in vain, he is bearing physical suffering patiently, and in his outlook, his thoughts, and his attitudes, he is exhibiting characteristics daily, and he is bearing contrasts between himself and the world gladly.

There is one further thing to say that seems to round it all up concerning this appeal for consistency. I have admitted—and perhaps you have too—that in terms of experience Paul has left us a long way behind. However, in the principle of the thing, by the grace of God, I think I can say that I am following in his track—are you? I see in this passage what I would call the principle of dispensing the grace of God. There is not only the peril of dissipating it and throwing it away, not only the characters of the platform upon which I can display it in every area of life, but the principle upon which God dispenses grace.

In this tremendous, open-hearted statement concerning God's dealing with him, Paul has shown us what a contrast there is between the Christian and the unbeliever—different contrasts and different phases of life—and if there is one thing that seems to me to stand out, it is the spirit of his absolute detachment from the world around him. He holds the things of time so lightly and is concerned about one supreme thing: a life of consistency in which there is detachment in every area of life. This consistency includes several

characteristics. It is exhibiting characteristics that are totally contrary to the spirit of the world. It is bearing these things patiently
while the world would be impatient. It is suffering contrasts where
otherwise he would feel himself so out of place, and doing this
because in his spirit he is a man who is detached.

What do I mean by that? God expends His grace day by day, not
in the public arena or in the crowd, but as He sees His child alone
with Himself. He observes his reactions and his thoughts to suffering
and depression, to pressures, and to the whole spirit of the world
in which he lives. He is advancing in his study and reading of the
Bible; he is advancing in his prayer life; he is advancing in his
witness. In all these contrasts and under all these pressures God
watches this man and sees the discipline of his life.

You may be a woman—He watches you in the kitchen and as the
mother of children; He watches you in your home and longs to see
one in whose life His grace is not being dissipated, but rather a life
where grace is being received gladly, as you live day by day on the
platform of the world.

I want to ask you this very personal question: I do not know
what your life has been like during the past week, or what your
circumstances are at all, but have you advanced? Have you advanced
in your prayer life and your devotional life? Have you gone deeper,
and has there been progress behind the scenes? Has the grace of
God dissipated this week, or has it been laid hold of? Amid all the
pressures that have come upon you and the contrasts you observed
because you are a Christian, and the afflictions which have been
yours, have these things caused you to advance in the things of God?
Has that housewife advanced in grace in her kitchen, in her home,
as a mother of children? Has that businessman, in his office with all
the problems that beset him, experienced a week of progress? God
has been watching and has seen you upon the platform that only
He can see. God dispenses fullness of grace every day to the man
who is (do not misunderstand me) learning to squander it and to
come to Him day by day for more. Such a man is not dissipating
God's grace because he is relying on the past. But he is going deeper
every day into the Word and into prayer, deeper into the Lord,
that there may be further and greater supplies of grace. Thus he is
advancing.

If ever there was a time when the church of Jesus Christ needed
to advance like this, to take root downward and to bear fruit upward,

it is in these days. What has your Bible study been like this week? Just a little casual reading with a casual time of prayer, hurried, unbalanced, unmeaningful, which has not put anything into your life and has not helped? Have you been dissipating His grace by saying to yourself, "Well, I remember at the last Keswick Convention I got a blessing. I will rely upon that and ask the Lord to make it real again"? He will not. It has gone forever, but there is Jesus Christ, who is the same yesterday, today and forever, waiting to dispense grace to those who are prepared to live on this principle, to those who bear outward circumstances patiently, to those whose lives express certain characteristics daily, and in whose lives there is the glad acceptance of the contrast between the spirit of the world and the will of God.

Are you making progress in a life of true consistency?

O ye Corinthian Christians, our mouth is open unto you, our heart is enlarged. Ye are not straitened in us, but ye are straitened in your own bowels. Now for a recompence in the same, (I speak as unto my children), be ye also enlarged. Be ye not unequally yoked together with unbelievers: for what fellowship hath righteousness with unrighteousness? and what communion hath light with darkness? And what concord hath Christ with Belial? or what part hath he that believeth with an infidel? And what agreement hath the temple of God with idols? for ye are the temple of the living God; as God hath said, I will dwell in them, and walk in them; and I will be their God, and they shall be my people. Wherefore come out from among them, and be ye separate, saith the Lord, and touch not the unclean thing; and I will receive you, And will be a Father unto you, and ye shall be my sons and daughters, saith the Lord Almighty.

II CORINTHIANS 6: 11-18

1.2

A CALL TO CONSECRATION

I AM sure that a minister never appears in so forbidding a form, especially to young people, as he does when he comes to deal with this subject of separation, and with the relationship of the Christian to the world in which we live. Many people are almost ready to account him an enemy of their happiness, and call him a kind of promoter of gloom and misery. Immediately they will put up all sorts of defenses, and there springs to their minds a torrent of ideas to refute every argument from the pulpit. For instance, "Narrowness! Legalism! Why shouldn't I? What is the harm in it?"

Now before any of you withdraw into a bomb-proof shelter, I would show you the spirit of Paul when he wrote these words to the Corinthian Christians, for at this point in the letter he suddenly breaks into a passionate appeal for them to separate themselves from every worldly entanglement. They simply must maintain the fundamental opposition which exists between the Christian way of life and that of the world. The two are as irreconcilable—and Paul uses some tremendously graphic contrasts—as light and darkness, God and the devil, faith and unbelief. He well knew that the Christians lived daily in heathen surroundings, and were in grave danger of falling prey to the spirit of the world around them.

This appeal immediately follows the most wonderful outpouring of love from the heart of the Apostle that you would find anywhere in the New Testament, so much so that he almost seems to apologize for it. "Oh ye Corinthians, our mouth is open unto you, our heart is enlarged" (v. 11). In other words, we have told you about our life and how we live it in the opening part of this chapter. We have spoken to you about conditions that we bear patiently, characteristics that we reveal daily, contrasts that we accept gladly, for Jesus' sake and for your sake. We have opened our heart to you completely, not to boast of our spirituality, but to show you that we love you and long for God's best in your lives. "Ye are not straitened in us, but ye are straitened in your own affections [bowels]" (v. 12). In other words, there is no coldness in our hearts towards you; we love you. "I beg of you as my children," Paul says, in effect, "do not be cold in your response! Do not be suspicious of our motives! Let your heart be as wide open to the message of the Word as ours is to you."

It is in that very same spirit that I would minister to you in the things of the Lord, as one member of God's family to others. As one member of a family would warn another member of the family of the things that are likely to throw him off-center in relation to his service for God, so I would speak to you in His name, and ask that you, too, might be enlarged. Do not hide behind some shelter as we come to think of this great subject. Come prepared to receive everything that God has for you in His Son, who purchased you at Calvary. Come as believers, persuaded that there is an experience of fullness of blessing in Christ if we are prepared to walk God's way.

A text like this, if it is to be understood, has to be seen in a far wider context than in its local meaning to the Corinthian church, or even in the immediate situation surrounding us today. If you use these verses simply as an argument for negative approach to almost anything, resulting in a Christian's shutting himself away in a nice little corner all his own labeled "Separated," you do a gross injustice to the whole teaching of the Word of God. I want you to see the greatness and dignity of this text, and therefore to see the greatness and dignity of the Christian life. I want you to see something of its urgent application to your life today.

Is it not a wonderful thing that God has made us a part of His great program of redemption? Surely that is something that must compel our uttermost response in love to Him. Therefore here is a word that is based upon an Old Testament command. It is as old as the dawn of redemption, rooted in Old Testament history. Indeed, it is the substance of the call of Isaiah the prophet: "Depart ye, depart ye, go ye out from thence, touch no unclean thing; go ye out of the midst of her; be ye clean, that bear the vessels of the the Lord" (Isaiah 52: 11).

It was the call of the prophet to the exiles in Babylon. It was the

Word of God to Solomon as he dedicated the Temple: "If my people, which are called by my name, shall humble themselves, and pray, and seek my face, and turn from their wicked ways; then will I hear from heaven, and will forgive their sin, and will heal their land" (II Chronicles 7: 14).

In essence it is the subject of innumerable prophetic appeals in the Word of God, and underlying them all is God's conception of His people as a peculiar treasure for His own enjoyment. He claims Israel for Himself, and He sets them apart from all others. He began it, of course, in a covenant with Abraham, but it was initiated in that day when they were brought out from Egypt under the covering of the blood, and brought through the Red Sea, guided through the wilderness, and brought into the land of fullness of blessing. This was the people who were bound to God by solemn obligation and by sacred rights. He gave them first of all His commandment which was, "I am the Lord thy God, which have brought thee out of the land of Egypt, out of the house of bondage. Thou shalt have no other gods before me" (Exodus 20: 2, 3).

God and His people have always been intended to be all in all to each other. Nothing must ever come between them, and if anything threatens to break that bond, it must be destroyed. Therefore the Canaanites must be rooted out; the high places of idol worship must be cast down; there must be no intermarriage with the heathen. This principle was enforced by prophetic teaching and by bitter experience, until it became the passion of the heart of every Jew. This applies to the appeal of God in Isaiah 52 that carries the conviction—often, I am afraid, in a fanatical spirit—that they stood above all other nations in their separation to God.

You might ask why should this be so? What is God's motive in it all? Well, it is twofold. First, it was for their preservation. They were to be hedged in like a walled garden in order that it might be kept from weeds and from thorns that would choke it. If they were not so sheltered, it would not be long before they would lose their faith, adopt heathen customs, and walk in heathen ways until they became as corrupt as the heathen people around them, and nobody could distinguish the difference between them.

The whole history of Israel is a powerful testimony to that very danger. Time after time, you recall, they were seduced from their real faith, to their own sorrow and bitter experience. Even Solomon had his heart turned away by the fascination of heathen women.

How much more easily then could it happen to the ordinary people? Here was the lifelong struggle of the Jewish people with their tragic failure and downfall; against this the voices of the prophets were raised consistently. It is this that gives a wonderful sense of pathos to the prayer of Ezra. As he came back from captivity and chastisement into the land, and found God's people mingling again in marriage with the heathen, he says with a broken heart as he prays to God, "And after all that is come upon us for our evil deeds, and for our great trespass, seeing that thou our God hast punished us less than our iniquities deserve, and hast given us such deliverance as this; Should we again break thy commandments, and join in affinity with the people of these abominations? wouldest not thou be angry with us till thou hadst consumed us, so that there should be no remnant nor escaping? O Lord God of Israel, thou art righteous: for we remain yet escaped, as it is this day: behold, we are before thee in our trespasses: for we cannot stand before thee because of this" (Ezra 9: 13-15).

It was for the sake of their preservation that God marked them out as a separated people.

But not only so. Second, it was because—may I say it reverently, in the presence of the Lord, and with such a sense of awe in my soul? —of the exclusiveness of God's love. You see, love is possessive, and when the whole heart is given, then the whole heart must be returned. It will be satisfied with nothing less. When God empties heaven of all the glory and gives Himself to the point of bankruptcy, as He gave everything in Jesus Christ at the cross, He will not accept less than all in return. That was the demand that God made upon His redeemed people. His love would have no rival: " . . . the Lord thy God is a jealous God. . . ." In case you think that is an ugly thing to say about God, may I remind you that He was not jealous of other rivals for His sake, but because of what the rivals would do to His people. It was for their sake.

In Old Testament picture language, how wonderfully that love is portrayed to us. It is the love of a father: " . . . Ephraim is my firstborn" (Jeremiah 31: 9). It is the love of a husband: " . . . I am married unto you, saith the Lord" (Jeremiah 3: 14); " . . . thy Maker is thine husband . . ." (Isaiah 54: 5). And that wonderful love of God could stand the strain of His people's sin apparently without limit. It could forgive and restore, because in the amazing drama of Hosea, He says, " . . . behold, I will allure her, and bring her into

the wilderness, and will speak unto her; . . . I will even betroth thee
unto me . . ." (Hosea 2: 14, 20). Can ever that love of God be satisfied
with less than the whole heart, that His people should keep themselves for Him alone?

You see that this great text is rooted in Old Testament revelation,
in the purpose of God for our preservation, and for the satisfaction
of His loving heart. But there is the New Testament interpretation
also, and in this sense the same call is made upon the Christian. The
Jew, of course, gave it a meaning that ministered to their racial
pride, as an excuse for contempt of other people, but all that is done
away in Christ. Yet the same call for separation—not racially or
socially, but in spirit and manner of life—runs right through the
Book. Jesus said, "If the world hate you, ye know that it hated me
before it hated you. If you were of the world, the world would love
his own: but because ye are not of the world, but I have chosen
you out of the world, therefore the world hateth you" (John 15: 18, 19).

That is the whole significance of the cross, the place where Jesus
died! It reminds us that the Lord whom we follow was rejected and
cast out because the spirit of His life, His way and manner of life,
were so totally contrary to the spirit of the world. He said to His
disciples, " . . . if any man will come after me, let him deny himself,
and take up his cross daily, and follow me" (Luke 9: 23). We are
called to take sides with Him against a world that crucified Him.

The New Testament church had no misconception of what He
meant. The writer to the Hebrews says, "Wherefore Jesus also,
that he might sanctify the people with his own blood, suffered
without the gate. Let us go forth therefore unto him without the
camp, bearing his reproach" (Hebrews 13: 12, 13). The Apostle
James takes up the theme, saying, "Pure religion and undefiled
before God and the Father is this, To visit the fatherless and widows
in their affliction, and to keep himself unspotted from the world"
(James 1: 27). Almost in a burst of indignation—which I feel, not
knowing him personally but reading between the lines, James was
quite capable of—he writes, "Ye adulterers and adulteresses, know
ye not that the friendship of the world is enmity with God? who-
soever therefore will be a friend of the world is the enemy of God"
(James 4: 4). I think his pen nearly took fire when he wrote like that!
He was indignant at the possibility of a Christian's getting mixed
up with worldly things.

Paul's whole view of the Christian life rested upon this principle.

"But God forbid that I should glory, save in the cross of our Lord Jesus Christ, by whom the world is crucified unto me, and I unto the world . . . let no man trouble me . . . for I bear in my body the marks of the Lord Jesus" (Galatians 6: 14, 17). And to Paul the gulf between himself and the world was as wide and as final as was death itself.

The Christian is to reckon himself dead unto sin and alive unto God. He is a soldier on active service and therefore he must not entangle himself with the affairs of this life. He is part of a colony of heaven living in an alien, enemy country. He must be subject to the laws of the kingdom of which he is a member, and if you want to know what they are, read the Sermon on the Mount.

The motive in the New Testament is exactly the same as the motive in the Old Testament. First, for our preservation, not racially but spiritually, Jesus prayed—oh that you would catch the anguish in the heart of our precious Lord as He prayed in the last days of His earthly life: "I pray not that thou shouldest take them out of the world, but that thou shouldest keep them from the evil. They are not of the world, even as I am not of the world" (John 17: 15, 16). I was included in that prayer, so were you; is not that wonderful?

God's motive is not only for our preservation and purity, but it is for the satisfaction of the heart of God, for Jesus declared that the first and greatest commandment is, " . . . Thou shalt love the Lord thy God with all thine heart, and with all thy soul, and with all thy mind. . . . Ye cannot serve God and mammon." There can be no rival in the heart to this supreme passion of the love of God, and as Christ loved His own unto the end, He must have our whole love in return. The Holy Spirit uses, in the New Testament, exactly the same symbol of marriage as He uses in the Old Testament: " . . . I have espoused you to one husband, that I may present you as a chaste virgin to Christ. But I fear, lest by any means, as the serpent beguiled Eve . . . so your minds should be corrupted from the simplicity that is in Christ" (II Corinthians 11: 2, 3). What daring language!

Our text is as great, as deep, as wide, as long as all the revelation of God. It is a part of God's mind, heart, and purpose for His people, from the day when He flung the stars in space until the day when we shall see His lovely face, and we are part of that great plan. Therefore, come ye out from among them and be ye separate, saith the Lord Almighty.

Now, wait a minute, that is all very well, but what is the modern significance? The great question is, how are we to apply it today? I hope you read John Bunyan's books: *Pilgrim's Progress, Grace Abounding, Holy War*. Do you remember how Bunyan describes his pilgrims in Vanity Fair? He says of them that they were so different from all the others in their dress, in their speech, in their behavior, and in their contempt for the merchandise of the Fair. Is that relevant in our day? Many would reply no! Oh, that was all right in the dark ages of ancient civilization, but when Christian principles are applied to society in which we live, the call is obsolete.

That is the most dangerous attitude a Christian can take today. It is an attitude that pulls the dynamic power of the church of Jesus Christ right down to the level of a godless, sinful, Christ-rejecting world until she is powerless to lift the world up. We have set aside the call to separation.

To what extent do you think Christian principles are really applied in modern society? I suggest to you that the veneer is very thin, not even more than skin deep. It is the same world that rejected Christ, and it does so still. It is a civilization which is under the judgment of God, and it is doomed to destruction. The Babylon of the Old Testament has its counterpart today, and in the great last Book of the Word of God, in the picture of the overthrow of world civilization, God says: " . . . Come out of her, my people, that ye be not partakers of her sins, and that ye receive not of her plagues. For her sins have reached unto heaven, and God hath remembered her iniquities" (Revelation 18: 4, 5).

It is fantastically absurd—it is worse than that, it is sheer downright sin—for one generation for the sake of its worldly convenience to imagine that it can lower the bars of separation, which are rooted in divine history, and revealed in divine prophecy, when we live in a world that is under God's judgment and doomed to destruction, and when Jesus Christ is returning to take His people home. Yet most Christians are satisfied to conform to custom, to dress, and to the opinion of the day in which we live, and the great command, " . . . be not conformed to this world: but be ye transformed by the renewing of your mind . . ." ceases to grip our hearts, and is regarded as archaic. Indeed, it even creates resentment on the part of those who argue that you must conform if you would live. I wonder who spread that devilish doctrine into the church of Christ today? The great church historian, Honeck, records this: "The church never had so much influence on the world as when she kept herself aloof from it. A church conformed to the world will never lead it; she must be separate if she would live."

Now if that principle is true for this day—as it has certainly been true in every other, and it is certainly yet to be true in those to come till Jesus comes again—then how do I apply it in daily life? Do you know where we have gone wrong, and why we have brought down upon us the scorn of an unbelieving world? We have laid down mechanical rules and lifted a whole row of things that are taboo. Life is far too complex for that. You cannot lift certain things and make separation from them a mark of Christian discipleship. Let me be careful to say, nevertheless, that what Christian people found to be harmful in days gone by, they are most likely to find harmful today. On the other hand, separation such as I am talking about is not a negative thing; it is a positive thing. It is not simply living contrary to the world, as I have said before, putting yourself in a little compartment labeled "Separated," and making everybody mad at you. It is living in harmony with the passion in the heart of God for a world that is lost. That is separation.

Separation is investing every moment of your day, wherever you may be, in the ministry or in secular life (and that is a ministry anyway), to the glory of God in a commitment to His authority and power in your life without reservation. This means that day by day you live in such a way that you refrain from doing anything which would disturb your harmony with God. I am not concerned if people do not like me, and I am unpopular down here. But I am very concerned if I lose the harmony of my relationship with the Holy Spirit. He is a very sensitive Lord.

It is not a question simply of trying to empty your heart and life of every worldly desire—what an awful impossibility! It is rather opening your heart wide to all the love of God in Christ, and letting that love just sweep through you and exercise its expulsive power till your heart is filled with love.

One would think that a fundamentalist group of Christians ought never to need to be told this, but they do! Surely the all-sufficient incentive for a holy life is not legalism but grace, not saying to a young Christian, "Thou shalt not do this or that; thou shalt not go here or there." No, it is saying, "Do you not recognize what God has done for you in Jesus Christ, the privileges that are yours, what it cost Him to forgive you? That which you have taken so easily as

God's gift was purchased with a broken heart, with the God of all the universe giving His life for you outside Jerusalem. You are the temple of the living God."

You see, this is Paul's basis for it (v. 16). A temple is set apart for holy use. In Old Testament days it was in three parts: the outer court of service, the holy place of sacrifice, the holiest of all of worship. You are the temple of the living God and the outer court of your body (the place of service), the inner place (the holy place of your soul where you make decisions, the place of sacrifice), and the holiest of all (your spirit, the place of worship), every bit of you, is set apart in the sight of heaven for holy use. The conduct of the people in the outer court and in the holy place of the Temple was regulated twenty-four hours, day and night, by the awful sense of the presence of the living God in the holiest of all. "I will dwell in them, and walk in them; and I will be their God, and they shall be my people." The whole temple is set apart for His glory.

Are you going to argue about motion pictures? Do not be so absurd! You are set apart for His glory, every bit of you, every minute of every day. Bunyan—forgive me for quoting a favorite author again—says of his unconverted days, "I well remember that though I could myself sin with the greatest delight and ease, yet even then if I saw wicked things practised by those who professed godliness, it made my spirit tremble."

I am not going to lay down any rules for you for it is not law but grace, but I am going to suggest principles about anything in your life which is a problem: Is it to the glory of God for you to do that (I Corinthians 10: 31)? Has it the appearance of evil (II Thessalonians 5: 22)? Is it a stumbling block to a weaker Christian? Beware how you use your liberty in Christ lest a younger brother be caused to offend. Is it a weight? Does it drag you down? Does it make your prayer-life more difficult? Does it dim the vision of your wonderful Saviour? Does it make you less than your best when you are praying and reading the Word? Does it destroy all that, or does it help you see His lovely face? Can you ask His blessing upon it? "The blessing of the Lord, it maketh rich, and he addeth no sorrows. . . ." If you are honest and concerned enough, and deeply devoted enough to the Lord Jesus, when you apply those principles, you will have no doubts whatsoever about anything.

What a promise there is here for obedience (v. 18). What does the Lord offer to His child who is really prepared to face this? Relationship with God is established by faith and commitment to Jesus Christ as Saviour and Lord; but sonship and friendship are the rewards of obedience (John 15: 7). Such a reward is the result of an intimate relationship with the Lord that makes us sensitive to sin. Nothing else matters too much except that there may be in your heart an intimate sense of His nearness and love, His protecting care, His presence and joy. How urgent it is that you might hear His word, for the church of today has lost its savor because it is conformed to the pattern of the age and is no longer marked out as being a separated church. The spirit of the world has poisoned our life and paralyzed our testimony, and on that level the church of today is powerless to do a thing. In the light of the majesty, dignity, and greatness of this text at the very heart of divine revelation, respond to His great love in terms of the cross, and say to Him, "Father, I yield"!

Having therefore these promises, dearly beloved, let us cleanse ourselves from all filthiness of the flesh and spirit, perfecting holiness in the fear of God. Receive us; we have wronged no man, we have corrupted no man, we have defrauded no man. I speak not this to condemn you: for I have said before, that ye are in our hearts to die and live with you. Great is my boldness of speech toward you, great is my glorying of you: I am filled with comfort, I am exceeding joyful in all our tribulation. For, when we were come into Macedonia, our flesh had no rest, but we were troubled on every side; without were fightings, within were fears. Nevertheless God, that comforteth those that are cast down, comforted us by the coming of Titus; And not by his coming only, but by the consolation wherewith he was comforted in you, when he told us your earnest desire, your mourning, your fervent mind toward me; so that I rejoiced the more. For though I made you sorry with a letter, I do not repent, though I did repent: for I perceive that the same epistle hath made you sorry, though it were but for a season. Now I rejoice, not that ye were made sorry, but that ye sorrowed to repentance: for ye were made sorry after a godly manner, that ye might receive damage by us in nothing. For godly sorrow worketh repentance to salvation not to be repented of: but the sorrow of the world worketh death. For behold this selfsame thing, that ye sorrowed after a godly sort, what carefulness it wrought in you, yea, what clearing of yourselves, yea, what indignation, yea, what fear, yea, what vehement desire, yea, what zeal, yea, what revenge! In all things ye have approved yourselves to be clear in this matter. Wherefore, though I wrote unto you, I did it not for his cause that had done the wrong, nor for his cause that suffered wrong, but that our care for you in the sight of God might appear unto you. Therefore we were comforted in your comfort: yea, and exceedingly the more joyed we were for the joy of Titus, because his spirit was refreshed by you all. For if I have boasted any thing to him of you, I am not ashamed; but as we spake all things to you in truth, even so our boasting, which I made before Titus, is found a truth. And his inward affection is more abundant toward you, whilst he remembereth the obedience of you all, how with fear and trembling ye received him. I rejoice therefore that I have confidence in you in all things.

II CORINTHIANS 7: 1-16

13

REVIVAL THROUGH REPENTANCE

AT this point in our studies a remarkable transformation has taken place in the church at Corinth. What wonderful blessings, what things have been happening, how this church has been revived! Once it was carnal, though not when it was founded. No Christian is ever carnal when he begins his Christian life, but he can sink into carnality. And this church had sunk into carnality, but now it is living in great blessing and victory, so that Paul can say, "I rejoice therefore that I have confidence in you in all things" (v. 16).

What a contrast! You remember in I Corinthians he said, " . . . there is among you envying, and strife, and divisions, are ye not carnal . . .?" (I Corinthians 3 : 3). And in chapter 4 he said, " . . . some are puffed up . . ." (v. 18). Phillips uses the expression "like inflated gas bags"! In chapter 6 Paul says: " . . . ye do wrong, and defraud, and that your brethren" (v. 8). But now, " . . . I have confidence in you in all things." What a tremendous transformation! What has happened?

Let Paul tell us in his own language, as I paraphrase the opening verses of this chapter. In the fourth verse he says, in effect, to them, "I speak to you boldly and I glory in you, for you have given me so much comfort. I am joyful in the midst of all my testings and afflictions and tribulations in the ministry. What has happened to you has filled me with joy, and I can tell you when it happened.

"One day I was in the very depths of despair. I was in Macedonia at the time, actually in Philippi, and while there I had no rest for my body, and I was attacked on every side. Without were fightings and within me were all kinds of fears. I was at low ebb. I was really with my back to the wall. But God knows just when to bring us a word of encouragement when we are like that. And at that moment,

Titus arrived on the scene, having come to me from Corinth. Not only was I refreshed because he came to talk and pray with me, but I was so refreshed because of what he told me about you. He told me how you had received my first letter. It had rocked you, and grieved and hurt you. But it had brought you down not in anger, but in utter repentance—not merely sorrow, but real godly repentance. You dealt with the thing about which I had spoken to you, and you have borne ever since all the marks of repentance and the fruit of it in your lives. Because of this, I am both refreshed and encouraged. Why? It's worth all that I have been through in my ministry," says Paul, "to know that this has happened to you."

In other words, here is a church that had existed for quite a while which had slipped from the vision into carnality, but now was living in victory and revival because it had taken a shattering blow in the power of the Holy Spirit from the preacher who himself loved those people so deeply that he says of them in the third verse: "You are in our hearts to die and live with you"—or as the *Amplified New Testament* says: "You are nestling in our hearts, we love you so much."

Paul, who spoke to them like this and loved them so deeply, nevertheless had to face them with some important issues, but they had accepted his rebukes, had listened to his word, and had responded with broken-hearted repentance. Because of this, God had brought them right through into revival. What a wonderful thing true repentance is! Indeed, I believe that all of the gospel can be included in this simple statement. " . . . repentance toward God, and faith toward our Lord Jesus Christ" (Acts 20: 21). True repentance is not only a momentary act, but a constant attitude of the heart.

Do you know this in experience? Do you understand it? You cannot separate faith and repentance. True, repentance inevitably must lead to saving faith. But saving faith can never exist without constant repentance. The gospel which talks much about faith and little about repentance will be free from offence, and will certainly be much easier to preach, but it will be deprived of all heavenly power. For the preacher to say, "peace, peace," when there is no peace is to make himself an ally of unrighteousness, and to make himself guilty of allowing indulgence in sin.

Let us look, therefore, at the significance and the qualities of true repentance. Keeping closely to the context of this chapter, see first the root of repentance. But let me say, by way of explanation, that in thinking about the root of repentance in the Christian life you can never have uniformity of experience. No two people are alike. Perhaps it is just as well! But you are unique, you are different from every other person, and because you are different, your experience with Christ is different.

Isn't it wonderful to think that in the eons of eternity—it will take all eternity to tell—as you meet people in heaven, each one will be able to tell you about the road he came along to meet God in Christ at Calvary, for everyone has come along a different road. There will not be two people with the same testimony in heaven, even among the countless multitudes. There are as many roads that have led people to faith at Calvary as there are Christians. Inevitably there is a big difference between the life of a man who has spent most of his life on Skid Row before his deliverance, and the boy or girl who has had the privilege of the sheltered home and a Christian upbringing. Yes, there may be big differences, but there is always, in every true experience, an element of what Paul calls in this chapter "sorrow toward God" (vv. 9-11).

Quite evidently it is possible for us to be sorry, to be chagrined, to be full of remorse without ever being repentant. It is possible for sorrow to have nothing at all to do with God. That is the difference between true and false repentance. The one puts our sin in the light of God's judgment; the other ignores God altogether. The one grieves with a broken heart over the sin itself; the other is embittered with the consequences of sin, but has never been made to grieve over the act.

You see, crime is one thing, wrongdoing is another, and sin is still another. Crime is an offence against the law of the nation, wrongdoing is an offence against the law of your conscience, but sin is an offence against the law of God. If there is a God and I have personal relationships with Him and His law, to break God's law is much more than offence, it is much more than crime; it is sin!

Repentance begins when a man faces the law of God—the Ten Commandments as amplified in the teaching of the Lord Jesus on the Sermon on the Mount—examines his life alongside that law, and begins to recognize the awfulness of his sin. Nobody ever enters into grace before he has felt the thunder of the law of God and the condemnation of guilt which he cannot escape by any effort of his own. I want to speak confidently in the name of the Lord Jesus, although it is not easy to say: until I have seen sin in the light that

God sees it and have repented of it, I have never entered into the straight gate and the narrow way that leads me to life. No matter how much I have stressed my faith in Jesus, or how much I have said that I believe in Him and His work on the cross, unless I have seen my sin as He sees it and have repented of it, I have never entered into His kingdom.

It is failure not to submit to that truth, and that failure has led to some desperately superficial expressions of so-called conversion. It is like the parable of the sower and the seed of which the Lord Jesus spoke in St. Matthew 13: 20. The seed fell on stony ground and for a while it sprouted and grew, but then was shriveled by the heat of the sun, and having no root, it withered away. As He explained the parable, the Lord said these are they that have received the Word and for a time have rejoiced in it and are thankful for it, but because they have no root in themselves, they have withered.

Unless a man's faith in Jesus Christ is rooted in a soil which is bathed very often with tears, soil that has been broken up from its hardness, soil that has felt the melting and moving of God's Spirit in conviction of sin and has cried, "Oh, God be merciful to me a sinner"—unless faith in Christ is grounded on that soil, it has no root and it will die.

Someone might say to me, "That's all very well. I understand that but, you see, I don't ever feel that I am sorry enough for my sin."

How sorry do you think you have to be? What is the purpose of your sorrow for sin? It is to bring you to trust in the atoning work of our Lord Jesus Christ. It is not your sorrow that cleanses you from sin, but His blood. It is the goodness of God that leads a man to repentance. Has your sorrow for sin led you at one time or another to fling all the burden of it at the feet of a crucified, risen Saviour? If it hasn't, anything short of that is what Paul here calls sorrow that leads to death. This is the root of repentance.

Let me take you to the next step in what Paul has to say about this. Consider the reality of repentance. Clearly this text separates sorrow and repentance. This sorrow is not merely for sin. There are some passages in Scripture which actually attribute repentance to God. For instance, you will recall in the story of Jonah that after he had recovered himself, and set his face again toward Nineveh, he preached there in the power of God and Nineveh repented. And so what happened? " . . . God repented of the evil, that he had said that he would do unto them; and he did it not" (Jonah 3: 10).

Godly sorrow that leads to repentance, therefore, is a sorrow that leads to a change of purpose, of intention, and of action. It is not the sorrow of idle tears; it is not crying by your bedside because once again you have failed; nor is it vain regret, wishing things had never happened, wishing that you could live the moments again. No, it is not that. It is a change of purpose and intentions, a change of direction and action.

Here is the whole difference between the sorrow of the world and that of godly sorrow. The sorrow of the world, the sense of remorse, the sense of failure, the sense of defeat which has come upon everyone of us many times I am sure in the course of our lives—that kind of sorrow leads to despair and unbelief. It often leads to an attempt at reformation, . . . when you set out bravely into a new day saying, "It's never going to happen again!"

But it has happened again. Frustrated by inner corruption and the hopelessness of the battle against inbred sin, many people have been driven to the extreme limit of taking their own lives. When I read in the daily paper the verdict that is passed by the court, "Suicide while the mind was disturbed," my heart aches. I wonder if on that day when the truth is known, it will be the story of some poor fellow or girl who has battled with himself, with his temperament and the downward drag of a sinful nature, who has given it all up as hopeless, and has ended it by committing suicide. That kind of sorrow leads to death.

When sorrow for sin has swept over your heart, and you have been deeply convicted of that which you have done and you have cried like David of old, "Against thee, thee only, have I sinned"; when you have seen your sin not simply as an offence against the law of the land or a rejection of the voice of conscience, but as sin against God; when it is all over and your heart has been broken about it, will you then still be facing the same way? Is it right-about-turn or is it as you were? Has there been a right-about-turn and a complete switch around and now an upward look into the face of the Lord Jesus? This is the reality of repentance—something that has led you to His feet, that has changed the direction of your life, that has caused you to turn right around, and with a broken heart come to Him for cleansing and forgiveness. What is the result of it all? The next step is the main thrust of what Paul has to say: "Godly sorrow worketh repentance to salvation not to be repented of."

What do you think is the connection between repentance and

salvation? Let me answer that question by two sentences which may seem to be contradictory, but which nevertheless get into the heart of the matter. First, you cannot have salvation without repentance. Second, you are not saved because you repent. Does that sound like a hopeless contradiction? Is it simply picking at words? No, it is touching at the heart of the whole matter. You cannot be a Christian without repentance, but you do not become a Christian because you repent.

Let me deal with the first: there is no salvation without forsaking of sin. Beware of making a scapegoat of the grace of God in order to permit you to continue living in personal failure. This is not in our Bible. It is no use for a preacher or for anybody else to say, "Believe! Believe! Believe!" unless he also says, "Let the wicked forsake his way, and the unrighteous man his thoughts: and let him return unto the Lord, . . . for he will abundantly pardon."

It is an absolute, absurd contradiction, a denial of the great purpose of redemption. Surely, it is impossible for God to save a man and to give him deliverance from his sin while at the same time the man insists on holding on to it. Unless you turn from sin as resolutely as you would turn from a serpent if it crept into your room, you cannot enter into the kingdom of God. May the Spirit of God write that upon your heart!

But you do not get salvation by repentance.

> Could my zeal no respite know,
> Could my tears forever flow,
> All for sin could not atone;
> Thou must save, and Thou alone.

We fight and struggle with this, and we will do everything under the sun rather than see this precious truth, that there is repentance in one hand and faith in the other, and repentance hand-in-hand with faith leads a man into the presence of a crucified Christ from whom peace will come immediately into the darkest and lowliest of hearts.

It is not my repentance but His death that is the ground of my salvation, and yet repentance is a condition of being saved. There is no true repentance which does not lead you to a complete trust in a crucified, risen Saviour and the committal of your life to Him. But there is no trust in Him such as that trust without the absolute forsaking of all the things that you know to be wrong.

Now see the result of this in experience, expressed by Paul in the language of verse 11: " . . . behold this selfsame thing . . ."—here is the evidence that you sorrowed after a godly sort. What carefulness! Since that day how careful you have been of the company you keep, of the places you go, of running ahead needlessly into temptation! You have steered clear. You haven't given up friends; they have given you up. You have refused to get yourself involved or entangled again in a situation which would lead you back into the path. What carefulness!

What clearing of yourselves, not in any sense to vindicate yourself by self-justification, but by putting the whole business away forever, dealing with it, finishing with it without compromise. You have been careful not to leave one possible line of retreat. You may have written the letter stopping a friendship or a correspondence, ending the whole affair. You have dealt with it at depth drastically and finally without compromise.

And what indignation! I am glad the Bible allows me to get mad, mad with the devil! To think that he had the audacity to pull me down and make me do that! What indignation, what fury at sin and all the agencies of Satan!

What fear, what reverence, what watchfulness! People will notice a difference in the way you walk and talk, for this experience with God has knocked the flippancy out of your life. It has removed the superficiality and froth from it, and it has made you one who walks in godly fear that Satan might trip you up again.

What a vehement desire, what hunger for a deeper relationship with God! Your concern now is that you might walk with God. And what zeal, what love, what anger for sin, and what zeal for Christian service! Why, the lethargy in service is all gone now. What zeal, what passion is being put into you!

What revenge against sin in all its ways and against your own folly! You are determined that, even though the hour be late, the Lord will restore the year or years that the locust has eaten. These, says Paul, are the things that have happened to you. I rejoice that I have confidence in you in all things. It has been worth all the buffeting that I have taken in my ministry to be able to say this of you again.

If these words have touched your heart, I beg of you do not trifle with the conviction of the Spirit. For if you do, you will only be hardened and will come one step nearer to the sorrow which worketh unto death. Do not trust to your tears, or your resolves, but yield yourself today to the Holy Spirit who convinces of sin and points you to Jesus' blood, and to a trust in Him. Let Him bring you to such repentance that you cast it all at His feet, One whose death for you and life in you by His Spirit gives you deliverance. Then you will have a salvation never to be repented of.

Moreover, brethren, we do you to wit of the grace of God bestowed on the churches of Macedonia; How that in a great trial of affliction the abundance of their joy and their deep poverty abounded unto the riches of their liberality. For to their power, I bear record, yea, and beyond their power they were willing of themselves; Praying us with much intreaty that we would receive the gift, and take upon us the fellowship of the ministering to the saints. And this they did, not as we hoped, but first gave their own selves to the Lord, and unto us by the will of God. Insomuch that we desired Titus, that as he had begun, so he would also finish in you the same grace also. Therefore, as ye abound in every thing, in faith, and utterance, and knowledge, and in all diligence, and in your love to us, see that ye abound in this grace also. I speak not by commandment, but by occasion of the forwardness of others, and to prove the sincerity of your love. For ye know the grace of our Lord Jesus Christ, that, though he was rich, yet for your sakes he became poor, that ye through his poverty might be rich.

II CORINTHIANS 8: 1-9

14

HEAVEN'S MISSIONARY PROGRAM

IN this last half century we have seen two world wars which have rocked civilization to its very foundation; if ever we stood at a critical moment in world history we do today. One crisis seems to follow another until we live in such a moment when either the Lord must soon be coming back, or disaster confronts us. There is just one other alternative and that is, that the Protestant church must recover its vision of God's plan for missionary enterprise that the gospel may reach out to every land in this generation. Another generation would be too late! The return of our Lord, the ruin of our civilization, or the revival of our Protestant faith, resulting in an outpouring of men, money, and equipment to the uttermost parts of the earth while there is yet time—these, I firmly believe, are three alternatives which face us at this moment.

Such revolutionary world changes as have taken place in these last years have left missionary enterprise lagging behind, both in terms of method and in terms of men. Never has there been a time when the church needed more than now a word from the Lord in heaven as to His will, plan, and strategy for this tremendous hour. So much of our Christian living these days lacks any sense of goal or of heavenly directed motive: so much of it is haphazard, without concern, and indifferent to the vital issues of the day.

I was interested to read that the United States spent no less than four billion dollars on what is called "religious and welfare activities," but it spent sixty and a half billion dollars on tobacco and alcohol a year. I wonder if there is any connection between that shattering statement and the fact that they spend seven times as much on church buildings as they do on foreign missions. In a poll of seventy Bible colleges, seminaries, and institutes for the past ten years of about thirty-three thousand graduates, only $9\frac{1}{2}$ per cent have gone to the foreign mission field, $36\frac{1}{2}$ per cent to the home ministry and no less than 53 per cent to secular work. I wonder if there is some connection between indulgence in tobacco and drink in the world, and the lack of vision and of real Holy Ghost concern and a lack of a sense of spiritual values that exists in the church today. The task is overwhelming, but we have a God-given opportunity to seek His face concerning His plan for His people at this moment. God grant we may not miss it, and God grant that as He speaks to us, we may not only hear but that we may respond and take action.

The most vital issue of all is to see to it that our lives are totally adjusted to the principles of heaven's missionary program, and that therefore the over-all missionary enterprise is in line with the pattern and purpose of the mind of God. Only as that is so can we expect to see the unfinished task completed, because He gives His Holy Spirit without measure to them that obey Him, and only Holy Spirit strategy can be adequate for a day like this. In this task we are engaged in a total spiritual campaign against a ruthless and powerful enemy: a spiritual enemy and a powerful foe, whose only superior—let this be noted and underlined—is God the Holy Ghost.

Our text, originally given as the motive for the Corinthian church in a matter of financial responsibility, is in fact the whole principle of the Christian life, and the secret of our strength and strategy for this great moment of missionary opportunity. Paul has spent a good deal of time in appealing for funds for the church in Jerusalem. This is evidence, incidentally, that the church is one and has a world-wide responsibility. Paul quotes the example of the churches in Macedonia, of whom we read in the second verse, in the rather startling paraphrase in Phillips' *Letters to Young Churches*: "Somehow, in most difficult circumstances, their joy and the fact of being down to their last penny themselves, produced a magnificent concern for other people." What a statement! But how did they come to have such a concern, to give so recklessly and in their poverty? It was because they were gripped by the principle of heaven's program as outlined in the ninth verse. It was nothing less than that, and the understanding of what was involved in it, that brought them to the uttermost in surrender and sacrifice. For they " . . . first gave their own selves to the Lord, and unto us by the will of God" (v. 5). Not only did they give themselves to the Lord in commitment but

then, and only then—after having made a total commitment to the
Lord in response to the grace of our Lord Jesus Christ—they gave
themselves to His church as His ambassadors and His servants in
total availability for whatever the will of God might be. Surrender
to Christ was followed by abandonment to the church of Christ
in carrying out the church's program for world evangelization.

Now that same spirit of all-out dedication on every level must
somehow catch all of us, for it lies at the very heart of heaven's
strategy, and for lack of such dedication the cause of Christ is in a
tragic condition today. But how can these things be accomplished?
How can Christian people be stabbed awake and into alertness?
Is it by the high pressure of financial appeals? Is it by masses of
impressive statistics of world needs? Is it by fearful and horrifying
stories, albeit true ones, of the advance of Communism?

No, not by any of these things will you stab the conscience of a
Christian to get into the will of God. You will never do it by impressive statements concerning the need of the world, or of the shortness
of funds. You will do it only when every child of God catches the
glow and the fire which is in the heart of God in His love shed
abroad by the Holy Spirit. You will do it only as you see the grace
of our Lord Jesus Christ that He launched at Bethlehem, continued
at Calvary, and continues today from the throne of heaven, and one
day will complete when He returns. We shall only catch the glow
and fire, and be stabbed awake, when we see what was involved in
God's mighty counterattack against sin and Satan. No, if the church
is going to arise to the tremendous opportunity and challenge of
these days, it will be only as we see and know the grace of our Lord
Jesus Christ, who though He was rich, yet for our sakes became
poor, that we through His poverty might be rich.

Think first of the position of Christ, the pre-eminence of Christ,
if you like. " . . . though he was rich. . . ." How often I have tried
to peer through the mystery of that statement; I have tried to plumb
the depths, but I have to confess to you that my effort has been
in vain. At least this much I can say: He was rich, rich in possession,
the whole universe was His. He had only to speak one word and a
new world would be created. He could put His finger on every star.
He could put His finger on anything and everything throughout
all of His great creation and He could say, "Mine!" " . . . by him
were all things created, that are in heaven, and that are in earth,
visible and invisible, whether they be thrones, or dominions, or

principalities, or powers: all things were created by him and for him: And he is before all things, and by him all things consist" (Colossians 1: 16, 17).

Jesus Christ was rich in honor. I think of the multitude of heavenly hosts that bowed before Him in praise and adoration. From time to time you catch a glimpse of it in the Word of God. Isaiah saw something of them, the Lord sitting upon the throne high and lifted up, and His train filling the Temple and above it the seraphim. Each one had six wings, and with twain he covered his face, with twain he covered his feet, and with twain he did fly—fly to the rescue of this spoiled and corrupt humanity that it might be cleansed from sin. Jesus was rich in honor with a great heavenly host around Him. A host only too eager to fly at His bidding.

He was rich in love, the love of His Father and of the Spirit. What human being could ever speak of the love which existed within the Trinity, between Father, Son, and Holy Ghost? The love of the Father—the Lord Jesus prayed in John 17: 26 that " . . . the love wherewith thou hast loved me may be in them. . . ." He was loved by the whole host of heaven. I sometimes wonder (and if this is but a flight of imagination, forgive me, but I am quite sure that when we speak on a text like this, one day when we meet the Lord, we shall be ashamed of our efforts) if heaven has held in history what we might call "a court day," when hosts of angelic beings and those who have not fallen into sin like this human race, visit some planets and stars, and return into the courts of heaven to bring their tribute of honor and glory and worship to the Lamb who was slain and who liveth again. Words fail me, but I know that He was rich, and the best place that heaven affords is His by sovereign right.

Oh, the pre-eminence of Jesus Christ! He was rich, yet He became poor. Oh, let us speak with bated breath! What amazement there must have been in the courts of heaven when the announcement was made that He was about to depart. Can you see Him stripping Himself of His glory? Can you see Him preparing for that journey? Can you see how they followed Him as far as they could into outer space, and even into the heaven around us, crying, "Glory to God in the highest, peace on earth, good will to men"?

Then see Him upon whose shoulders all this universe rested—for all things are upheld by the word of His power—being carried as a Babe in the arms of a peasant woman in Bethlehem. See Him in a dirty stable, and see Him in a carpenter's shop; no ray of glory now, none so poor as He.

We are told that His garments were woven from the top throughout—a mark of extreme poverty. See this wonderful Lord Jesus, who one day long ago in the councils of eternity dug the bed of the ocean, go to a sinful woman and say, "Give me to drink." He saw the foxes and the birds going back to their nests and resting-places, and He had to say, "I have nowhere to lay My head." Once He had been honored by the "Hallelujahs!" of heaven, and all the courts of glory had shouted His praise. Now He is stripped naked; He is put upon a cross to bleed and die; He is spat upon and struck.

Who can measure the gap between the throne and the cross? "He who was rich became poor": and poverty is always worse when you have known better days. If you want to know extremes of poverty, visit India and the cities of Calcutta and Madras and Bombay and other places, and you would see the poor outcasts in their thousands all suffering, perhaps getting two or three meals a week. But they have been like that since their birth; they have lived with it, and are used to it, and everybody else seems to live with it too. But one day Jesus was rich and He became poor. Oh, the grace of our Lord Jesus Christ! Cursed by everybody, for He became a curse for us.

What was the purpose of it all? For your sake, " . . . that ye through his poverty might be rich." For your sake, not just a certain group, not Christians *en masse*, but you, husband and wife, parent and child, young man and lady, one by one, for your sake, "He who was rich became poor."

Those eyes of yours, which He gave for vision, have seldom looked upon Him. That tongue of yours, which He gave for speech, has rarely spoken a word in His name. That life of yours, which He gave for His use and to be available for His purpose, is being used for anything but that. That heart of yours, which He gave that He might love through you, has loved anything and anybody except the Lord—for your sake, He who was rich became poor that you through His poverty might be rich.

When I have responded to this tremendous truth and to His mighty work, I discover it in possession. He became poor that you might have within your heart a fountain of life that would never dry up: not simply a little cistern or pool, but a fountain that would overflow in blessing to the world—God the Holy Ghost incarnate in your life that you might be rich in possession, that out from you might flow rivers of living water. Rich in promises, for every promise in the Book, sealed by His precious blood and absolutely unbreakable, is yours to claim by faith! "Go ye," He says, "into all the world and preach the gospel to every creature." Rich in promises and rich in power: " . . . ye shall receive power, after that the Holy Ghost is come upon you: and ye shall be witnesses unto me. . . ."

Through His poverty you might become rich, and this is heaven's counterattack against sin, and this is still the only principle of heaven's missionary program—the grace of our Lord Jesus Christ, communicating Himself, a love that was never turned away by sin, a love that never held back because of unworthiness, a love that is not moved by anger, that is not easily provoked, content to give nothing less than a total, complete surrender and an absolute impartation of itself—that is heaven's counterattack. Oh, that we might know the glow of that love in our hearts!

> Fill me with gladness from above,
>   Hold me by strength divine;
> Lord, let the glow of Thy great love
>   Through my whole being shine.

Heaven's missionary program was that He became poor, assumed all the poverty of our manhood in order that through His poverty we might be made rich. He stooped to earth, veiled His deity in His humanity, in order that He might lift us right up into heaven, and clothe and veil our humanity in His divinity. He became like us that He might make us like Him; and "the Son of man came not to be ministered unto, but to minister, and to give his life a ransom for many."

This is not only an object for our worship, but it is the pattern and principle for our lives if we are to get into the heart of God's program today; for this same necessity that brought the Lord Jesus down to our level to lift us up to His level, to communicate Himself, to give nothing less than all for our sakes, to love and never to be turned away by sin, or by anger, or by provocation, is the principle upon which you and I are to live our lives if we are ever to get into God's plan for the world. For Jesus said, "Except a corn of wheat fall into the ground and die, it abideth alone: but if it die, it bringeth forth much fruit." Unless somehow this principle gets into the heart of Christian testimony before it is too late—when really and truly, not as a theory but as a principle for life, we die to ourselves for the sake of others—we are in solitude and in fact die while we think we are living, utterly fruitless; but if we die, then He lives in us to communicate His life and power and principle through us.

It was this principle of which the Lord speaks that had taken hold of the church in Macedonia. If you glance at the opening verse of this chapter again, notice how these churches were plunged into sorrow and trouble and deep poverty, that they gave far beyond what they could afford, for they could afford nothing. They gave far beyond prudence, and without waiting to be asked or pleaded with, they begged Paul that he would receive the gift. Just think of it! A church, financially bankrupt, unable to do a thing, so poor and unable to afford to keep themselves, yet this church comes with a gift and begs Paul that he might receive it on their behalf! Why? Because they had yielded themselves to the Lord, and they had seen and known the grace of the Lord Jesus Christ. They had given themselves up to Him entirely, and when a man comes to a place where he knows he does not own himself, when he comes to that moment in his life when he knows that the grace of the Lord Jesus is such that it did all that for him and therefore he does not own himself, he will never again say that he owns his money. He will never again say that material things belong to him. He belongs to the Lord Jesus himself and therefore everything that he has is Christ's also.

And yet we argue about a tithe. God forgive us! We argue about how much we should give. Christian giving is never by commandment, by human pressure or by appeals—what an ugly, paltry level all that is—for the giving of money and of life! If the Holy Spirit is talking to us now, we are moving in an area far above all vulgar appeals for the raising of funds to meet the need of missionaries. We are in a place where we know the grace of our Lord Jesus Christ, and therefore we give ourselves in utter self-surrender to Him and, not only that, we follow through in the commitment of our lives to the church of Christ for His use wherever He may lead. In other words, we become poor in every bit of self-confidence that we might make others rich.

I believe with all my heart, though I put this case so inadequately, that this principle of the cross lies at the very heart of heaven's missionary program. Alas, it is a principle to a large extent discarded and gone out of use, and in place of it we major in higher education, better techniques, and development of talent, only to find ourselves in the thick of the spiritual battle tragically and helplessly inadequate to take the pressure of the hour. But alas again, instead of recognizing the reason for our failure, we leave the mission field or retire from Christian work and service for a prolonged furlough, and take further studies and more degrees, and we are bent on the same devil-misguided goal to educate the self-life till we fondly imagine we shall have what it takes. Then often after one term on the field and more often still, after two, we are added to the list of casualties.

When the grace of the Lord Jesus Christ captures the heart, and when you yield yourself with total, complete motivation which has stemmed from a revelation of His grace, to the Lord and to the church, what happens then? You begin then to say (if I may take this word as applied to the Saviour and apply it in another setting to your own life), though you were rich, yet for the sake of others you became poor that they through your poverty might be rich. Once you were rich, not as Jesus was rich, but in self-esteem, in self-importance, in self-righteousness, in pride, and in arrogance, but now having known the grace of the Lord Jesus Christ, who though He was rich became poor, and having marveled at that mighty dynamic counterattack against sin, you have become poor. For what things were gain to you, those you counted loss for Christ: reputation, education, religion, everything; " . . . I count all things but loss for the excellency of the knowledge of Christ Jesus my Lord. . . ." Then out of that utter poverty of spirit you desire that others too might become rich. Paul puts it—"For we which live are alway delivered unto death for Jesus' sake, that the life also of Jesus might be made manifest in our mortal flesh. So then death worketh in us, but life in you" (II Corinthians 4: 11, 12).

Only when that principle gets back into the heart of our living, nothing on earth or in hell will prevail against another counterattack from heaven in the name of the Lord Jesus, for it is upon such a principle of life that there will rest all the authority of the Holy Ghost. "Blessed are the poor in spirit: for theirs is the kingdom of heaven." Blessed are they who have renounced all their self-life, important as it was, and have come in poverty to the foot of the cross with nothing to offer but their desperate need. Blessed are they who have given themselves like that in total poverty of spirit, and have then followed through and have abandoned themselves to all the sovereign purpose of God until one day they meet Jesus face to face. Oh, that God in these days would bring His church back on to resurrection ground, to give every one of us a new vision, a new venture, a new faith, and a new obedience up to the hilt, until one day Jesus comes and reigns as King of kings! " . . . the grace of the Lord Jesus Christ, that, though he was rich, . . . he became poor, that you through his poverty might be rich," and therefore, "Lord Jesus, all I have and all I am, without argument, without debate, without committee, without question, without any possible contradiction, all of this is Yours now and forever."

I believe that will loosen purse strings. I believe that will warm hearts and cause to go out, while there is yet time, a great recruitment to the mission fields to intensify heaven's counterattack in this day. God grant that you and I might be found part of heaven's program.

And herein I give my advice: for this is expedient for you, who have begun before, not only to do, but also to be forward a year ago. Now therefore perform the doing of it; that as there was a readiness to will, so there may be a performance also out of that which ye have. For if there be first a willing mind, it is accepted according to that a man hath, and not according to that he hath not. For I mean not that other men be eased, and ye burdened: But by an equality, that now at this time your abundance may be a supply for their want, that their abundance also may be a supply for your want: that there may be equality: As it is written, He that had gathered much had nothing over; and he that had gathered little had no lack. But thanks be to God, which put the same earnest care into the heart of Titus for you. For indeed he accepted the exhortation; but being more forward, of his own accord he went unto you. And we have sent with him the brother, whose praise is in the gospel throughout all the churches; And not that only, but who was also chosen of the churches to travel with us with this grace, which is administered by us to the glory of the same Lord, and declaration of your ready mind: Avoiding this, that no man should blame us in this abundance which is administered by us: Providing for honest things, not only in the sight of the Lord, but also in the sight of men. And we have sent with them our brother, whom we have oftentimes proved diligent in many things, but now much more diligent, upon the great confidence which I have in you. Whether any do enquire of Titus, he is my partner and fellow helper concerning you: or our brethren be enquired of, they are the messengers of the churches, and the glory of Christ. Wherefore shew ye to them, and before the churches, the proof of your love, and of our boasting on your behalf.

II CORINTHIANS 8: 10-24

15

THE TIME TO ACT IS NOW

AT this time in his missionary service Paul was especially concerned about the condition of the church in Jerusalem, a church which had grown poor. There might have been spiritual reasons for its material poverty, but that is another issue. He was concerned that other churches which he visited, and through which he passed in the areas in which he traveled, should recognize their sense of responsibility to the church at Jerusalem. A prominent part, therefore, of Paul's teaching in the two following chapters has to do with the great subject of Christian giving, and I trust you will ask the Holy Spirit to speak to you upon this important matter of Christian stewardship from this portion of God's Word.

For those of you who are following the teaching of this letter, will you please notice that this chapter is really divided into three separate sections. This is an automatic division of the chapter, in no way artificial. You find in the first six verses what I have called the principle which we must follow. From verses 7-15 there is a promise we must fulfill; and in verses 16-24 there is a practice which we must foster.

First of all, the principle to follow in this matter of giving. There is one word which occurs over and over again here, and when the Holy Spirit repeats Himself frequently, it is always because He desires this to be the emphasis. And the word which finds frequent repetition in this chapter is the word *grace*.

Note the repetition. In chapter 8: 1, " . . . we do you to wit of the grace of God . . ."—we want you to know of the grace of God bestowed on the churches of Macedonia. Then again in verse 4: "Praying us with much intreaty that we would receive the gift . . ." —and that word *there* is the same word that is translated *grace*, "receive the grace." Again in verse 6: "That [Titus] would . . . finish in you the same grace also." Verse 7: " . . . that ye abound in this grace. . . ." In verse 9: " . . . ye know the grace of our Lord Jesus Christ, that, though he was rich, yet for your sakes he became poor, that ye through his poverty might be rich." In verse 16 we read: "But thanks be to God, . . ." and again in verse 19: " . . . but who was also chosen of the churches to travel with us with this grace, which is administered by us to the glory of the same Lord. . . ." So seven times in this chapter you have the repetition of the word *grace*.

Now what does that word *grace* mean? You have often heard it defined as the unmerited favor of God. Well, that is a definition, but it is only a limited definition of the word. It is the word from which we get our English word *charity*.

Now the word has taken on many different meanings down through the years. When this word was used in the early stages of history, it meant a desire to bring to other people goodness, health and strength, beauty, and loveliness. Later it became a little more pregnant in its meaning and began to mean the actual activity which expresses the desire to bring to others goodness instead of evil, health instead of sickness, beauty instead of ugliness, glory instead of punishment. This of course is outstandingly so as we think about the manger and the cross: " . . . the grace of our Lord Jesus Christ [as it is mentioned here in verse 9] who, though he was rich, yet for your sakes he became poor, that ye through his poverty might be rich."

Here then is the activity of heaven, desiring to bring to all that which is good, that which is wonderful, that which is glorious in place of all that is unpleasant and unsavory and unhappy. What a wonderful word is this word *grace*! Once you see the matter of giving is centered in this lovely word *grace*, it lifts the whole act away from mechanics, from pressure and duty, from obligation and mere legalism. It lifts us up into the most lovely atmosphere of an activity which seeks by giving to convey to others all that is lovely, all that is beautiful, all that is good, and all that is glorious. What a lovely word this word is!

Paul, you notice, quotes a human example of *grace* in the opening verses of this chapter as he refers to the churches in Macedonia, where he speaks of their action as " . . . the grace of God bestowed on . . ." them. And you notice the measure of their giving, "How that in a great trial of affliction the abundance of their joy and their deep poverty abounded unto the riches of their liberality." What glorious language that is!

The title of this series of messages is *Blessings Out of Buffetings*, and there is no area in the Christian life in which there is greater blessing coming out of severe buffeting than in the area of Christian giving. For there is no area in the Christian life in which grace shines out so much, so beautifully, so delightfully, and so happily as when giving comes from the background of poverty.

The churches of Macedonia, who had been so poor, had been through so much affliction, and, out of their poverty, had given so generously. This was the measure of their giving, and you notice that they gave far beyond the bonds of discretion, far beyond what they could afford. Paul says, " . . . I bear record, . . . and beyond their power they were willing of themselves, . . ." (v. 3). This was the measure of their giving. They were rash. They went far beyond the limit of discretion. They gave out of what they could not afford; they gave out of deep poverty. The grace of God was upon them.

You will observe what merit their giving had, because we are told that far from any pressure being brought upon them to give, they were the ones who put the pressure on Paul to receive their gift: "Praying us with much intreaty that we would receive the gift, and take upon us the fellowship of the ministering to the saints" (v. 4). What a refreshing atmosphere! There was no pressure put upon them to give. It was those who were giving who were putting the pressure on the others that they might receive their gift and take it from them.

What was the method by which they did this? And they did even more than I expected, says Paul, in effect, because first of all they " . . . gave their own selves to the Lord, and then unto us by the will of God" (v. 5).

Here then, is the principle to follow. It was giving out of poverty; it was giving without any pressure; it was giving by a specific method, by which, before they gave anything to others, first of all they gave themselves to the Lord and then having done that, everything they had belonged to Him. So they gave to the fellowship of the church. Here then is the background for our message, the principles which we must follow in this whole grace of giving.

Now see, in the second place, the promise that has to be fulfilled. Paul is referring here in verses 10 and 11 to an occasion about a year previously, apparently, when the Corinthian church had made what we would call "a faith promise." They had indicated their willingness to help the church in Jerusalem. They had given their faith promise, but now was the time to act.

Twelve months had passed by and while they had been willing, they had not acted upon their willingness; there had been no performance. So I am very interested to know how Paul goes about the task of seeing to it that people who have promised and yet have not fulfilled that promise, actually put their promise into action! How does he persuade people that being merely willing to give does not get one anywhere. It must be followed by action? Well, this is how he does it.

What do you know about tact? Well, here you have it, for in the first place he gives a word of praise. "Therefore," says Paul, "as ye abound in every thing, in faith, and utterance, and knowledge, and in all diligence, and in your love to us, see that ye abound in this grace also" (v. 7). Here is the acme of tactfulness, is it not? He begins by praising them for all their good qualities rather than exacting their promise by pressure.

He tells them they excel in faith, which is a great quality. They excel in utterance, having the gift of speech and expression. They excel in knowledge, knowing the doctrines of the Bible. They are diligent and sacrificial in their service and supreme in their love for the Apostle. He was so grateful for this, and for their warmth in fellowship, and in all these things he praises them. Now see to it that you abound in this grace also!

There is a complete absence of any pressure upon the people, for he says, "I speak not by commandment, but by occasion of the forwardness of others" (that is, the example of the Macedonian churches) "and to prove the sincerity of your love" (v. 8). In other words, I am not going to say you must do this, I am not going to issue a command. No, not at all; but I give you my advice. Paul continues, " . . . for this is expedient for you, who have begun before, not only to do, but also to be forward a year ago. Now therefore perform the doing of it . . . " (v. 10). Following the word of praise, there is a reminder here of the necessity of performance: " . . . perform the doing of it. . . ."

In what measure must they give? Now, I want you to notice this gift. Listen very carefully, for this goes to the very heart of the whole matter. Therefore, " . . . as there was a readiness to will, so

there may be a performance. . . ." I want you to perform. This is
my advice to you, he says, out of that which you have. "For if there
be first a willing mind, it is accepted according to that a man hath,
and not according to that he hath not." So I am expecting, says Paul,
in effect, that you would give, not according to what you have not
got—that is not expected of you—but according to what you actually
have.

This hits very hard at the modern idea of tithing. I have no
objection to tithing, but I would suggest to you that in the light of
the atmosphere of this teaching and in the grace that centers here
in this chapter as the whole principle of New Testament living,
tithing in many instances would be totally inadequate.

Let me give you a simple example. Supposing a man in this
country, living in this country permanently, earns $3,000 a year.
And let us assume that this man gives $300.00 to Christian work,
not necessarily to his own church, but to Christian work. Well, I
would suggest that this man was being generous. But let us suppose
there is a man somewhere earning $10,000 a year, and this man
gives $1,000 to Christian work. I would suggest to you that he is
not being very generous. And if you have another man who is
earning $20,000 a year and he is giving $2,000 to Christian work,
that man is being quite mean!

I am suggesting to you that tithing is totally inadequate. And you
cannot preach a gospel of tithing in the light of New Testament
principles and views, because tithing simply means to suggest that
having given my tenth, I keep the 90 per cent and everything is
lovely. I am to give according to what I have, not what I have not.
And this I believe necessitates that at least once a month a man will
sit down with his bank book, he will examine it and say to himself,
"Now this past month I have made so much more or so much less
than the previous month. Therefore I will regulate my giving
accordingly. I will give according to what I have."

This, then, is to be the performance of our giving. Not giving by
the standard of the mechanical, legalistic tithe which may be totally
inadequate, but by a standard whose character is grace and love,
giving in the consciousness that having first given myself to the
Lord, I am altogether His. And because I am altogether His, then
nothing I have is my own. I must give according to what I have.

The basis of this gift is simply that of a recognition of partnership.
You see, in considering this promise that Paul must fulfill, he has

begun by praising the people, then he has reminded them of the necessity of their performance on that basis, and now he shows giving is the result of one's recognition of partnership.

What do I mean by that? Look at Paul's words: "For I mean not that other men be eased, and ye burdened: But by an equality, that now at this time your abundance may be a supply for their want, that their abundance also may be a supply for your want: that there may be equality: As it is written, He that had gathered much [and of course he is going back to the wilderness journey and the gathering of the manna] had nothing over; and he that had gathered little had no lack" (vv. 13-15).

Now here again let me ask you to notice a very important principle on this matter of giving. I do not believe God ever intended all men to possess equally of everything of this world's goods, because this would immediately dispense with the whole principle of charity and of sacrificial giving on the behalf of others. But Paul is teaching here that there needs to be a recognition that the church is one, that there is a need for fellowship, and that there needs to be a recognition that this is a partnership for life.

Paul then says, " . . . your abundance . . . their want . . . " (v. 14). Then following in the same verse, " . . . their abundance . . . your want. . . ." Your abundance; that is the abundance of the Corinthian church. Their want; that is the church of Jerusalem. Their abundance; that is the abundance of the Jerusalem church; your want; that is the want of the Corinthian church.

We might ask ourselves, what abundance had the church at Jerusalem? It had a great deal of want, it was very poor. What abundance had it? If it had not been for the church at Jerusalem, there would not have been any other church at all. Other missionary churches were formed because from Jerusalem they went everywhere scattering the Word. I think that it could be substantiated that the Jerusalem church failed in its responsibility as it hugged itself too much, and probably lost a great deal of its missionary zeal. But nevertheless, the truth remains that had it not been for the disciples from Jerusalem who scattered the Word everywhere, there would have been none of the other churches, who owed everything they possessed of spiritual life, of vision, and of understanding of the gospel, all their spiritual wealth, to what had happened in Jerusalem.

This is not simply the strict confines of one little church family.

THE TIME TO ACT IS NOW

It is the partnership of the whole church everywhere. And here, then, because of this recognition of partnership, there must be, says Paul, an immediate performance of what you promised a year ago. So then, there is our promise to fulfill.

Now let us look at the third thing I have called a practice we must foster. I am now interested to know how Paul carries this performance out in terms of its practical outworking. How does he collect the money? How does he make sure that people give? How does he regulate it? For there must be some administration of the whole matter, and indeed you find that this is just exactly so.

In the first place in the closing portion of this chapter, there is an immediate delegation of responsibility, and here we have mention of the name Titus: "But thanks be to God, which put the same earnest care into the heart of Titus for you" (v. 16). "And we have sent with him the brother, whose praise is in the gospel throughout all the churches . . ." (v. 18). "And we have sent with them our brother, whom we have oftentimes proved diligent in many things . . ." (v. 22).

So Paul, recognizing that this was not his task, delegates to three people the responsibility of the gathering of the funds on behalf of the Jerusalem church. The first of them is named Titus; the second and the third are not named. Tradition has it that the second one, whose praise is in the gospel throughout all the churches, is none other than Dr. Luke. And the third one, " . . . our brother, whom we have oftentimes proved diligent in many things, . . ." is Apollos. But this merely conjecture. However, we can be quite sure that here is one young man whom Paul has entrusted with this sacred responsibility, Titus.

I want to leave the thought with you, because it is worth following through in your own personal study: in the course of Paul's journeys and preaching he was used of God to bring many young people to Christ. Two outstanding men were Titus and Timothy, two very different types. And at this particular moment in his life he says, "Titus, he is my partner and fellowhelper concerning you . . ." (v. 23).

Why should Paul entrust this man with such tremendous responsibility? As we think about this young man, Titus, he is not mentioned in the Book of Acts at all, but he is found in the second chapter of Galatians, where he is the test case which Paul used concerning the whole matter of a Gentile convert submitting to the rite of circumcision. Paul refused to allow Titus to go through this:

he was a Gentile by background, and so Paul says no, this man must not be submitted to a Jewish ceremony.

This is in distinction, incidentally, to Timothy. When Paul won Timothy to Christ, one of the first things he did was to see to it that he passed through this rite of circumcision. Timothy's father was a Gentile, his mother and her ancestors were Jews. And so in order to validate his testimony, to authorise it and give it approval among Jewish circles, Paul has Timothy circumcised.

Later on, you will recall, it was Titus who was entrusted with one of the most difficult tasks of all missionary enterprise, because he became bishop of the church of Crete. And there as its first bishop was entrusted with looking after a situation in which he needed all heavenly wisdom and grace and understanding. But to train him for that great task which would require all heavenly strategy and wisdom and understanding, this man was the one to whom Paul delegates the responsibility of raising funds from the church at Corinth. Titus, Luke, and Apollos (if we accept what tradition tells us) were the three chosen of God to whom Paul delegates responsibility.

Furthermore, he does it because he has something in view: he has a reputation to safeguard. "Avoiding this, that no man should blame us in this abundance which is administered by us" (v. 20). In other words, says Paul, in effect, I am not going to lay myself open to any charge of dishonesty because I as one individual would handle so much money on my own. This is going to be a big offering, so I am going to see to it that responsibility for handling it is going to be handed over to someone I can trust, and someone you can trust also.

Titus had already been to Corinth. They already knew him, they trusted him, they loved him, and he had meant much to them. And so Paul makes his wise choice of men whom he could entrust with this sacred responsibility in order that he might guard his reputation, for he says this must be done: "Providing for honest things, not only in the sight of the Lord, but also in the sight of men" (v. 21). This is to be a matter of absolute integrity. It must be above reproach or suspicion; the accounts must be beyond any possible cloud of doubt, and so it must be undertaken by men of transparent honesty.

To ensure that the Corinthian Christians will receive them, Paul now gives them their references: concerning Titus, he says, " . . . he is my partner . . ."; and Paul says, in effect, "if you want to know who the other brethren are, they are messengers of the churches, and they are men indeed who are the glory of Christ."

Here is the whole question of Christian giving put before us without any human mechanism, without any pressure, without any prolonged appeals. It is lifted up into an atmosphere of heavenly grace. You are brought face to face with an example of another church which gave out of poverty, and most of all the supreme example of our Lord Jesus who for our sakes became so poor that we might be made rich.

Then very tactfully, graciously and lovingly, Paul reminds them that now is the time to act: you promised, you have intended, you willed, you decided, you declared; now is the time that you must perform. And you must give not according to some legalistic percentage, but you must perform out of that which you possess. In order that this may be collected I am going to delegate responsibility. There will be a treasurer, and others who will be chosen for this task, men of integrity, so that everything will be done in the open without any suspicion; and the accounts will be audited and available for your inspection. This is the whole principle of giving.

Let me tell you a story. In the country of Palestine there are two seas, both fed by the same river, the river Jordan. If you went alongside one of those seas, you would find children playing by the banks, trees growing alongside, and life apparent everywhere. But you would find people avoid traveling anywhere near the other sea; they take another route and go in another direction. There is no sign of life or vegetation—there is nothing at all but barrenness.

What is the difference between the two? There is no difference in the source of supply, for the same river supplies both. But the difference is this: that for every drop of water that goes into Galilee (that, of course, is the first sea) another drop goes out. What it receives, it gives. It takes in, it gives out. And all around it is life, blossoming fruit, abundance. But the other sea jealously hoards its resources and refuses to let out a single drop. It keeps everything it takes in. And its name is *Dead*.

To give is to live. To restrain, to hold, to guard, to hoard, is to die. The same river of life in the power of the Spirit of God comes into your heart and into mine, and I would leave that parable with you. Freely you have received; the Lord help us to freely give.

For as touching the ministering to the saints, it is superfluous for me to write to you: For I know the forwardness of your mind, for which I boast of you to them of Macedonia, that Achaia was ready a year ago; and your zeal hath provoked very many. Yet have I sent the brethren, lest our boasting of you should be in vain in this behalf; that, as I said, ye may be ready: lest haply if they of Macedonia come with me, and find you unprepared, we (that we say not, ye) should be ashamed in this same confident boasting. Therefore I thought it necessary to exhort the brethren, that they would go before unto you, and make up beforehand your bounty, whereof ye had notice before, that the same might be ready, as a matter of bounty, and not as of covetousness. But this I say, He which soweth sparingly shall reap also sparingly; and he which soweth bountifully shall reap also bountifully. Every man according as he purposeth in his heart, so let him give; not grudgingly, or of necessity: for God loveth a cheerful giver. And God is able to make all grace abound toward you; that ye, always having all sufficiency in all things, may abound to every good work: (As it is written, He hath dispersed abroad; he hath given to the poor: his righteousness remaineth for ever. Now he that ministereth seed to the sower both minister bread for your food, and multiply your seed sown, and increase the fruits of your righteousness;) Being enriched in every thing to all bountifulness, which causeth through us thanksgiving to God. For the administration of this service not only supplieth the want of the saints, but is abundant also by many thanksgivings unto God; Whiles by the experiment of this ministration they glorify God for your professed subjection unto the gospel of Christ, and for your liberal distribution unto them, and unto all men; And by their prayer for you, which long after you for the exceeding grace of God in you. Thanks be unto God for his unspeakable gift.

II CORINTHIANS 9: 1-15

16

HEAVEN'S LAW OF SUPPLY AND DEMAND

THIS gem of a text comes right at the heart of an earnest appeal which Paul is making on behalf of the Christians at Jerusalem for financial help from the church at Corinth. He has boasted everywhere of the generosity of the Corinthian believers, and now he writes very tactfully about the matter in case his boasting proved empty, and to ensure that their promised contribution would be ready when Titus arrived and not be exacted and wrung out of them by pressure. God loves, as Paul says here, a hilarious giver, and each one must give as he purposed in his heart.

But finance is certainly not the burden of this message: that is secondary. Nor was it the burden of Paul's message. He is lifting up this secular matter, if you could call it such—though it is certainly a deeply spiritual one—into a wonderful spiritual area of truth, and he is laying down a principle which lies at the very heart of our Christian life, that I have called "heaven's law of supply and demand."

Notice first, a provision which is inexhaustible: " . . . God is able to make all grace abound toward you . . ."; a practice which is inevitable, " . . . that ye always having all sufficiency in all things, may abound unto every good work"; and third, a principle which is inescapable: " . . . He which soweth sparingly shall reap also sparingly; and he which soweth bountifully shall reap also bountifully" (v. 6).

Consider first the provision which is inexhaustible. The Christian life, as depicted in the New Testament in all its various experiences, is no more and no less than the outflow from a fountain of life which has its source at the very throne of heaven, an outflow that comes from the great giving of the heart of God in Jesus Christ our Lord (John 4: 14). Such is God's plan for you.

Notice how Paul piles on the superlatives here: " . . . God is able to make *all* grace abound toward you." This word *abound* is exactly the same word that the Lord used when He said, " . . . except your righteousness shall exceed the righteousness of the scribes and Pharisees, ye shall in no case enter into the kingdom . . ." (Matthew 5: 20). In paraphrase, Paul says, "God is able to make *all* grace exceed toward you; abound toward you that you always might have *all* sufficiency in *all* things." This is the provision for your life from heaven today, right now in your immediate circumstances, a provision that is inexhaustible; it is all grace and it is, moreover, abounding grace.

What does Paul mean by grace? It is just one word which sums up all the blessings which come to our lives undeservedly from God through Jesus Christ our Lord. Primarily, the word *grace* describes a disposition in the very nature of God, in His character, which is revealed in His eternal, unchanging, and pardoning love. This is grace: a kindness, an overflowing disposition in the heart of God. But then God's dispositions are never passive or inactive, and grace therefore means love that is expressed and displayed in action: "Love knows no limit to its endurance, no end to its trust, no fading of its hope: it can outlast anything" (I Corinthians 13: 7-8, PHILLIPS).

It is still more than this. Grace is never fruitless. It is always fruitful, and therefore the greatest meaning of grace is all the blessedness that comes, and all the lovely and beautiful things that take place and happen in the life of a man who has come to know the indwelling Christ and the very nature of God dwelling in Him by the Holy Spirit. Grace is love, joy, peace, longsuffering, gentleness, goodness, faith, meekness, self-control. Thus, Paul, in effect, says, "And God is able to make *all* grace abound toward you; in order that you might have all sufficiency in all things."

Very briefly and inadequately, that is the New Testament meaning of grace: love in action in the heart and passion of God expressed supremely at Calvary's cross. Love in action as expressed in the passion of each of God's own redeemed family, expressed in redemptive living, in sacrificial, sacramental living, in a life that is broken bread and poured out wine.

God is able to make *all* grace abound toward you. You see, there are not many graces. There is only one. What is it that God gives to each one of us and calls grace? It is not an "it." It is a Person, and His name is Jesus. When God gives grace, He gives Jesus, and that grace in Jesus Christ has many-sided expressions in our living, but it has only one source. It is from the throne and from the heart of God that there is poured out, in the name and virtue of Jesus Christ, by the power of His indwelling Spirit, grace; and it is abundant grace, for Paul says, He is able to make all grace abound toward you.

When God gives grace, He does not reluctantly open a little finger and maintain a clenched fist full of gifts. I would tell you today that God's hands are nail-pierced hands and they are wide open. This fountain of grace is always pouring itself out with no limitation on heaven's side at all. No wonder Paul concluded this chapter with a doxology: "Thanks be unto God for his unspeakable gift"! God's grace is a provision that is inexhaustible.

Because this provision is inexhaustible, and is to be found and expressed by love in action, to be demonstrated by every member of God's family—that means you and me, if we are redeemed by the precious blood of Christ—then, in the second place, there is a practice that is inevitable. " . . . God is able to make all grace—all the fullness of His grace in Jesus Christ—abound [exceed] toward you; *that ye* always having all sufficiency in all things, may abound to every good work."

The inevitable result of this constant and exuberant giving (may I use the word in relation to heaven? I don't wish to be irreverent, but when God says He loves a hilarious giver, He has set the example Himself and He has given hilariously; He has given gladly, happily, thankfully, and with exuberance in Jesus Christ) —from the fountain of life in the very throne of God—is that the basin of my life, which receives from the fountain in heaven, must always be full.

Now that is God's intention: "The water that I shall give you shall be in you a fountain springing up, bubbling up, overflowing into everlasting life." "He that believeth on me, . . . " out of his belly shall flow rivers of living water." The man redeemed by blood and indwelt by the Spirit is receiving from a fountain that is inexhaustible, from a provision that is limitless, and therefore God expects him always to be full. God says in this word to our hearts " . . . that ye having all sufficiency, . . ." in other words, His grace is sufficient.

Is that rather an anti-climax? Certainly in days when we have to exaggerate everything to make anybody believe anything, it sounds rather like it. Sufficiency—couldn't He have used a stronger word than that? But then, how much more do I need for my life than sufficiency, and where else do I get sufficiency for anything except I get it from the very heart of God? He " . . . is able to make all grace abound toward you; that ye . . ." may have *all* " . . . sufficiency in *all* things," and the grace of God and the supply from the fountain of heaven is always proportioned to the need of each one of His children.

Could you not bear testimony with me when I say that there is nothing in life so wonderful and so satisfying as day by day to receive from the fountain strength for the task? Strength to carry the cross, to bear the sorrow or the persecution, strength to stand in the day of adversity, strength sufficient for every demand that could ever be made upon me, as I live in God's will, and all this out of the fullness in Jesus Christ.

> He giveth more grace when the burdens grow greater,
> He sendeth more strength when the labors increase,
> To added affliction, He addeth His mercy,
> To multiplied trials, His multiplied peace.

Thomas Fuller once prayed, "Lord, please either lighten the load or strengthen my back." The word from heaven is, " . . . as thy days so shall thy strength be." God has never hurled a battalion of His soldiers into a blundering attack against some impregnable situation to stand and watch them defeated and discomfited. He lays His command upon them to do this or that, then He infuses His strength and His power adequate for the task, and He makes the back to carry the load. There is never one bundle of affliction that can come into the life of any of His children, but that when you unwrap it, you will discover sufficient grace. For every increasing responsibility in life, God gives spiritual maturity and manhood. Therefore, the basin should always be full, full because it isn't there simply for your own enjoyment of grace, but for the blessing of other people.

" . . . the service rendered . . . does more than supply the wants of the saints, it overflows with many a cry of thanks to God. This service shows what you are, it makes men praise God for the way

you have come under the gospel of Christ which you confess, and
. . . they are drawn to you and pray for you, on account of the surpassing grace which God has shown to you" (vv. 4-12, MOFFATT).
Grace, all sufficient and abounding, in order that I may abound to
every good work and supremely that I might become an attractive
person! I don't mean necessarily physically, but I mean that, by a
character transformed by the surpassing grace of God, other people
will see this that is caused to rest upon us, and they will be drawn
to us because of it. The church then glows with a spiritual attraction
because every basin is filled up. That is why God gives grace, that
we may abound unto every good work.

Now please follow me very carefully. There have been terrible
evils arising from the way in which some evangelical preachers have
talked as if the end of God's dealings with us is a vague sort of
experience which we call salvation, which means little more than
dodging hell. The New Testament declares that the purpose of
God is that we should be filled with all the fullness of God, and that
the basin of our life should be full because of the fountain being
inexhaustible. We have received of His fullness that we may abound
unto every good work. " . . . we are . . . created . . . unto good works,
which God hath before ordained that we should walk in them"
(Ephesians 2: 10).

A correct creed is intended to become a Christ-like character, and
if it does not do so, then the creed is worthless. The avalanche of
grace that rushes down 'upon us from the throne of God in Christ
is supremely for the reproduction of character and conduct which
will make men see our good works and glorify our Father which is
in heaven. We are not saved *by* our good character. We are saved
from our character to demonstrate our salvation. The evidence of
it will be in the display of the character of Jesus Himself whose
grace abounds in His children. Any profession of salvation which
does not issue in this is certainly not authentic.

How could it ever be possible for the grace of God in Jesus
Christ to be in Him and not in His people, when He is actually
living within them? It is fantastic to think about it. This inexhaustible
provision—all grace abounding that you might have all sufficiency,
and all things abounding to every good work, reaching the life,
touching the heart, filling the soul—must result in this inevitable
practice.

I suppose every preacher, if you asked him, has a burden on his heart. He is not worthy to be a preacher if he doesn't, for he has a major concern which brings him constantly to God, upon his face in prayer, a burden that is with him not merely days but nights as well. I can truly say before the Lord I have that, and if you want to know what it is these days—it changes, I suppose, but this has lain upon me now for some years with increasing heaviness—my soul is burdened for all those whose lives are a complete contradiction of this principle, who profess to glory in the fact that salvation is all of grace and who claim to rejoice in forgiveness by grace, but whose lives are utterly bereft of that quality in which they boast.

To claim to have experienced the grace of God in forgiveness and yet to be ungracious is a fantastic contradiction of New Testament thought. To claim to have experienced the grace of God in forgiveness, yet fail to display the grace of God in action is a total contradiction of New Testament truth, and let me say it, though I die in the saying of it, such a man is as lost as a man down on "Skid Row," in fact, more so, for in that memorable, immortal parable of the prodigal son, the man who was in the far country knew it. When he was starving and knew (as Paul later came to know) that in his flesh dwelt no good thing, he said, "I will arise and go to my father." But there was an elder brother who geographically was very near his father and under the sound of his father's voice all his life, but spiritually he was in a far country, far worse and far more final than that of the prodigal. He was in the far country of self-righteousness and religious formality and correctness of creed which was unsupported by the passion in his heart for his brother who was without God. Oh, you who are so near geographically to the sound of the gospel, who have been brought up under the sound of fundamental teaching, who claim forgiveness by grace, are you really saved?

So we see, there is a fountain that is inexhaustible, and because of that there is a basin which is my life, and it must always be full. Because it is filled up from the fountain, that which is in the basin must be of the same quality and character as that which is in the fountain, and therefore it will be displayed in love, in joy, in peace, and in the grace of Jesus Christ. Now observe the principle that is inescapable, because there is something in our text that is quite shocking: "God is able to make all grace abound toward you. . . ." Paul does not say, God *will do* this: he says, God *is able* to do it. He puts the whole weight of responsibility upon us to make God's ability to do this mighty work an operating factor in each life, seven days a week.

God is able! I pause to think about the marvel of it, that He is able to make all grace abound toward me that I might have all sufficiency in all things. But there are conditions. I may have access to this fountain from the throne in heaven, but it may gush by my side and pass me by, and the reason is not that I am straightened in God but that I am straightened in my own life.

Does not what I have said to you make you ask the question, as it certainly does me, why the breakdown? Why the lack of display in your life of all this which heaven supplies in Christ? Why the ungraciousness? Why the un-Christlikeness? Why the doctrine without the practice? Why the defeat and emptiness? Ask why until He gives you the answer.

You have learned something, I trust, about heaven's law of supply, but what about the demand? There is a principle here, and it is that of harvest. I cannot take a text like this out of its context. " . . . He which soweth sparingly shall reap also sparingly; and he which soweth bountifully shall reap also bountifully." Here is a principle of harvest, of sowing, and of reaping. " . . . he that soweth to his flesh shall of the flesh reap corruption; but he that soweth to the Spirit shall of the Spirit reap life everlasting" (Galatians 6: 8). If you want God's supply, this great harvest of grace—or to change the metaphor for a moment, if you want this fountain of life and want to be supplied with an all-sufficiency—then you must show God that you are desperate for it, and you must sow, and sow that you might reap.

Oh, how sparingly we have sown in the Spirit! How little we pray, how little time we give to meditating upon the Word, how rarely do we witness to others. Examine your sowing, and if your sowing is poverty-stricken, no wonder the supply is held up. Even in Christian work, you can sow to the flesh and reap a harvest of corruption. You can make the church the opportunity to demonstrate your authority, and you can use it in the flesh and substitute service in the house of God for nourishment of your own soul in quiet alone.

God is able to make all grace abound toward you that you may have all sufficiency in all things and abound unto every good work, but does heaven hear you knock and knock at the door? " . . . Ask, and it shall be given you; seek, and ye shall find; knock, and it shall be opened unto you." God's supply is there, but the door is shut because He has never heard the cry of your heart.

Consider God's principle of supply and demand: " . . . concerning the work of my hands command ye me" (Isaiah 45: 11). He is able, but His doing depends upon your sowing; His supply depends upon your demand. "Let us therefore come boldly unto the throne of grace, that we may obtain mercy, and find grace to help in time of need" (Hebrews 4: 16). You see, you don't ask and demand and knock until heaven's door is opened and the fountain gushes out, do you? God is not going to display and dispense heaven's treasury upon a self-satisfied individual.

Perhaps someone says, quite frankly, "If I would be honest with you, I've lost every bit of desire to sow to the Spirit. I have no heart concern for other people. I just couldn't care less. As a matter of fact, from all practical realities, I'm learning to live without God, even though I profess to be a Christian." In other words, my dear friend, you are prepared to settle for the delusion, for the mockery and travesty of a salvation that is not real or genuine, one that will land you in a lost eternity, simply because you profess such and such a thing and have been in a fundamental church, but now you don't really care.

You say to me, "Are you telling me that for this fountain to flow into my life, then there must be desire and demand? I haven't got it, so I am lost and it is hopeless." Is it? Listen to Paul: " . . . he that ministereth seed to the sower both minister bread for your food, and multiply your seed sown, and increase the fruits of your right-eousness" (v. 10). When you have no desire and no heart for God, when your appetite for the Word has turned sour, when your prayer life has gone shattering apart, when you have shown to everybody and to God especially that you don't really care, when you neither witness nor really pray nor show any deep heart concern, what does God do about it? Does He leave you to perish eternally? No, He ministers seed to the sower. If that isn't the overplus of grace, I do not know what is.

When He sees someone who has lost his spiritual appetite and concern, one who has recognized the provision as being inexhaustible, but one who has seen that the basin of his life is so empty—he has no desire and no heart for the things of God any more, and therefore the supply to his soul has broken down because the demand is never going up to heaven—does God deliver him up completely to perish? No, He holds out His hand with the overplus of grace, and He ministers seed to the sower.

There was a corn of wheat that fell into the ground and died that it might not abide alone, and because it died, it shall bring forth much fruit. That seed which fell into the ground and died and rose again is the seed which He offers to us in our desperate spiritual poverty in the overplus of His grace. He does not leave the sour appetite of the professing believer, who settled for a salvation that is not real, to descend to a lost eternity. He gives the seed of His life, and if you will come to Him today with all the sourness of your appetite, the ungraciousness of your life, the evidences that have abounded, that show you are not a genuine Christian at all in spite of all your profession, if you will come like that, He will put into your heart the seed of His crucified, risen life and create within you the hunger which is the longing of the Holy Spirit Himself to express Himself through life.

Now I Paul myself beseech you by the meekness and gentleness of Christ, who in presence am base among you, but being absent am bold towards you: But I beseech you, that I may not be bold when I am present with that confidence, wherewith I think to be bold against some, which think of us as if we walked according to the flesh. For though we walk in the flesh, we do not war after the flesh: (For the weapons of our warfare are not carnal, but mighty through God to the pulling down of strong holds;) Casting down imaginations, and every high thing that exalteth itself against the knowledge of God, and bringing into captivity every thought to the obedience of Christ; and having in a readiness to revenge all disobedience, when your obedience is fulfilled. Do ye look on things after the outward appearance? If any man trust to himself that he is Christ's, let him of himself think this again, that, as he is Christ's, even so are we Christ's. For though I should boast somewhat more of our authority, which the Lord hath given us for edification, and not for your destruction, I should not be ashamed: That I may not seem as if I would terrify you by letters. For his letters, say they, are weighty and powerful; but his bodily presence is weak, and his speech contemptible. Let such an one think this, that, such as we are in word by letters when we are absent, such will we be also in deed when we are present. For we dare not make ourselves of the number, or compare ourselves with some that commend themselves: but they measuring themselves by themselves, and comparing themselves among themselves, are not wise. But we will not boast of things without our measure, but according to the measure of the rule which God hath distributed to us, a measure to reach even unto you. For we stretch not ourselves beyond our measure, as though we reached not unto you: for we are come as far as to you also in preaching the gospel of Christ: Not boasting of things without our measure, that is, of other men's labours; but having hope, when your faith is increased, that we shall be enlarged by you according to our rule abundantly, To preach the gospel in the regions beyond you, and not to boast in another man's line of things made ready to our hand. But he that glorieth, let him glory in the Lord. For not he that commendeth himself is approved, but of whom the Lord commendeth.

II CORINTHIANS 10: 1-18

17

VICTORY IN THE BATTLE

I AM sure that nobody would dispute the statement that the Christian life is essentially a conflict, and in various areas and in different ways this conflict expresses itself in the experience of every one of us; but when we begin to think about the real nature of the conflict, what it is basically, and the secret of victory in it, then we would have various ideas upon that subject. As we consider from this chapter the conflict of the Christian life, I would seek to show you what is the real basic nature of it, what it stems from, and, therefore, the secret of victory in it

" . . . the weapons," says Paul, "of our warfare . . .": our warfare, and right from the very beginning you will recall that the Lord Jesus Christ always made plain to His disciples that He was calling them to a battle, and if we are to understand this text, we must not only see it in its context, but we must compare Scripture with Scripture.

When Jesus began to speak to a group of people who were seeking to commit themselves to Him and to follow Him, He said, "Blessed are they which are persecuted for righteousness' sake: for theirs is the kingdom of heaven. Blessed are ye, when men shall revile you, and persecute you, and shall say all manner of evil against you falsely, for my sake. Rejoice, and be exceeding glad: for great is your reward in heaven: for so persecuted they the prophets which were before you" (Matthew 5: 10-12).

At the very moment when He was beginning to gather together a little group of disciples, He announced that this was what discipleship would involve. He enlightened them on this subject and elaborated on it again when He commissioned them: " . . . I send you forth as sheep in the midst of wolves. . . ." He spoke to them about kings and governors being against them, but they were to take no thought of what they would say, for in that hour He would give them what to speak, and then He said, "And ye shall be hated of all men for my name's sake: but he that endureth to the end shall be saved" (Matthew 10: 16, 22).

Then for further enlightenment He told them the parable that we know as the wheat and the tares (Matthew 13: 24-30), and spoke to them about the reality of the wheat and the counterfeit of the tares that looked so like the wheat in its early growth, but ultimately there was no possible mistake as they were so different. His method of teaching them was to say, "Now, let them alone. Don't try to root up the tares, don't counterattack in that manner, but leave them alone until harvest time."

He did not only enlighten His disciples, however; He explained Himself to them, and you find the Lord Jesus using words like this to that little group of men, "If ye were of the world, the world would love his own: but because ye are not of the world, but I have chosen you out of the world, therefore the world hateth you" (John 15: 19). And then He gave them a word of encouragement: "These things I have spoken unto you, that in me ye might have peace. In the world ye shall have tribulation: but be of good cheer; I have overcome the world" (John 16: 33).

So from the very beginning the Lord Jesus was calling out to Himself a little group of men, of whom you and I claim to be in direct succession as His representatives here on earth, and He enlightened them concerning the conflict to which He called them. But He also said, " . . . my yoke is easy [or, my yoke fits] and my burden is light" (Matthew 11: 30)—don't be afraid of it; this is the kind of life to which I am calling you! He gives them a word of enlightenment, a word of explanation as to why this is so, and then He gives them a word of encouragement proclaiming that He has overcome the world.

In this way our Lord calls His disciples to a new principle of life altogether. What a strange kind of battle it was, and as He spoke to them about it, there seems to me to be one thing that stands out perfectly clearly: they were to win the battle by apparent defeat. By crucifixion they were going to be crowned. By refusing to counterattack they were to find the way of victory. By apparent failure they were going to conquer; and by allowing themselves to be identified with His cross, they were going to find the way of triumph. The

paradoxes of the Christian life! Thus the Christian faith had, in its
birth, a new principle at the very heart of it—the principle of sacrifice,
the principle of love, the principle of non-retaliation, the principle
that was to lead to absolute victory.

So we come to our text, because we find Paul explaining this more
fully. If that is the fact of conflict, what is the nature of it? The
strange thing that we notice about this verse is that it is written to
a Christian church, and it soon became apparent in the early days of
the Christian faith that the simple issues were godliness on the one
hand and godlessness on the other; but not simply godlessness in a
pagan world, but godlessness found inside the sphere of the Christian
church.

It is interesting to notice that these verses come in a context in
which Paul is defending his apostleship. The Corinthian church
had challenged his authority! "For his letters," say they, "are
weighty and powerful; but his bodily presence is weak, and his
speech contemptible" (v. 10).

Here was Paul, finding himself faced with contention and dispute
and a questioning of his authority in the church at Corinth, so he
answers them in the words of our text and says, in effect, "I want you
to understand that the weapons of our warfare are not carnal, but
mighty through God to the pulling down of strongholds; casting
down imaginations, and every high thing that exalteth itself against
the knowledge of God, and bringing into captivity every thought
to the obedience of Christ."

What is the nature of this Christian battle? Paul spoke of it to
the church of Ephesus in these words, "For we wrestle not against
flesh and blood, but against principalities, against powers, against
the rulers of the darkness of this world, against spiritual wickedness
in high places" (Ephesians 6: 12). The conflict into which the
Christian is introduced is first a spiritual one, and in its essence it
is one which stems from our minds and from our thought-life. So
the child of God, responding to the call of Jesus Christ, and duly
warned by Him that he is entering into a battle, finds himself in a
warfare, the nature of which is spiritual and the source of which is
in his thought-life. Paul describes the problem of carnality in the
church as that which stems from corruption in the mind and which
results in captivity of the soul.

We will consider these things in their setting. First of all consider
carnality in the church. The Christian church is a very wonderful

body, composed of a group of people who have received Jesus Christ as Saviour, who have been redeemed by His precious blood, and who share together in the fellowship of His Spirit. Therefore, they are a group of people who share, or ought to share, in each other's burdens, who comfort each other along the journey of life, and who stand together in the name of the Lord against a common enemy. The problem is that although they have been born again, although they have entered into the fellowship of the Christian church, they don't come by some magical process to be saints all in a moment! Paul's concern for the church at Corinth (as it would indeed be for us) is simply that the imagination of the mind, the process of thinking, the way of reasoning, the method of logic, the understanding of things which a man adopted in his unconverted days, become projected into the fellowship of the church, and the church begins to fail in its spiritual battle because it adopts carnal procedures. Alas, there is so much carnality in the church, but Paul says, " . . . the weapons of our warfare are *not* carnal. . . ."

The process of victory which our Lord taught His disciples was this: that if you cease to resist in the realm of carnality, then you are resisting automatically in the realm that is spiritual, and in this way you overcome the enemy. Resist, counterattack, deal with the situation upon the same level that the world deals with it, and you are defeated. But refuse to follow that principle of life; take up rather the principle of the cross, and by non-combat in carnal levels you are combating the enemy in spiritual levels and therefore you will overcome.

To illustrate this, turn to Simon Peter and the incident in which the Lord Jesus began to show to him this principle of the cross (Matthew 16:21-23). Christ spoke to him about the cross, about the blood, about the way of sacrifice and death. He had spoken earlier about the corn of wheat falling into the ground and dying, and if it die, it brings forth much fruit, but if it did not die it would abide alone; and Peter's answer was, "Not so, Lord, not that way, not the way of the cross and death!"

Christ's reply was shattering: " . . . Get thee behind me, Satan: thou art an offence unto me: for thou savourest not the things that be of God, but those that be of men."

But Peter did not learn his lesson. In the Garden of Gethsemane up goes his sword, out goes his arm, and off goes the man's ear. He is still resisting the principle of the cross, still following the

VICTORY IN THE BATTLE   177

procedure of carnality, and taking the line of resistance instead of the line of meekness and submission. He did not learn his lesson until after Pentecost (and it took him some time then), but this is the lesson which the Lord Jesus sought to teach him, and the very lesson which Paul is bringing to bear upon the church at Corinth.

You find this principle today in the church in terms of the theological outlook upon the Bible, though I have no wish to get involved in a controversial issue. The difference between what we call today the fundamentalist or the conservative evangelical and all others in their approach to the Book is that we as conservative evangelicals submit ourselves to the criticism of the Word of God, whereas all others submit the Book to their own criticism. This is the basic difference of approach to the whole subject of theology, so much so that in some circles it is said that if you are orthodox you are out-of-date; you are an obscurantist, and it is an impossible position to hold in the light of modern theology and modern science.

These are some of the high things that Paul said exalt themselves against the knowledge of God, and because the evangelical conservative holds to a position in which he submits all his criticisms and life to the authority of Scripture, and refuses to move from that position, while he is only too glad to discuss and consider all enlightenment upon the Book, he is therefore called out-of-date.

Now this I believe is the form of carnality in the church which stems from corruption of the mind; not necessarily moral corruption, but the mind which insists in submitting the Word of God to its own criticism and only accepting that which the human intellect can understand and believe. This corruption of mind leads to carnality in the church and to captivity of spirit, for by that means there is that which exalts itself against the knowledge of God. That, in the theological area, is exactly the modern counterpart of our verse.

I wish to come much closer home than that, as I bring this right down to where we live. What is the nature of this conflict? It is the battle which goes on in the personal life of every one of us in ordinary, everyday, down-to-earth, practical living—the battle to forsake the principle of carnality and to accept the principle of spirituality. It is the battle to take the line of refusing to resist along the human level, and by so doing, resisting in terms of spiritual warfare, and therefore overcoming. This is something which works itself out in terms of our relationships with one another, as well as in terms of our relationship with God.

If, therefore, it is true that the weapons of our warfare are not carnal, if God in calling us to be His followers and to live the Christian life here and now on exactly the same principle as that which was followed by His disciples—in other words, the line of non-resistance, of meekness and crucifixtion and death, the line of submission one to another in the fear of God—what then are the weapons a Christian must use, and how does he use them?

I remind you of words which Paul wrote in his letter to the church at Ephesus. We must arm ourselves, because in paraphrase he says, " . . . the weapons of our warfare, though they are not carnal, are mighty through God to the pulling down of strongholds." In other words, there is a way of life, there is an armor, there are weapons which the Christian church (and by that I mean any group of Christians) can use today in ordinary everyday life which will be so invincible that, to quote the words of our Lord Jesus, " . . . the gates of hell shall not prevail against them."

If this is true, then it behooves us surely to give very prayerful attention to this fact, because the fact of the matter is that apart from a mighty awakening and revival in the church, we are fighting a losing battle because we are resisting on carnal levels. This is not something you settle at denominational headquarters or in the high courts of the ecclesiastical world. It is something you begin to settle here and now that causes the tide of Holy Spirit power and life to flow once again through the church, which has been blocked because we as individual believers have rejected God's principles.

What then are the weapons which are mighty through God? " . . . take unto you the whole armour of God, that ye may be able to withstand in the evil day, and having done all, to stand . . . your loins girt about with truth, and having on the breastplate of righteousness; . . . your feet shod with the preparation of the gospel of peace; . . . taking the shield of faith, . . . And take the helmet of salvation, and the sword of the Spirit, which is the word of God: Praying always with all prayer and supplication in the Spirit, . . . for all saints" (Ephesians 6: 13-18).

Here is the Christian armor. Now will you please notice this: it is not armor to protect the body, for it is not designed to keep the Christian from physical harm, but it is armor designed to protect him against all spiritual attack. It is not something with which he clothes his body, but something with which he clothes his soul. It is hidden from the outward scrutiny of others, but its existence in the realm of a man's soul will be revealed in his daily life. That is why Paul says " . . . though we walk in the flesh, we do not war after the flesh . . ." (II Corinthians 10: 3). Yet our whole activity and our actions in the flesh, in the body, in daily conduct, are governed by this inward clothing, the armor of the spirit.

Let a man neglect putting on this armor and he will soon reveal carnality to everybody else in his conduct and behavior. But let him go into the robing room each day with God in the name of the Lord Jesus, and let him there in prayer put on the whole armor of God —truth, righteousness, faith, peace, the helmet of salvation, the Word of God as the sword of the Spirit, and the armor of all-prayer, clothing that the world cannot see—and it will soon be evident to all by his daily conduct in his daily life that he has clothed himself with the whole armor of God. The absence of a time he takes to clothe himself with the armor of God is revealed in his approach to the Bible, in his criticism of everything, in his refusal of every authority, in his hesitancy to accept the Word of truth, and in his carnality of daily behavior. Here, then, is the answer to the area within the church where the greatest battles are to be fought, in the weapons of our warfare that are not carnal, but mighty through God to the pulling down of strongholds.

You may ask, how do they work? They work in the realm of the mind. How is the victory won? It is won in the realm of the thought-life. Does this mean merely asking God to do something while we do nothing at all ourselves? No, indeed. What then is the secret of it? Jesus said, "As a man thinketh in his heart, so is he," and it is our leisure thoughts, our meditative life, that decides our conduct.

Alas, how much time we give to the life as it appears before men, and how little do we give to the life that appears before God! Yet it is that life that shines through everything, it is that life which is lived with the Lord Himself and which is clothed with heavenly armor that reveals itself in spirituality. It is that life, when it is lacking, that displays itself in carnality. The world, you see, sees the expression on a man's face, hears the tone of his voice, studies his actions whether they are selfish or unselfish, and by these he is judged inevitably and rightly. In spite of all his efforts to hold it all in check, he is conveying transparently to other people that his

Christianity is all in the shop-window, and he is painfully lacking in being clothed with the armor of God in the soul.

To be specific, it works something like this. Somebody says an unkind word about you, or you are accused falsely of something you have not done, or somebody is spiteful in his comments and critical in his attitude. You begin to think about it, you repeat it to yourself over and over again with increased indignation, and because it begins to fill your mind, you tell your friends (with additions of course) until at last, by frequent repetition, you have been insulted twenty times instead of one. You have determined to counterattack, to retaliate, to answer back, to vindicate yourself, and to prove that they are wrong and you are right. This is the carnality in the life which has happened because of corruption in the mind, because in the thought-life you have been defeated before you have to counterattack.

What then is the answer? As a Christian engaged in this conflict, knowing that the weapons of our warfare are not carnal but mighty through God to the pulling down of strongholds, there is the law of exclusion. How does it operate? When the thought comes and the person is reported to have said what he has said, and the un-kindness has been passed over to us, and the criticism has been made, whereas carnality would say, "Counterattack!" spirituality has the mind which was in Christ Jesus and humbles itself and recognizes that nothing that any person could ever say about any of us is really one hundredth part as bad as the truth if he only knew it. Therefore, we have no reason to counterattack, but one good reason to submit and to forget. That is the law of exclusion.

But there is the law of attention. " . . . whatsoever things," says Paul, writing to the church at Philippi, "are true, whatsoever things are honest, whatsoever things are just, whatsoever things are pure, whatsoever things are lovely, whatsover things are of good report; if there be any virtue, and if there be any praise, think on these things." When carnality arises in our hearts, causing us to answer back, to retaliate, and to fail to follow the principle of discipleship laid down by the Master, then at that moment we must think on these things, and answer the enemy by saying, "I'm sorry, my house is full, I have no room for you and I have no time to listen to you." That is the law of attention.

I quote some lovely words from that wonderful book, *The Imitation of Christ* by Thomas à Kempis: "Many thoughts have risen up against me, and great terrors which afflict my soul. How shall I pass through them without hurt? How shall I break them in pieces before me? I will go before Thee, O Lord, and I will bring low the proud boasters of the earth and I will open the gates of the prison and reveal to Thee the hidden secret. Do, Lord, as thou saidst and let all wicked thoughts flee from before Thy face. This is my hope and only consolation—to put my trust in Thee, to call on Thee from my inmost heart, and to wait patiently for Thy help and for thy strength."

Yes, truly, the weapons of our warfare are not carnal, but they are mighty through God to the pulling down of strongholds; and they cast down imaginations and every high thing that exalts itself against the knowledge of God and bring into captivity every thought into the obedience of Christ. That is the principle upon which the church was founded; that is the principle that was followed by the Master when He stepped from the throne to the manger and from the manger to the cross. That is the obedience He expects from each of His followers. But let us confess with shame, today in the realm of the intellect, the mind, the thought-life, the church—that is, you and I as believers in Christ—has followed the carnal method, and therefore she has divested herself of spiritual power.

God grant that you and I everyday may go into our personal robing room alone with Him, and put on all the armor of God which is mighty to the pulling down of strongholds of the enemy.

Would to God ye could bear with me a little in my folly: and indeed bear with me. For I am jealous over you with godly jealousy: for I have espoused you to one husband, that I may present you as a chaste virgin to Christ. But I fear, lest by any means, as the serpent beguiled Eve through his subtilty, so your minds should be corrupted from the simplicity that is in Christ. For if he that cometh preacheth another Jesus, whom we have not preached, or if ye receive another spirit, which ye have not received, or another gospel, which ye have not accepted, ye might well bear with him.

II CORINTHIANS II: I-4

18

THE JEALOUSY OF GOD

THIS statement of Paul's is very unusual, striking, and somewhat challenging. Of all things that has brought misery upon the human life it is jealousy. There is nothing that has done so much harm in homes, in personal and national relationships, in international situations, in church life, as the ugly, devilish poison of jealousy. This has been true all through history, not only in secular history, for at the beginning of the story of redemption, as you will recall in the Word of God, Cain is jealous of Abel and slays him; the children of Israel are jealous of Joseph and sell him; Saul's jealousy of David results in his trying to murder him.

In the New Testament, to carry the picture through, the disciples become jealous of the man who cast out devils in the name of the Lord, and try to destroy him; the scribes and Pharisees are bitterly jealous of the Lord Jesus Christ and stirred up the emotions of the crowd to crucify Him. Everywhere in the story of God's Book and in the story of human life, you have this fearful, ugly business of jealousy, which is the seed of murder, and which usually has led to it, pre-eminently in the case of our Saviour Himself. Against this background, therefore, I find these words of the Apostle Paul very striking. " . . . I am jealous over you with godly jealousy. . . ."

I would never have dared to think it possible that God could be jealous, and yet I am reminded that the moment God begins to lay down the pattern of His relationships with human people, He reminds them, " . . . I the Lord thy God am a jealous God. . . ." And if I might carry the analogy further, in laying down the basis of human relationships by the implication and standard of the Ten Commandments, the Lord not only declared His jealousy but He said, "Thou shalt have no other gods before me."

In other words, it is as if Jehovah in effect says, "I refuse to consider the possibility of a rival, I must be master, I must be supreme. I must be Lord, total Lord of all, or I will not be Lord at all. I am not going to compete with another for a place in your affection, I am not going to attempt to bargain that you should decide upon a syndicate or by the resolution of a committee that you should follow Me. I will be your sovereign, I will be your Master, your God, or I shall be nothing."

But this is surely the very thing that has wrecked human living, that has broken marriages and wrecked homes, and this ugly business has smashed its way into churches. "I will have no other friends nor will I allow other friends to come into your life, but me," says one to another. Is this the thing of which God is responsible? Oh, no, but at least I have said enough to make you realize that this word *jealousy* needs examination and explanation.

What is the jealousy of God? I will answer that question in the first place by reminding you of the character of God revealed to us in His Book, and then I will answer it for you by reminding you of the context from which our verse is taken.

First of all, what does the Bible say about the character of God? It has always been the belief of non-Christian religions that their gods are jealous and must be appeased by sacrifice. But this is not our God. The Bible reveals that our God is essentially moral and just, essentially pure and holy, and His jealousy—which is the greatest flame that burns in the heart of deity—is the flame of love in action. His jealousy is a concern for the purity, the holiness, the greatness, the glory of His people. His concern—and you need only refer to your Bible and you will see there His purpose to call out a peculiar people unto Himself who will be His witnesses, and whose lives will demonstrate His beauty to the world—is a consuming flame, burning eternally in His heart, the flame of love in action.

No sooner does He lay down the law in the Ten Commandments than He declares His jealousy for His people. His eyes are too pure to behold iniquity, yet He declares that the whole basis of His people's holiness and happiness is centered in their loyalty to Himself.

In case I am getting on debatable theological grounds, let me say this to make myself clear, that the ceremonial law of the Jew was finished in Jesus Christ. God made the first sacrifice in the Bible, and God made the last. The first He made in a garden; the last He made on a rugged cross outside Jerusalem; and there the thin trail of blood which has flowed from Genesis all through human history was stopped. Christ's finished final work was the last complete sacrifice for the salvation of the human race. But the moral law of God as defined by the Ten Commandments was not put away by Christ. It was fulfilled in the person of Jesus Christ completely in order that in the twentieth century, in civilized "Christianized" lands as well as in the uttermost parts of the earth, there might be a great company of people redeemed by the blood of Jesus Christ, indwelt by the Holy Ghost, in whose lives the righteousness of the Lord is fulfilled by the Spirit (Romans 8: 4).

God's jealousy, therefore, is a concern for the holiness, integrity, purity of ethics, and Christian standards for His people. Because of this, He will refuse to brook a rival in our affections for Him, not because of a selfish greed which wishes us all for His own possession, but simply because He knows that His great purpose for us of purity and holiness of life depends on our personal surrender and submission to His purpose, and because God would make it known (and we are very slow to believe) that happiness without holiness is impossible.

God is fearful lest His people bestow their affections on some alien thing or on some other master, and therefore I say to you that the jealousy of God stems from a tenderness and passion that burns in the heart of God for the welfare of His people.

To put it another way, the jealousy of man is selfish and self-centered. It usurps the rights of others, it is blind to their happiness, and it involves their ruin by leading to tyranny, and it cares nothing for anybody else as long as he gets through.

Observe carefully that God is not jealous *of* you; He is jealous *for* you, and that is the big difference. If you want proof and demonstration of this in reality, I take you to the cross and ask you to remember that there God, instead of destroying the race that deserted and rebelled against Him, has allowed that very race to rebel against Him in order that through that very act He might win back their love. That is the jealousy of God.

Think about that; let it get into your heart and into your soul: God jealous for His people and displaying it. Instead of wiping out of existence those who had deserted Him and treated Him so basely, He allowed them to murder Him on the cross of Calvary that He might win back their hearts. Glorious, life-giving jealousy!

Does this then throw some light upon this passage? I believe it does, for it introduces us in the second place to the jealousy of Paul. What an amazing thing that here is a man who says, in writing to a group of Christian people, " . . . I am jealous over you with godly jealousy. . . ." He says, in effect, "I wish that you could bear with me in my folly; please understand, for this flame that burns in my heart for you and eats up my life, possessing my personality and gripping my soul, is something that has got hold of me until nothing else matters." " . . . I am jealous over you with godly jealousy. . . ."

Elsewhere Paul said, "My little children, . . . I travail together in birth . . . until Christ be formed in you." I am jealous, not of you, but I am jealous for you. I care nothing for anything else, says Paul, except that those to whom I minister might fulfill God's purposes in their hearts.

I would remind you at this point of the terrific thing that has taken place in this man's life. Consider for a moment what happened as he went down the road that led to Damascus. In Acts 9 is the account of this experience, and as this great Pharisee went on his way, he was just eaten up with anger and fury. What was the matter with him? He had secured letters of authority to slay every Christian, and to put to death everyone who followed Jesus of Nazareth. Paul's whole life was a consuming jealousy against every Christian, so much so that he was determined to wipe them out. That was all that was wrong with him: he was eaten up with jealousy and bent on murder. Ah, but on that road he came face to face with the risen Lord. "Who art thou, Lord?" he asked.

" . . . I am Jesus of Nazareth, whom thou persecutest; and in your attempted destruction of my people, you are fighting against me."

"Then, Lord, what wilt thou have me to do?" and from that moment a wonderful revolution took place in Saul's personality. He was still jealous, he was still consumed with the passion of jealousy as a Christian. Ah, but it had been transformed into a jealousy not of people, but for them. " . . . I am jealous over you with godly jealousy. . . ."

Has that transformation ever happened in your life? People are so afraid of what they call "the crucified life," and when they hear it taught that we must die to ourselves that we might live unto God, they say, "What a miserable thing to die like that! This is negative teaching, this is passive—this is agony! Fancy dying!" Does this mean that God wipes out your personality? No, indeed. He does not; but I will tell you what He does, much to the discomfiture of the devil: He takes hold of that twisted, warped life of yours that is eaten up with jealousy, and He fills it with Holy Ghost jealousy. Instead of your being jealous of people, you become jealous for them. You live with one great burning motive that others might be blessed and helped along life's road. God takes hold of the tongue that has been so critical and maliciously talkative, and what does He do—cut it out and silence it? No! He gives you a new tongue that speaks with love and gentleness, grace and meekness. Here is the fruit of the gospel, when a man's weakest point is transformed by the Holy Ghost, taken to the cross, brought into resurrection life, and purified for the glory of God. What a gospel!

Oh, what discomfiture in the regions below! What awful panic in hell when a man who has served the devil successfully (often, alas, in good fundamental churches) by his jealousy, by his tongue, and by his gossip, and for long has been a wonderful vehicle of the enemy right inside the camp of the King of kings—what discomfiture when the devil finds such a man suddenly revolutionized by the power of the Spirit of God, with a new flame burning in his heart—the flame of love—and a new tongue talking through his lips, a tongue that has been touched by the grace of the Holy Spirit!

The jealousy of Paul has been transformed, but now in this Scripture passage is seen the subtlety of Satan: " . . . I fear, lest by any means, as the serpent beguiled Eve through his subtilty, so your minds should be corrupted from the simplicity that is in Christ" (v. 3)—the simplicity that is in Christ.

That is an arresting phrase because in these days there is scarcely anything that is simple; everything is so complicated. What am I to believe? What is right? What is wrong? In every area of life the old simplicities have vanished from us until even this word *simple* has changed, and I do not think people like being called *simple* because it has an association that is a little unpleasant! It would mean that you are not quite one-hundred per cent! That is not the meaning of the word in the New Testament, for simplicity means single-hearted, crystal clear. As a matter of fact, the actual word would be "like a bit of cloth without a crease in it."

All the great men of God have been so simple, just as little children. I could bring an array of them (I wish I could in person) to your mind—Isaiah and Paul from the Word of God, Bunyan, William Carey, Handley Moule, Hudson Taylor, D. L. Moody,

Adoniram Judson, to mention just a few, but these men with brilliant minds were basically as simple as little children in their walk with God. A man may be a saint without having many of the qualities which the world today rates very highly, but he will never be a saint without the simplicity of soul, a simplicity that is in Christ. It was this that burned in the heart of Martin Luther in the days of the Reformation when he said, "Let us get through to God. Give us a basic, dynamic, personal simplicity of faith in Jesus Christ."

Let me put in a warning here. When people go around saying, "All we want is the simple gospel," let us be careful. That could be an excuse for sheer mental laziness. The gospel is simple, but it is profound; and when Paul speaks about the simplicity that is in Christ, we will see that the *Revised Version* alters it slightly.

Look first at the simplicity that is in Christ. How simple was His life! He had nowhere to lay His head. The only legacy He left was a seamless robe that His mother made Him. There was no connection in the life of Jesus between wealth and happiness. And His speech, never shallow, was always simple. He could stand against the best intellects of His day and confound them, but He was never above people's heads. Is it not significant, the common people heard Him gladly. His way of salvation, too, is so simple, only two words, "Follow me."

His cross was so simple, so clear, yet we try to improve on it today, of course. It is not enough to say, some people would tell us, that "there is life for a look at the Crucified One." This needs a new intellectual approach to the gospel for these days. Rubbish, my friend! What this world needs is an enlightenment of the Holy Ghost, such a breathing upon our hearts of His conviction that we recognize that it is revelation and not education that gets a man into the kingdom. Yes, so simple was Christ's way of salvation; so simple was His whole soul, His inner life.

Have you ever thought about how worrying the life of Jesus could have been? What about the disciples who just would not learn their lessons, who were so slow, so disobedient, so backward? How worrying! But He was never distracted. How loud were other voices that dinned upon His ears: " . . . come down from the cross!" " . . . Art thou then the Son of God . . .?" But through all the contention and strife that surrounded His person, He was never dismayed. How threatening and dangerous was the whole situation, but He was never disturbed. " . . . my peace I give unto you, . . ." that is the simplicity that is in Christ. If you ask me the reason, I would give it to you in the words that He Himself spoke when He said, "My meat is to do the will of him who sent me, and to finish his work." In other words, you see, in the person of Jesus our Lord the jealousy of the heart of God the Father was completely satisfied. No rival claims at all to the will of God can be found in His life, and godly jealousy found perfect satisfaction in the total submission, total commitment, and single-heartedness of our precious Saviour.

Now look at the *Revised Version*: "I fear lest Satan should corrupt your minds from the simplicity that is toward Christ." In other words, our attitude which is the governing relationship of everything else toward the Lord Jesus is to be utterly simple. Here is the only thing that will work in the rush of modern life and glorify God in the tremendous controversies and testings that face us today There is one thing that will end simplicity, and that is divided loyalty.

What is the simplicity that is toward Christ? I give it to you in a nutshell: it is a faith that looks to Christ crucified and risen exclusively as the source of salvation and life; not Christ plus the church, not Christ plus ritual, not Christ plus ceremony, not Christ plus works, but Christ: crucified, risen, glorified, coming again. It is a faith that looks to Him exclusively and says, "Lord, in days like these to whom shall I go? Thou alone hast the words of eternal life." A faith that is exclusively resting in and centered upon Jesus our Lord alone, a love that is clear from every competing affection: "I am jealous over you with godly jealousy: for I have espoused you to one husband that I may present you as a chaste virgin to Christ" (v. 2). God's purpose for His people is union with Himself as between man and woman like this: a chaste, pure, spotless bride, absolutely separated and devoted to the claims of Jesus Christ.

I suppose one of the greatest delights of a bride or a bridegroom is to keep himself or herself chaste for the other, and neither of them would brook the incoming of a third party who would take away that sweet, precious, sacred relationship. No, and neither will heaven. That does not mean that in my love to Jesus I am not to love other people. Of course not. But it does mean that if I cannot take any human love into His presence and have His smile, or if that love deflects me from my devotion to the Lord Jesus Christ, that is the end of simplicity, that is the end of sweetness, that is the end of power, that is the end of graciousness, that is the end of reality in my Christian life. It must be a love that is clear from every rival affection.

Is that true of you? You love other people rightly, but are you being presented, as Paul says, as a chaste, pure virgin to Jesus, washed in His blood, consecrated, dedicated to His service, yielded to His loving heart? Can you say that every other affection that you have has been taken into His presence and He has smiled upon it, or if He has said "no" then you have put it away? Every human love that is real, far from taking away from devotion to your Lord, is being sanctified, made pure, beautiful, lovely, just because Jesus is in the midst of it.

There must also be an obedience, unqualified obedience to His commands, for the Lord Jesus said, "If ye love me, keep my commandments." This is the simplicity in Christ. Have you got it? This is what we need, this is the only answer in Christian living today—a faith, I repeat, that looks to Him exclusively, a love in which He is totally supreme, an obedience which is unreserved. Anything short of that is totally unworthy of the cross.

So many people today have got enough religion to prick and sting their consciences, but not enough to make them forsake their sins or bend their wills in submission to the will of God and say "no" to the thing that is wrong. How much of a dose of Holy Spirit authority do we need that people's consciences may not merely be pricked, but that their wills may be broken to the will of God?

In the days of the First World War, in London, a regiment of soldiers was about to go out to France. In those days war was slaughter, and before they went, they were entertained at a concert in a theater in London by a group of people who wished them well. When the concert, which was given very well, was ended, the captain in charge of the regiment stood up, thanked the people for their kindness, and then with a broken voice said, "Ladies and gentlemen, is there anybody here who can tell us how to die?"

There was a moment's embarrassed silence until one lady, an artist in the concert, a Christian, came forward, stood up before the whole regiment of men and sang, "Oh, rest in the Lord, wait patiently for Him." There were few dry eyes that night.

In what you say to other people, have you so lost your way in theological argument that you can no longer tell people how to die? For the simplicity that is in Jesus Christ is to rest in the Lord like a little child rests in the arms of a mother. Are you there?

For I suppose I was not a whit behind the very chiefest apostles. But though I be rude in speech, yet not in knowledge; but we have been throughly made manifest among you in all things. Have I committed an offence in abasing myself that ye might be exalted, because I have preached to you the gospel of God freely? I robbed other churches, taking wages of them, to do you service. And when I was present with you, and wanted, I was chargeable to no man: for that which was lacking to me the brethren which came from Macedonia supplied: and in all things I have kept myself from being burdensome unto you, and so will I keep myself. As the truth of Christ is in me, no man shall stop me of this boasting in the regions of Achaia. Wherefore? because I love you not? God knoweth. But what I do, that I will do, that I may cut off occasion from them which desire occasion; that wherein they glory, they may be found even as we. For such are false apostles, deceitful workers, transforming themselves into the apostles of Christ. And no marvel; for Satan himself is transformed into an angel of light.

II CORINTHIANS 11: 5-14

19

TRANSFORMATION OF THE DEVIL

In the course of our studies we now come to words of Paul's which I cannot possibly pass by. They are almost terrifying as well as tremendously challenging. When seen in the context of the whole teaching of the Word of God and in the light of current events, these words expose the true nature of the battle in which you and I are engaged: " . . . Satan himself is transformed into an angel of light." Therefore, instead of looking at the chapter itself, I want to bring to bear upon this one verse other passages from the Word which will illuminate it for us. At the same time, may God help us to understand, as perhaps we have never understood before, the desperate plight of modern civilization, the awful grip of the devil upon the world at this time, and the one hope that yet remains for us who are God's children.

There is no need for me to argue for the existence of Satan, or his personality, not simply as an influence or as an evil thing, but as a person who is just as real as Jesus Christ Himself. Indeed, if we accept the personality of Christ upon the revelation of the Word of God (and that is how we do accept it), we must also accept the personality of the devil upon the same evidence.

In Isaiah 14 he is revealed as one of God's heavenly host long before the existence of civilization on this planet, who set himself against the will of God and said, "I will ascend into heaven, and I will exalt my throne above the stars of God. . . ." Before there was rebellion on earth, there was revolt in heaven.

Satan stepped into the record of human history as the serpent seeking to ally the human race in his purpose to become self-centered, self-sufficient, independent of God (Genesis 3). He was one hundred per cent successful, and ever since then submission to that principle of life, as he calls it, has become the very nature of the human race as we know it, transmitted down from all posterity to this generation.

. Further, Satan is seen as one who has access to the throne of God (Job 1: 6). Then we find him in face-to-face, direct combat with Jesus the Son of God, offering to Him all the kingdoms of this world if He would only worship him, and acknowledge that there is a possibility of life that can yet be achieved for the human race out of relationship with the Lord of all creation (Luke 4).

Now please notice that it is perfectly plain from the teaching of Scripture that it is not the aim of the devil to destroy humanity. That may surprise you, but his plan rather is to realize his ambition for world dominion through men yielded to him. To such he promises that they shall know good and evil. On the other hand, God, the Lord of all glory, power and authority, upon a throne above all His created universe, far above Satan, declares that life on that principle will bring doom. Satan says it will not. God says it will. God says one thing, Satan says another thing. Satan says, "Believe me, yield to me, accept the principle of self-existence, self-sufficiency, independence of God, and I will show you life." God says, "Believe him and you will die, but believe on the Lord Jesus Christ, and you shall be saved." The whole of your life here and your destiny in eternity depend upon whom you believe.

In this great spiritual warfare there is one factor that weighs heavily in the devil's favor, for because the human race basically has submitted to this principle he has an ally in every human heart; there is that within each of us that will assent to this principle of evil. Because of a nature that is born in sin and therefore demands its self-existence and self-dependence, Satan has a powerful ally in the heart of each of us today.

There is also another factor in this spiritual warfare that weighs heavily against him. It is the course of human history which has abundantly proved, never more so than today, the awful tragedy and disaster which God said would happen if we rebelled against Him, and allied ourselves with the enemy. Furthermore, human history records that heaven has launched a full-scale counterattack against this hellish principle of life in the person of Jesus Christ, and in spite of all the efforts of the devil—in that he fought and battled with Jesus face to face—at the cross our Lord has stripped from Himself principalities and powers and made a show of them openly, and ascended into heaven to the right hand of all power, from whence He shall reign till every enemy becomes His footstool.

This mighty counterattack from heaven against all the powers of darkness is a factor which weighs heavily against the enemy. Yet in spite of it Satan successfully blinds the minds of them who believe not, lest the light of the glory of the gospel of Christ shines into them. He holds the whole of modern civilization, as the *Revised Version* renders I John 5: 19, "he holds the world unconscious in his arms." What a plight for a soul made in the image of God, unconscious in the arms of the devil!

It follows, therefore, that the enmity of Satan is never with the unbeliever—they are already his—but it is with the man who has revolted from his rule, turned to God in Christ, and found himself by that blessed act of turning inspired by the Holy Spirit, and wonderfully free from the grip of the enemy. He is free to do the will of God, free not for license or lust, not to live as he pleases, but free to live in submission to the whole principle God has laid down, and in living that way to find His liberty. All the fiery darts of the enemy are hurled at the child of God simply because the Christian is indwelt by His divine nature, Satan's deadly enemy. The attack of the enemy against the Christian is not against flesh and blood, but it is against our relationship to Jesus Christ. Satan is not primarily concerned to make a Christian descend into moral filth. Oh no, for, in fact, that would rather defeat his object. But he is concerned to make the child of God fail in prayer, be bankrupt in his testimony, defeated in his spiritual life, deprived forever of being a channel of communication of God's principle of light into this world. Now it is just here that we see the transformation of the devil.

" . . . your adversary the devil, as a roaring lion, walketh about, seeking whom he may devour" (I Peter 5: 8). I somehow feel that kind of language rather suited the man who wrote it—Peter is of a lion-hearted temperament! In Bunyan's immortal book he writes of Apolyon in this way: "Now the monster was hideous to behold, clothed with scales like a fish, wings like a dragon, feet like a bear, and out of his belly came fire and smoke; his mouth was as the mouth of a lion." And that is how Satan comes upon us sometimes, as an undisguised, hideous, evil monster, ready to devour us and throw us down. But he is easy to detect, and if he always came like that, the Christian could take his sword and beat him off.

Paul speaks of the devil much more seriously, and in many passages of Scripture he refers to him as a serpent, who comes with subtlety and guile. Listen to his language, " . . . we are not ignorant of his devices" (II Corinthians 2: 11). "Put on the whole armour of God, that ye may be able to stand against the wiles of the devil" (Ephesians 6: 11), " . . . the snare (or trap) of the devil . . ." (II Timothy 2: 26). To Peter, a roaring lion; to Paul, a serpent which beguiles and still fascinates men with his glittering eye, and then slowly winds his slimy length, coil after coil, around their lives, because he fashions himself as an angel of light.

That is exactly what he once was, an angel of light, and that is what he pretends to be today. That is what he was before creation when he rebelled; that is what he pretends to be while still living in rebellion. He offers men light on that principle, and by every counterfeit imaginable he offers a way of life without any relationship to God.

As you observe Satan's basic place of attack and his counterfeit, notice that his master-stroke in this twentieth century, as far as an ungodly world is concerned, is the strategy of communism. Never has Satan achieved anything so powerful, so successful and so overwhelming as this in all history. It was practically unknown fifty years ago, and is now sweeping the world, threatening to engulf western civilization. The fear for lands of freedom and civilization, as we know it, is not from an onslaught of nuclear bombs, but from the collapse of the whole moral fiber from inside. The thing we are fighting today is not over in Moscow or Peking, but right here where we live. Our enemy is not flesh and blood, but a spiritual foe.

If this be so, notice the strategy of the devil. He has the world blinded by this devilish system, but where is the focal point of his attack? It is upon the Christian church, for his only enemy really is the divine nature, Jesus Christ, who only lives in born-again people. Therefore Satan's first and priority target is the church of Jesus Christ.

He attacks in three ways: first, in the realm of the Spirit by false teaching. It is this which Paul has strictly in view in this passage: " . . . if he that cometh preacheth another Jesus, whom we have not preached, or if ye receive another spirit, which ye have not received, or another gospel, which ye have not accepted, ye might well bear with him" (v. 9) " . . . such are false apostles, deceitful workers, transforming themselves into the apostles of Christ" (v. 13).

In other words, the first basic attack of the enemy upon the church of Jesus Christ is in the realm of our souls by false teaching.

There is no doctrine of the church which is free from abuse. When Satan attacked the Lord Jesus Christ, you will recall, he turned himself into a preacher with a text from the Bible (Psalm 91) and dared to use the Word of God to attack the Lord of glory. Satan is adept at preaching a form of religion based on Scripture tests and incorporating many of the doctrines of the Christian faith; indeed every doctrine of the faith except one. There is one he is afraid of, because he knows it is this one which will defeat him.

We read in Revelation 12: 11, as the whole of this universe celebrates the triumph of our risen and returning Lord Jesus, " . . . they overcame him by the blood of the Lamb, and by the word of their testimony." If there is one doctrine that Satan cringes before, it is redemption by blood. It is justification by faith and not by works. It is atonement by the blood of Jesus. It is the free grace of God that puts a man right by God's unmerited favor, and not by our working to achieve salvation. Because Satan is afraid of this, he does his deadliest work not by ignoring this cardinal doctrine, but by perverting it. Then he makes this wondrous, precious, glorious truth of the gospel an excuse for self-indulgence until you have the antinomians saying today, "It does not matter how I live; all my sins will be washed away by the blood of Christ." So Satan would, if he could, deceive the very elect.

There were very few things that could make Paul cry like a child. He had the Roman scourge upon his bare back, but he ignored it and was glad that he was counted worthy to suffer for Jesus. He could be in the midst of a Mediterranean storm, driven to shipwreck, but he praised God and believed Him for deliverance. He could have the executioner's sword raised above him, about to behead him, and he could say, "I have fought a good fight, I have finished the course, and kept the faith." Ah, but there was one thing that made him sob, that broke his heart—it was when he saw men take the gospel of the grace of God and make it an excuse for sin, saying, "Let us continue in sin that grace may abound!" for of such, Paul says, " . . . I tell you even weeping, they are the enemies of the cross of Christ: Whose end is destruction, whose god is their belly, and whose glory is in their shame . . ." (Philippians 3: 18, 19).

Satan's masterpiece in the church today is an attack upon the stronghold of evangelical testimony to make us abuse the gospel of grace, and make us permit it to allow us to continue in disgusting sin, and yet say, "I am a Christian." Friends, in the name of heaven, this has to stop before it is too late, or else the church will be doomed! That is what is happening in fundamental circles in western lands today, when people exploit the grace of God, make use of it to say, "By grace all is well!" and then live like the devil. The thing is a sheer impossibility.

Second, the enemy attacks in the realm of the imagination, by unholy thinking. Here it is that temptation is dressed up in its most attractive garb. There is no gift so exalting as that of our imagination; it can rise to great heights. But there is no curse so debasing, so degrading, as an imagination which is defiled by the enemy. Therefore, Satan, who knows exactly the moment to attack, will come with full force at the best time. At times of sickness and depression, when low in spirit and health, he fills our mind with doubt, with questionings, with self-pity. When we are well, strong and prosperous, he fills our mind with self-confidence, self-love and self-admiration. In times when we relax and seek rest to our mind, he will fill an empty mind with foul thinking and imagination. When we seek the face of God in prayer, he will invade the holy place with thoughts of which we are desperately ashamed. For every mood or condition he has his weapon.

But most subtle of all are the moments when he withdraws altogether from the field of action and you are left numb, no longer with any love for God's work, doing it because you have to do it. No sweetness is found in God's word; you may be stirred by the sermon occasionally, but never stirred into action—that is dealt with five minutes after the service by the conversation that takes place. You are completely without any susceptibility to the things of heaven, immoveable by the most powerful message except vaguely stirred in your conscience. Life is just a round of duty, and there is a dead calm in the soul, with no hunger or longing for God and heaven, you seem to be just cruising along spiritually without life, without any semblance of concern, and Satan has conveniently withdrawn. He stands back and watches the soul that he has ceased to tempt because he does not need to bother.

You say temptation is hard. I know, but I tell you what is worse; when Satan has stopped bothering, and he leaves the soul without troubling about anything, and with no heart-concern for the things of God. If you are just going through life with no reality, no power, no grace, no hunger for God, everything a duty and performance, I plead with you, go to God and say to Him, "Lord, let the devil loose on my life again!" It is a dangerous thing to pray, for He will do it.

Satan's transformation into an angel of light is, in the third place, in the realm of conscience by self-interest. Oh, how subtly Satan puts on the apparel of an angel of light! As he is well dressed in the garb of heaven, he makes himself to appear in the soul as the very voice of heaven. You sometimes find it hard to know whether it is the devil or the Lord talking to you—of course you do, if you are honest. It is not always so easy to know when you are being "clearly led" about this or that. Satan is always working in the realm of conscience to cloud the issue, and when self-interest would call for me to go in a certain direction, he would tell me that is the path of duty. Have you ever heard him say this: "Friend, there is no harm in it! It does not pay to follow Jesus too far. After all, you have got to have a good time, you know"?

So by false teaching, by imagination, by conscience, the Christian is deceived by the devil transformed into an angel of light. I would say that one of the most amazing things about him is that he is so united. He has a thousand agencies all ready for his use, and while the church of Jesus Christ is always quarreling and indulging in the luxury of civil war, I never learn of any civil war in hell. All Satan's hosts are united on one full-scale attack upon the place where he can find the nature of Christ indwelling a child of God. God help us, for when the church fights within its own ranks, Satan has a field day.

What is the answer to it? Have I uncovered Satan in your own life? Is this your experience? Then how do you think he can be detected and overcome? I would remind you that the ultimate doom of the devil is certain (Revelation 12: 7-11), but we do not have to look into a vague future. Go back to the cross and see there One who cast from Himself principalities and powers, and made a show of them openly (Colossians 2: 14, 15). The defeat that was predicted from the very moment the rebellion began, when the Lord promised that the seed of the woman would bruise the head of the serpent (Genesis 3: 15) has actually happened in human history as Jesus Himself said: "Now is the judgment of this world: now shall the prince of this world be cast out" (John 12: 31).

But what about today, this desperate hour in which we live? I tell you, there is victory for the Christian now! " . . . greater is he that is in you, than he that is in the world" (I John 4: 4). Ephesians 6: 10, 12 speaks to us about putting on the whole armor of God that we might stand against the wiles of the devil.

You may say that you see the desperate plight we are in, but you cannot find the answer for your own life. What can you do about it? You can lay hold of God in His Word as you have never done before, for a man who is soaked in the Word of God has always an answer ready for the devil in the moment of temptation. "Wherewithal shall a young man cleanse his way? by taking heed thereto according to thy word" (Psalm 119: 9). However, the Word of God is not magic. It all depends how you approach it. If you approach it to submit it to your intellectual criticism, then you will never know victory. But if you submit yourself to the criticism of the Book, then you will discover the power of God to defeat in you the power of the enemy.

More than that, you must not only soak yourself in His word, but you must run to Him, the living Word, who is made unto us wisdom. This battle is not with flesh and blood, but with spiritual forces, and therefore it requires spiritual weapons, and " . . . the weapons of our warfare are not carnal . . ." (II Corinthians 10: 4). The sheep are never so safe as when they are near the shepherd; we are never so secure from the fiery darts of Satan as when we are near to Jesus. What does that mean? It means to walk according to His example: " . . . Christ also suffered for us, leaving us an example, that ye should follow his steps" (I Peter 2: 21). It means walking in the way He walked. It means living daily in His fellowship: " . . . if we walk in the light, as he is in the light, we have fellowship one with another . . ." (I John 1: 7). It means trusting always in His blood, for the blood of Jesus cleanses from all sin. Jesus said, "Blessed are the pure in heart, for they shall see God."

May I suggest to you that promise does not only mean one day in heaven when we shall see Him face to face, but it means that *now*, in the heat of the battle, in the tremendous intensity of the spiritual warfare in which we are engaged, in the light of world conditions that constantly challenge us, it is not only that we *will* see God in heaven, but we will see Him *now*. In the midst of the battle we are able to see not only God, but also the devil, and we are given the spiritual discernment to know which is which.

We live today in a world that is on fire. We see national and political corruption, and worst of all, a church that is lethargic, disunited, worldly, tripped up by the angel of light. What can we do before it is too late? Shake off the shackles, break free from the fetters, snap the chains, and lay hold of God as we have never laid hold of Him before! The Lord wants a chance to answer the fire of hell with the fire of the Holy Ghost, and He will do this very thing for you, because it is the only hope, the only answer. You cannot answer fire by human reasoning or human intellect; you can answer fire with fire. Today, the Holy Ghost on fire in the lives of God's people is the only hope for fundamental Christianity.

I beg of you that you personally will give God the opportunity to answer the fire of the enemy with the fire of heaven, for then the power of Satan cannot prevail against you. Are you on the Lord's side in the battle? Go now into the very presence of Jesus our Lord, close to His wounded side, and say to Him, "Lord Jesus, please put on the armor for me, for I have no might and no power against all these who come against me, neither know I what to do, but my eyes are upon Thee." Like Gideon of old, He will clothe you with the armor of righteousness on the right hand and on the left, and you will go forth as a man who has gripped the Word of God and who has been gripped by the Spirit of God. Only as revival comes to individual hearts can disaster, in nation and in the church, be averted in our time.

Therefore it is no great thing if his ministers also be transformed as the ministers of righteousness; whose end shall be according to their works. I say again, Let no man think me a fool; if otherwise, yet as a fool receive me, that I may boast myself a little. That which I speak, I speak it not after the Lord, but as it were foolishly, in this confidence of boasting. Seeing that many glory after the flesh, I will glory also. For ye suffer fools gladly, seeing ye yourselves are wise. For ye suffer, if a man bring you into bondage, if a man devour you, if a man take of you, if a man exalt himself, if a man smite you on the face. I speak as concerning reproach, as though we had been weak. Howbeit wherein-soever any is bold, (I speak foolishly,) I am bold also. Are they Hebrews? so am I. Are they Israelites? so am I. Are they the seed of Abraham? so am I. Are they ministers of Christ? (I speak as a fool) I am more; in labours more abundant, in stripes above measure, in prisons more frequent, in deaths oft. Of the Jews five times received I forty stripes save one. Thrice was I beaten with rods, once was I stoned, thrice I suffered shipwreck, a night and a day I have been in the deep; In journeyings often, in perils of waters, in perils of robbers, in perils by mine own countrymen, in perils by the heathen, in perils in the city, in perils in the wilderness, in perils in the sea, in perils among false brethren; In weariness and painfulness, in watchings often, in hunger and thirst, in fastings often, in cold and nakedness. Beside those things that are without, that which cometh upon me daily, the care of all the churches. Who is weak, and I am not weak? who is offended and I burn not? If I must needs glory, I will glory of the things which concern mine infirmities. The God and Father of our Lord Jesus Christ, which is blessed for evermore, knoweth that I lie not. In Damascus the governor under Aretas the king kept the city of the Damascenes with a garrison, desirous to apprehend me: And through a window in a basket was I let down by the wall, and escaped his hands.

II CORINTHIANS 11: 15-33

20

COSTLY COMPASSION

Let us take time here to review some of Paul's statements which we have considered that emphasize the truth that blessing does come out of buffeting. First Paul says that he had the sentence of death in himself that he should not trust in himself, but in God which raiseth the dead (1: 9). Then giving testimony to his own experience Paul said, I have been "persecuted, but not forsaken; cast down, but not destroyed; Always bearing about in the body the dying of the Lord Jesus, that the life also of Jesus might be made manifest in our body" (4: 9, 10). Then he writes, " . . . death worketh in us, but life in you" (v. 12).

Summing it all up Paul says, " . . . our light affliction, which is but for a moment, worketh for us a far more exceeding and eternal weight of glory" (4: 17, 18). He speaks of himself "As sorrowful, yet always rejoicing; as poor, yet making many rich . . ." (6: 10). Then he says, " . . . without were fightings, within were fears. Nevertheless God . . ." (7: 5, 6). Finally, he states, " . . . the weapons of our warfare are not carnal, but might through God to the pulling down of strong holds" (10: 4).

Blessing out of buffeting—this has been the great principle of Paul's life, the principle that made the man who practised it the greatest missionary that the church has ever known, and this has been the great principle of every life that has truly known God ever since. It is a principle, of course, which has found its more glorious expression in the Lord Jesus Himself, who was wounded for our transgressions and bruised for our iniquities, who indeed was made sin for us. What buffeting, that we might be made the righteousness of God in Him! What blessing! And there is no spiritual blessing that is authentic which ever gets released from a child of God unless he has taken some of the buffeting. This is the principle of Christian living just because we are Christians.

Somehow in this chapter Paul seems to rise to a tremendous height of testimony, and excels himself as he recounts his experience as a servant of Jesus Christ. I know of no other place in the Bible where you could find this principle of blessing through buffeting more clearly outlined and taught than in these tremendous verses.

You will recall that there were those at Corinth who sought to undermine Paul's testimony, his influence, and his authority, who boasted of their own ancestry, their social position, their religious training, and for a moment in this chapter Paul meets them on their own ground, apologizing to heaven for doing so! "That which I speak, I speak it not after the Lord, but as it were foolishly, in this confidence of boasting" (v. 17). Again: "I speak as concerning reproach, as though we had been weak (v. 21). Howbeit whereinsoever any is bold, (I speak foolishly,) I am bold also"; and: "Are they ministers of Christ? (I speak as a fool) . . ." (v. 23). For a moment he departs, as it were, from the direct command of the Spirit of God and meets these men on their own ground. If they try to rebut his authority, refuse to recognize his spirituality, and claim that because of their tradition and social standing and religious education they stood head and shoulders above the great Apostle he says, in effect, "If that is your basis of evaluating a servant of Christ, then I can measure up with any of you. 'Are they Hebrews? so am I. Are they Israelites? so am I. Are they the seed of Abraham? so am I' " (v. 22).

Observe, however, that he forsakes such an attitude immediately and says, "If I must needs glory, I will glory of the things which concern my infirmities." The true test of discipleship, the mark of an authentic testimony, of a genuine saving experience of the grace of God is found in a totally different area from all of this.

After the Lord Jesus met Paul on the Damascus road, He spoke to Ananias concerning him and said, " . . . for he is a chosen vessel unto me, to bear my name before the Gentiles . . . For I will shew him how great things he will do in my name's sake." No! "What great success he will have as a missionary." No! "How many people he will move toward God." No! "What heights of fame and what a name he will make for himself." No! "I will shew him how great things he must suffer for my name's sake" (Acts 9: 15).

Paul says, in effect, "You challenge my authority! You dare to stand upon the ground of your religious training, your social position, your racial prejudice; you boast of this and say that is the mark of authority. I say to you, if I would glory, I will glory in the things that concern my infirmities, for the only valid test of my worth as a man of God is that the very thing that Jesus said would happen to me has happened."

When God began a good work in your heart and life at the moment He first met you at Calvary, I doubt whether there has ever been such a spiritual moment in your whole life. I wonder if there has ever been a moment since that day when, maybe with tear-stained face and certainly with a broken heart (if the experience was genuine) you first met God and gazed upon those nail-pierced hands and upon that thorn-crowned brow and said, as Thomas said of old, "My Lord and my God!" There was nothing of carnality or worldliness about you then. There was not a care for anything, except that the burden of sin had been lifted at Calvary, the condemnation of guilt had gone, and new life had started. You were right with God and the time of the singing of the birds had come. Oh, that was a spiritual moment! He who has begun that good work began it by breaking your heart and revealing the great intention that He would perform that work until that day when you see your Lord face to face. And the only platform for the performance of God's work is the platform of suffering.

See now, therefore, the price Paul paid (vv. 23-28). It is amazing how we can read a list like this and neither think about it nor apply it personally. There are twenty-three experiences mentioned, and as we, with Paul, go through them, I pray the Holy Spirit may impress them upon your heart and mind.

You say you are a minister of Christ? I speak as a fool. I am more than any of you. I have worked harder than any, I have taken more lashings than any, I have been in prison more often than any of you, I have been facing death more often too. In fact, nobody has experienced such trouble over sin but that I have become more involved because I am a Christian. There is no one who has suffered and been so persecuted as I have. I have had one hundred and ninety-five lashes on my bare back, which is the limit they could give me.

Paul continues. Contrary to all Roman justice, I have been beaten three times with rods. When I was in Derbe, I was stoned

and left for dead. Three times (I have only made public one instance)
I have been shipwrecked. Once I spent a night and a day on a raft.
And have I traveled! In journeyings often, and always I have been
in danger. I have been in danger on the seas; in danger of being
robbed, especially when I took the offering from the churches up
to Jerusalem. I have been in danger from my own countrymen, as
well as from nationals of other countries. I have been in danger
when I was in cities, and acutely so when I was in the wilderness
on the mission field. I have been in perils everywhere, and perhaps
the worst of all, I was in danger among people who called themselves Christians. That was the hardest thing to take.

Then I have been desperately tired, and I have had such pain,
not all physical pain, but pain because of speaking with brethren
who have lost out on the journey. It has been the exhaustion of
spiritual counsel, it has been the pain in my own soul as I felt the
pain in others, and as I watched people I loved so dearly fall apart
spiritually. I have often been in watchings: there have been nights
when I have not been able to sleep because of the burden. I have
sometimes not had enough food or drink, but regardless of this
I voluntarily went through times of fasting because I knew that the
kind of situations I was dealing with and the kind of people I had
to cope with would only be dealt with by prayer and fasting. So in
spite of my own necessary privations I went through times of
fasting, and sometimes I have been cold without clothes for my
back.

Such is the price that Paul paid. How does that react upon you?
Do you congratulate yourself that you have escaped it? One week
of such living and we would be done, but Paul went through it for
a lifetime and gloried in his infirmities.

Does this make you feel ashamed? Of course, I recognize that
the law of this country would protect its citizens from much of this
because of the religious freedom we enjoy, but I cannot let myself
off on that account. Investigating a little further, I must ask myself,
"Why is it that I have escaped, why have we all escaped this?"
What was it that made Paul live as he did? I ask you therefore to
notice the natural thought that comes here in the following verses,
the pressure that Paul felt in his spirit. Why did he live like that?
"Besides those things which are without, that which cometh upon
me daily, the care of all the churches. Who is weak, and I am not
weak? who is offended, and I burn not?"

" . . . that which cometh upon me daily. . . ." I have paraphrased twenty-three things that constantly hit this man from without, and I give you the one inclusive reason why any of them were allowed to touch him at all, for he could have escaped them all. Not one of them was necessary, and he could have avoided them all and lived in comfort and luxury—except for one thing. There was one thing internal in his heart that forced him to face all these twenty-three things that were external: " . . . that which cometh upon me daily. . . ."

I could not possibly convey to you adequately in the English language the force of that statement. I tried to picture it in terms of being smothered under a blanket, or by being attacked and crushed by some great animal, for he could not have used a stronger word when he said, in effect, "That which bears me down, that which is upon me as an intolerable load, that which is a burden, that which is something that I never shake off day or night. It is with me always. I have no vacation from it ever. It is upon me daily. The care, the compassion, the concern of all the churches." And please note, not the churches in an indefinite, vague, universal, world-wide sense, but Paul says, in effect, "Who is weak, and I do not feel for him; who is offended and it does not cause me to burn with anxiety on his behalf?"

This great man paid the price because he felt the pressure, and again I ask you lovingly in Jesus' name, how much of that do you know? I say it tenderly, and yet I say it firmly; we have escaped a great deal of the price of buffeting because we just do not care about other people. Although the law of the land would protect us from much of this, nevertheless, if we began really to live with no release and no vacation as those who care, as those who are pressed down under a burden which is intolerable, but for the grace of God, a burden cannot be shaken off—the burden of God's family everywhere, a burden that goes round the earth in concern for His blood-washed children—I say to you, if we lived as though we really cared and longed to rescue one soul from hell, the buffeting would begin at once. To our shame, we escape because we do not arouse ourselves to take up the fight, and we rarely launch a personal attack in the name of the Lord Jesus to rescue a sinner from his way. I am sorry to say it, but we just do not care, and therefore we never experience the pressure that Paul felt.

If you are being honest with the Lord as you hear Him speak, perhaps you are saying to yourself, "I know that is true, I don't really care, for I would not live as I do if I cared—then why don't I care? Why is it I have no compassion? Why is it my concern for the lost is so inadequate, and why do I rarely feel when I am under a burden or experience a real sense of concern? So often I exhibit that I don't care in my superficiality, in the way I behave when I am off-duty, in the things I do and in the places I attend. But *why* don't I care?"

"If I must needs glory, I will glory of the things which concern mine infirmities." What is the principle behind a statement like that? "I am going to glory," says Paul, in effect, "and boast only in the things in which God has made me weak, and in the infirmities which I suffer for His sake." What is the principle? I give it to you in three brief, simple statements. I give you the thought to pray over.

The first principle is that Paul had learned the value of a soul. "And unto the Jews I became as a Jew, that I might gain the Jews; to them that are under the law, as under the law, that I might gain them that are under the law; To them that are without law, as without law, (being not without law to God, but under the law to Christ,) that I might gain them that are without law. To the weak became I as weak, that I might gain the weak: I am made all things to all men, that I might by all means save some" (I Corinthians 9: 20, 21, 22).

Have you ever asked God in prayer to show you what it means for a soul to go out into a Christless eternity, into hell? I do not believe God would ever show us that completely, because if He did we would go out of our minds. We would become deranged if we knew that the person with whom we are rubbing shoulders every day, he who lives next door to us, maybe even he in our own homes, if he knows nothing of the grace of God in Jesus Christ, that he is going to hell to be lost for all eternity. We rarely dare think on these things because of the horror of the truth.

There are only two alternatives here. If the souls of men and women deserve no more attention than we give them, then Paul was a lunatic. But if we are truly to value the worth of a soul by his labors for them, then God forgive us! How sinful we are to value so much worthless and material things—things that we possess and then one day leave behind—and care so little for the undying souls of our fellow men! The first principle behind Paul's statements,

" . . . I glory in the things that concern my infirmities" is that he knew the value of a soul.

The second principle is that Paul knew the virtue of the gospel. Romans 1. 16: " . . . I am not ashamed [I am proud] of the gospel of Christ; for it is the power of God unto salvation to every one that believeth. . . ." In other words, I know that I have not simply *a* message to preach, but I have *the* message, and it is the only message that works in human lives. It delivers a man from the depths of his depravity, lifts him from the dunghill, and sets him among the princes in heaven. This is the only message that is adequate, and I am proud of it. I do not apologize for it. I do not talk in uncertain terms, nor does the trumpet blow with an uncertain sound. I am sure and positive of it because I have proved it in my own life. It has worked for me by transforming and turning me completely inside out! Therefore I do not go to people with any apology: I know the reality in my heart of the transforming power of the gospel of Jesus Christ, that there is no other way and no other answer. I know that for the lands where millions are without God and without hope today, there is a balm in Gilead, and that the gospel is God's final and only answer. Such was Paul's conviction.

When the Holy Spirit presses upon us the necessity for absolute commitment without reservation to Jesus Christ, no matter if people do say that we are narrow and fanatical, then something within us reveals the need for money and men for missions to get the task done in our generation, and to evangelize to a finish to bring back the King of kings. But there is too often another voice saying that it is too dangerous, too uncertain, doors are closing, and surely it is better to leave these heathen people to their own religions: God will not condemn them, for He is a loving heavenly Father!

Who would endure all that Paul endured if he had not known that the eternal destiny of the human race was at stake in the acceptance or rejection of his message? Who would have faced what he did if he had not known with an absolute conviction that nothing could shake him, that this message was totally adequate and it still is. He knew the value of a soul, he knew the virtue of the gospel, and he also knew the third principle, the victory of love.

If you asked Paul what inspired him to say, " . . . I will glory of the things which concern mine infirmities," he would answer, "The love of Christ constraineth me." From the buffetings in the

life of this Pharisee who became such a disciple, from the life of
this man who revolutionized the first century of the Christian
faith and to whom we owe such a large section of the New Testament, from the life of this man who blazed a trail as few others ever
have, there flowed immeasurable blessing—but, I do not preach
Paul: I proclaim Paul's Saviour, and would say that what he faced
in terms of buffeting was only a pale reflection of what the Saviour
faced to redeem our souls.

Open your Bible to Isaiah 23 and read it through again and again:
"We did esteem him stricken, smitten of God, and afflicted. He
was wounded for our transgressions, he was bruised for our
iniquities: the chastisement of our peace was upon him; and with
his stripes we are healed. . . . We have turned every one to his own
way; and the Lord hath laid on him the iniquity of us all."

Oh, precious Lord, what buffeting He endured to save such
wretches as we! Why did He endure it? Because He was moved
with compassion. He paid the price because He saw the multitude
as sheep without a shepherd, and as He went up the lonely road
to Calvary He said, " . . . weep not for me, but weep for yourselves,
and for your children," for He knew that eternal destiny depended
upon their attitude to Himself. Ah, what buffeting, what burden!
But oh, what blessing came out of His life! Let us say it to the Lord
with stricken spirits and broken hearts, we escape the buffeting and
we know so little of the burden, with the result that there is so
little of the blessing.

The Holy Spirit is waiting to work through the person who is
willing to take the buffeting because he has the burden, and out
from buffeting and burden comes the flow of Holy Spirit power.
It is when the rock is smitten that the water gushes out.

I think of David Brainerd who, though in a cool dry wind, sweated
and prayed, and hundreds of hard-hearted Indians were mowed
down like grass under the conviction of the Holy Ghost. I think
of Praying Hyde who shook a continent for the Lord. Does this
put you out of the picture? I think of two dear old ladies aged 81
and 82, who for two years prayed for hours a day in the Hebrides
of Scotland until one day the fire of God fell and revival came.

In Revelation 21 there is the picture of the New Jerusalem
coming down from God out of heaven prepared as a bride adorned
for her husband. Here is God's purpose for His children, to prepare
them to meet the heavenly Bridegroom, prepared through buffeting.

Then what does God say? " . . . God shall wipe away all tears from
their eyes; and there shall be no more death, neither sorrow, nor
crying, neither shall there be any more pain: for the former things
are passed away."

What does that mean? We have often read those verses in times
of sadness and loneliness, when friends have been going through
the valley of the shadow, and we have always found comfort in
them. But I do not think that is what the Holy Spirit is saying.
The bride is prepared, and how is she being prepared? The Captain
of our salvation was made perfect through suffering; He learned
obedience through the things that He suffered, and one day God
will wipe away all tears. What tears? The tears I have shed for a
soul. Will there be any? The times I have wept over someone who
has rejected Jesus. Have I ever wept? When I meet God face to
face, will He find dry eyes, and no tears to wipe away because I
have never really cared?

" . . . And there shall be no more death. . . ." I have had the
sentence of death in me all my life, says Paul. So have you and so
have I, if we have really cared. There will be no more buffeting,
no more sorrow, no more crying, and no more pain. The former
things are passed away.

Yes, there is coming a day, bless God, when the buffeting will
be over, and the last tear over a lost soul will have been checked,
the last sentence of death will have been concluded, and the last
pain of anguish over people who care nothing for our Lord Jesus
will have finished, and God shall wipe away all signs of sorrow and
concern. Let us covet a compassion that costs, so that on that day
He may have many tears to wipe away.

It is not expedient for me doubtless to glory. I will come to visions and revelations of the Lord. I knew a man in Christ above fourteen years ago, (whether in the body, I cannot tell; or whether out of the body, I cannot tell: God knoweth;) such an one caught up to the third heaven. And I knew such a man, (whether in the body, or out of the body, I cannot tell: God knoweth;) How that he was caught up into paradise, and heard unspeakable words, which it is not lawful for a man to utter. Of such an one will I glory: yet of myself I will not glory, but in mine infirmities. For though I would desire to glory, I shall not be a fool; for I will say the truth: but now I forbear, lest any man should think of me above that which he seeth me to be, or that he heareth of me. And lest I should be exalted above measure through the abundance of the revelations, there was given to me a thorn in the flesh, the messenger of Satan to buffet me, lest I should be exalted above measure. For this thing I besought the Lord thrice, that it might depart from me. And he said unto me, My grace is sufficient for thee: for my strength is made perfect in weakness. Most gladly therefore will I rather glory in my infirmities, that the power of Christ may rest upon me. Therefore I take pleasure in infirmities, in reproaches, in necessities, in persecutions, in distresses for Christ's sake: for when I am weak, then am I strong.

II CORINTHIANS 12: 1-10

21

THE MINISTRY OF THE THORN*

THE ministry of the thorn is a great subject: " . . . there was given to me a thorn in the flesh, the messenger of Satan to buffet me . . . . For this thing I besought the Lord thrice, that it might depart from me. And he said unto me, My grace is sufficient for thee. . . ." I would say at the very beginning that though we are considering something about which Paul has opened his heart to unveil as his own experience, we are really just considering a very faint reflection of the same experience that came to the Lord Jesus, Paul's Saviour. Paul's thrice repeated urgent prayer is but an echo of One who prayed in a garden, " . . . Father, if it be possible, let this cup pass from me. . . ." The answer which heaven gave to our Lord was the the answer given to Paul. The cup was left, confronting Him, to drink to the last drop. The thorn remained for the rest of Paul's life. But that was not the only answer, for in the garden angels came to strengthen the Saviour, and to the heart of the Apostle came the word, " . . . My grace is sufficient for thee: for my strength is made perfect in weakness."

Therefore, as we consider this great word, the Lord Jesus stands, as it were, in the shadows as He did when He heard Paul's prayer and answered it so unexpectedly, so differently, and yet so gloriously, to test his reactions and to equip him for all his ministry. In the same way the Lord stands in the shadows now to watch your reactions to a similar situation.

Perhaps you have looked into the face of a Christian who is always smiling, who never seems to have any worry, is always happy and radiant and, as you have thought about your own circumstances, you have said in your heart, "I wish I were he! He seems to have no problems. He doesn't have to take what I do." But perhaps you have lived long enough, as I have, to know that sometimes the most

*Based upon a booklet entitled *"The Discipline of Disappointment,"* by the Rev. G. B. Duncan, and reproduced by the author's kind permission.

213

radiant face hides great pressures, and often the man who is being most blessed of God is being most buffeted by the devil. I am glad, therefore, that we can consider now what I have called "the ministry of the thorn."

I notice, in the first place, what I am sure Paul would have called, at least for a time, a very frustrating experience, for to quote his own words: " . . . There was given to me a thorn in the flesh, the messenger of Satan to buffet me. . . ." For this thing, I besought the Lord thrice. . . ." What a comfort it must have been for him to address his urgent petition to the One who Himself had faced this all the more completely in Gethsemane! Quite evidently, therefore, we have here the pressure of a very severe trial in Paul's life. It was not just a little thing; it was a very big thing. The word which is translated in our New Testament *thorn* is not the kind of thing you might get in your finger while gardening, which is very painful. Then you can very quickly pull it out. Actually it is a word which is used for a stake upon which people were impaled to be crucified. Paul's experience, therefore, was a very severe trial.

It would be sheer speculation to imagine what it could have been. It might have been something in his own personal character and life which was constantly reminding him of the sinfulness of the flesh and which ultimately brought him to say, "I know that in me [that is, in the flesh] dwelleth no good thing." It might have been something in his environment or circumstances which seemed to be completely impossible for him to take any longer. It might have been some physical problem, and most people seem to think this was most likely. Some have suggested, and I think with a measure of authority, that Paul was suffering from partial blindness, if not total blindness. This is, of course, mere speculation, and what really matters is that when this thing hit him, he was absolutely convinced that it was the most restricting thing that had ever happened to him, and was inevitably going to affect and ultimately destroy his usefulness to the Lord.

Paul felt, therefore, that it must be dealt with, and the only way to deal with it was to remove it altogether. Paul went into the presence of God—not merely thrice, because that is simply the symbol of a persistent and consistent agony of heart—and said, in effect, "Lord, please take it away! It is the only thing to be done, for I just cannot live for You and serve You like this! O Lord, if only you would please remove this pressure! If only this opposition would cease; if only the pain and agony of this thorn would be removed, then I could do Thy will. If only. . . ."

I wonder if you have been saying this to the Lord in the past weeks and months, or even longer? "If only I were stronger in body!" "If only I did not have to work next to that difficult person in my office!" "If only my husband were an out-and-out Christian!" "If only my wife were really dedicated to Jesus!" "If only my job were different!" "If only . . ."

Yes, but notice that in spite of Paul's tremendous prayer and in spite of his agony the pressure was maintained. Paul prayed about it, as I am sure you have often prayed, and in his estimation of the the situation the only thing that God could do, if he was ever to be of any use to Him again, was to take this thing out of his life altogether, and set him free from it. " . . . I besought the Lord thrice," says Paul, with an intensity of desire and agony of soul, "Lord, remove this thing and cause it to depart!"

Is that how you and I have prayed? Do you share Paul's convictions concerning your own situation that the only adequate answer is that God must take the problem away, remove that person, or get you out of this situation and into another circumstance. You are so convinced that you have told God what He must do!

Observe carefully that the word is, "For this thing I besought the Lord thrice. . . ." In other words, there came a time in Paul's experience when he ceased to pray about this particular matter. He besought the Lord, and then he stopped praying about it. The pressure went on and was maintained because God did not remove it, but Paul ceased praying, because as he prayed and pleaded, God gave to him a most revealing explanation. After Paul stopped praying, the Lord said to him, as the correct rendering of that little phrase would be, "For this thing I besought the Lord thrice that it might depart from me." And Paul goes on, in effect, "he has been saying unto me. . . ."

I do not know how long this had been going on, certainly for fourteen years, because that is the period during which he speaks about the revelation which, as we shall see in a moment, is personally connected with this thought. But for all this time Paul had been praying, "Lord, take this thing away!" and for all that time the Lord had been trying to get through to him in vain.

Some of us are so busy telling God what He ought to do about our situation that we are incapable of hearing what He wants to do and say to us! We are so sure that the only thing to be done is to remove the problem altogether that we never give the Lord a moment to speak to our hearts about His alternative.

"I besought the Lord thrice, and when I stopped praying I heard Him say unto me. . . ." Well, what did He say? First of all it is clear that the Lord made plain to the Apostle Paul that there was a purpose in this. Did you notice that verse 7 begins and ends with exactly the same statement: " . . . lest I should be exalted above measure . . ."? In other words, Paul's estimation of what had happened to him was quite wrong. He had been sure that it was not merely useless but that it was a positive hindrance to him; but now he discovers that this has been right at the very heart of God in his life. " . . . lest I be exalted above measure . . ."—in other words, as long as this thing continues, it is impossible for him ever to be proud lest he be exalted above measure.

God had sent into this man's life something that came to him in a moment of spiritual ecstasy, in a time of wonderful revelation of the things of the Lord. At that very moment there came the pressure of the thorn to keep Paul humble. That is why many people suggest that when Paul said concerning himself that in speech he was contemptible and in bodily presence he was weak, these were his outward testimonies concerning this thorn. As people looked at him, there was no striking appearance, no big personality. Here was a man who, judged by every human basis of authority and power, was in a totally different area altogether, and the suggestion is that the reason for this was something that God had done to him, this thorn that had come into his life. For as long as the Apostle Paul was conscious of the old nature within him, he could only call himself the chief of sinners.

Truly God knows best how to deal with a man like Paul. I would say it very reverently, but when the Lord calls a man into a place of spiritual opportunity, into any place of leadership, be it as a missionary, as a pastor, as an administrator in some sphere of Christian work, whatever it may be, the Lord cannot afford to take any risks with him. There is too much at stake. God wanted to be sure that Paul's usefulness would never be marred and that he would be kept available, usable, and humble. When God's purpose is accomplished in your life, whatever that purpose may be, I can think of no better way of expressing it than by likening it to a greasy pan that you have taken and scrubbed, turned upside down, wiped round and round, and placed clean on the shelf. When God does that, His purpose is fulfilled, and the thorn is put into a man's life to turn him upside down, to wipe him thoroughly, and to leave him in a place where he says that he knows that in him dwells no good thing, for the flesh profits nothing.

I dare not speculate about the thorn in your life, nor presume to guess what it may be, but I know that behind it there is this ultimate purpose of God doing this very thing. However, I want to show you from this passage that there was not only a purpose in the thorn, but a wonderful provision. " . . . lest I should be exalted above measure" was the purpose. The provision, " . . . My grace is sufficient for thee," and then the explanation, "for my strength is made perfect in weakness."

Notice that the Lord did not say to him, "My grace will prove to be sufficient," nor "I will give you enough grace to get through." No! But He is saying, in effect, "Paul, as I put the pressure on and allow this thorn to remain, I want you to understand that at each moment now there is ample provision for your every need, for My grace is sufficient for thee."

Do you see the humor of this situation? God's grace: me. His grace sufficient for little me! How absurd to think that it could ever be any different! As if a little fish could swim in the ocean and fear lest it might drink it dry! The grace of our crucified, risen, exalted, triumphant Saviour, the Lord of all glory, is surely sufficient for me! Do you not think it is rather modest of the Lord to say *sufficient*? It is such a contrast, is it not?

I saw a most striking billboard in the State of New Jersey some time ago, and all it said was, "Our products are satisfactory." That did me good. So often we read that products are the world's finest, or the world's greatest, or the world's best, but this advertisement told us all we need to know to invite us to buy.

" . . . My grace is sufficient. . . ." Does that mean to say that in the midst of the pressure of the thorn we are only just going to have enough grace to see us through? Indeed it isn't! In the story of the feeding of the five thousand the common folk in the presence of Andrew said, " . . . Two hundred pennyworth of bread is not sufficient for them. . . ." Omnipotence said, "Bring the loaves and fishes and give them to me." Faith distributed them among the crowd. Experience gathered up twelve baskets that remained over and above. " . . . My grace is sufficient. . . ."

Then comes the word of explanation: " . . . for my strength is made perfect in weakness." Would you please notice the contrast here? His strength (and the word is *dynamis*, dynamite) is made perfect in my weakness (and the word is *neurasthenia*). His power, my weakness, and the connecting link is the word *made perfect*, which is the same word that the Lord Jesus used when He hung upon the cross and cried, "It is finished!" God's strength is completely made perfect in your weakness.

God does not work through those who think they are the pillars of the church. He works through weakness. There was a king in the Old Testament, Uzziah by name, of whom it was said, " . . . he was marvelously helped until he was strong . . ." but when weakness, personal insufficiency, and utter inability are consciously felt, realized, and known, then the power of God and His purpose for the thorn have been fulfilled.

When I see a young preacher begin to taste success, my heart trembles for him. When there is a Sunday School teacher beginning to see things happen, and where a Christian worker sees evidences of blessing, that is the moment to watch out. God works through weakness. I am reminded of the tremendous work Paul wrote of in his first letter to the church at Corinth, " . . . God hath chosen the foolish things of the world to confound the wise; and God hath chosen the weak things of the world to confound the things which are mighty; And base things of the world, and things which are despised, hath God chosen, yea, and things which are not, to bring to nought things that are: That no flesh should glory in his presence" (I Corinthians 1: 27-29).

Do you really think that the modern preparations for the education of young people for Christian work recognize that principle? God works through the man who has been wiped clean and turned inside out, his life emptied before the Lord until he is hopelessly weak, that no flesh might glory in His presence.

There is one other thing to say to make this picture complete, for there is not only a frustrating experience, then a revealing explanation for the thorn, but also the transforming estimate in Paul's life. Here is a wonderful double transformation: " . . . when I am weak, then am I strong. . . ." "Therefore I take pleasure in infirmities . . ." (v. 10). And "Most gladly therefore will I rather glory in my infirmities, that the power of Christ may rest upon me" (v. 9).

That word *rest* is interesting. When the Lord Jesus came, John says, He tabernacled among us and we beheld His glory, the glory as of the only begotten of the Father, full of grace and truth (John 1: 14). He tabernacled, He dwelt among us—that is the word. " . . . Most gladly therefore will I rather glory in my infirmities, that the power of Christ may [tabernacle] upon me." This means that weakness was turned immediately into strength.

Would it not be a wonderful thing if in the place where you have been so weak, where there has been a breakdown in your faith, where there has been the impetuous demand to heaven to shift your circumstances or remove this or that burden from your life, if in the place where you have failed to glorify God, you could remain strong?

How did it happen to Paul? I think I know, though he does not really tell us. It seems that there was a very deep and real relationship in the thorn that God gave to Paul and the cross that God gave to our Saviour. " . . . my strength is made perfect in weakness." This was the statement of the Lord to the Apostle. Was that a far-off statement, a truth not related to the Apostle's experience? Oh, no. He had only to think back a few years, to remember the coming of a little Baby; he had only to think about Gethsemane, about a mock trial, a cruel cross, a grave, and the death of One of whom he himself wrote: "He was crucified in weakness." Could anyone on earth be more meek than the Son of God to be hung on the cross, hung in our place that He might redeem us from our sins? As that point of absolute weakness was met by the mighty power of God as He raised Him from the dead, I wonder if the pressure of the thorn in Paul's life was a reminder of the power of the cross. Did it remind Paul that Jesus went down to the place of absolute weakness, and that God raised Him up to the throne? I wonder if at the very moment when Paul became aware of severest pressure, if he also became aware of the presence of God in Jesus Christ, who Himself had been weak but was raised up to the place of all power.

Herein lies a mystery, because Paul says, " . . . there was given to me a thorn in the flesh, the messenger of Satan to buffet me. . . ." But I am sure of this, that in every thorn and in every pressure like this, God and the devil are both equally concerned. If God gives it, Satan seeks to distort it; if Satan gives it, then the Lord seeks to sanctify it. If the pressure stems from heaven, Satan will seek to make it the opportunity to destroy it, whereas God sends it to prove us. It seems here that the very weapon which was the messenger of Satan, by which he was planning to overthrow the Apostle, was seized out of his hands and turned into a weapon to overthrow him.

When Satan sent that thorn to buffet, his desire was that the old nature might express itself and be stimulated and roused into sinful action by it. The pressure continues, and Satan watches to see that it might be the means of rousing the self-life and the flesh into rebellion against the will of God. That is why it is called Satan's messenger. But when Satan sent that trial to buffet Paul, he found that all it did, in fact, was to drive Paul to a new depth of trust and obedience and faith in God; and the pressure of the thorn and the power of Calvary became completely bound up together so that Paul could say, " . . . when I am weak, then am I strong."

Unseen by you, the Lord Jesus watches His children, and He does not take the pressure off. He intends it to remain, all the rest of your life probably. He does not intend it to go. He watches your reactions, and so does Satan. The pressure is there in the mind of the devil that he might drive the self-life into action that will prove sinful. The Lord Jesus watches because He allows the pressure to continue in order that, in the severest moment of testing, it may drive you to His wounded side, and teach you that for overwhelming pressure there is adequate grace. Oh, would it not be wonderful if that experience could be yours today! Stop praying for the removal of the thorn, and understand the transforming power of the cross!

Lastly, there is the transformation of misery into happiness: "Most gladly therefore would I gather glory in my infirmities, that the power of Christ may rest upon me." I am so thankful, he says, for this thing that keeps me humble and dependent as God's trusting and believing child. I am so glad of it all, for if God does grant me blessing and success in any measure, it drives me constantly back to Him.

Are you a dear child of God for whom the sunshine has departed from your life recently? Do you want it back? Life has become so hard and drab, so dry and uninteresting. Ah, but there was nothing lovely about the cross and the crown of thorns that God gave to the Lord Jesus, and I am sure there is nothing lovely about the thorn that you have either. The cross seems so cruel and so dreadful. Your trial is all that, I am sure, almost too much to bear. But you notice Paul says, " . . . there was *given* to me. . . ."—all the time I have been trying to thrust it away while the Lord has been handing it back to me, putting it on His hand and saying, "Take it, My child, this is from Me."

In Psalm 106: 15 we read a tremendous statement: " . . . he gave them their request; but sent leanness into their soul." If you keep saying, "Lord, take the thorn away!" and you refuse to submit to the discipline of it, then maybe He will do that very thing and send leanness to your soul. God forbid!

An old saint of God once prayed, "Lord, when wilt Thou cease to strew my path with trials and thorns?" The Lord answered him, "My child, that is how I prove my friends." The saint replied, "Lord, perhaps that is why You have so few of them." Yes, that may be the very reason. How often we seek to get from under the pressure, out of the will of God, when all the time He is holding out His hand and saying, "Take this thorn from Me."

When I was small, I used to get Christmas presents from my parents. Some of them I liked, others I disliked. I liked electric trains, kites, a toboggan, and interesting things like these. But how I hated getting a pair of gloves—fancy a pair of gloves for a boy at Christmas! What an infliction! But these were the useful things, and the thorn in the mind of the Lord is the gift that is useful, that is necessary when it comes from Him. The Lord Jesus holds out His hand of love and says, "Here is the thorn, my child. Will you lift up your hand tremblingly, yet in faith and accept it?" Look up as Jesus did when He said, "Father, not my will but thine be done."

A Sunday School child asked her teacher why it was that when the Lord Jesus came three times to His disciples in the garden and said, "Watch and pray," the third time He did not say that; He just said, "Sleep on and take your rest." The teacher was quite baffled to know the answer, and then the little child said to her, "I think I know. It was because Jesus had seen the face of His Father, and He didn't need their help any more!"

I trust that you have now by faith looked into the face of your heavenly Father, and are saying, "Most gladly will I glory in my infirmities!" At that moment you will begin to rejoice in the ministry of the thorn, and to see God's glorious purpose for it, for while He is prodigal in His riches of grace, He does not send any affliction unnecessarily to those He loves.

I am become a fool in glorying; ye have compelled me: for I ought to have been commended of you: for in nothing am I behind the very chiefest apostles, though I be nothing. Truly the signs of an apostle were wrought among you in all patience, in signs, and wonders, and mighty deeds. For what is it wherein ye were inferior to other churches, except it be that I myself was not burdensome to you? forgive me this wrong. Behold, the third time I am ready to come to you; and I will not be burdensome to you: for I seek not yours, but you: for the children ought not to lay up for the parents, but the parents for the children. And I will very gladly spend and be spent for you; though the more abundantly I love you, the less I be loved. But be it so, I did not burden you; nevertheless, being crafty, I caught you with guile. Did I make a gain of you by any of them whom I sent unto you? I desired Titus, and with him I sent a brother. Did Titus make a gain of you? walked we not in the same spirit? walked we not in the same steps? Again, think ye that we excuse ourselves unto you? we speak before God in Christ: but we do all things, dearly beloved, for your edifying. For I fear, lest, when I come, I shall not find you such as I would, and that I shall be found unto you such as ye would not: lest there be debates, envyings, wraths, strifes, backbitings, whisperings, swellings, tumults: And lest, when I come again, my God will humble me among you, and that I shall bewail many which have sinned already, and have not repented of the uncleanness and fornication and lasciviousness which they have committed.

II CORINTHIANS 12: 11-21

22

GOD'S ULTIMATE AIM

THIS is indeed a fascinating and challenging Epistle, for as we have reminded each other more than once in the course of studying it, in no other letter does Paul open his heart so completely as he does here, to reveal all that was involved to him in being a minister of the gospel or, if you like, a missionary. He tells us in this chapter, if you will allow me to paraphrase, that he almost feels he has made a fool of himself in boasting of all his experiences, but the Corinthian Christians have forced him into it! Instead of defending and standing by him, they had questioned the authority of his ministry. They had challenged the authenticity of what he had to say. They had even been questioning what right he had to speak to them as he did. "So," says Paul, in effect, "I have been forced to show you that though I am only a nobody, I am in fact not a little bit behind the very greatest of the apostles" (v. 11). To prove that he reminds them that they had seen in him a demonstration of the power of God given to all His true ministers in miracles, signs, and spiritual authority. It is interesting that the greatest evidence that Paul brought to the Corinthian church for the reality and genuineness of his life was his patience, and this they had seen with their own eyes.

Now he has just one last appeal to make to the church at Corinth which will succeed, perhaps, if nothing else has succeeded, in disarming their suspicion of him and winning their confidence. Again to paraphrase, "You must forgive me," he says, "if, because I have taken no money from you, I have made you feel inferior to other churches" (v. 13). Then, "But even though I have taken nothing from you, you thought I was being crafty, even then you questioned my motive and you thought I was taking you by guile. But did I

223

make any profit out of Titus, who came to speak to you, or the
brother I sent with him? They acted towards you in exactly the
same spirit as I have done, and you want to know why I have
behaved like this in my ministry, and why it is that I have acted
toward you in this way. Let me tell you. I have done it to prove to
you that I seek not yours but you. In other words, in all my life
and ministry I have no extraneous motives. I will most gladly spend
and be spent for you. In my ministry there is no limit to my expendability, and no reward expected for my services" (v. 16).

So in perhaps what is the climax of the whole principle of this
tremendous letter, Paul opens his heart completely, and we see
laid bare before us the selflessness of a man of God, which is indeed
a copy, a high standard, for all of God's servants for all time.

However, we have not come to magnify Paul, but to magnify
Christ. Paul is only a faint shadow of the Lord Jesus; and if these
qualities are found in his life, it is only because they were found
completely in the life of Jesus Christ our Lord. My concern, therefore, is that you should see these tremendous statements with which
Paul bares his heart to them: " . . . I seek not yours, but you. . . .
I will very gladly spend and be spent for you; though the more
abundantly I love you, the less I be loved." I trust that you will see
those statements as God's goal for your life, as God's grace in your
heart, as God's glory in your service.

Consider, first, God's great goal for your life. Our theme, you will
recall, has been *Blessings Out of Buffetings*, and that is the principle
which Paul has been revealing, the things which God has been
doing with him in order that He might bring Paul to this place in
his experience where he is completely selfless. This was God's goal
—and it is God's goal for you and for me—so that Paul was able to
say in relation to his ministry, " . . . I am ready to come to you. . . ."

In all the buffetings through which you and I have passed in life
—and who is there today who has not experienced some that are
inexplicable—what is God aiming at? What has God been doing?
What has He been trying to say to us? Though we have often been
so slow to listen, what is His goal for my life and yours? Surely it is
to enable us to say in relation to our service and in relation to Him,
"I am ready to come to you." You are ready, not because of your
academic qualifications, but because God has brought you through
many shattering experiences in life to a place of utter selflessness.
When He has brought you there, you can truly say in relation to

your testimony, "I seek not yours but you." In other words, as Oswald Chambers puts it in a portion from *My Utmost for His Highest*: "When the Spirit of God has shed abroad the love of God in our hearts, we begin deliberately to identify ourselves with Jesus Christ's interests in other people, and Jesus Christ is interested in every kind of man there is. We have no right in Christian work to be guided by our affinities; this is one of the biggest tests of our relationship to Jesus Christ." Your interest in another individual is to be centered in what is Christ's interest in them.

"I desire nothing from you," says Paul, in effect, "I do not want your money, your things, or your gifts; I want you. I am ready to come to you; and I am ready because God has brought me to this place of selflessness. My only motive is to lay down my life like a rug at the feet of the Lord Jesus that you may walk upon it and do what you like with me, if only the will of God may be wrought out in your life. I have become all things to all men that by all means I might win some." So this great Apostle, this tremendous Christian, has learned to live sacramentally as broken bread and poured out wine, and again quoting Oswald Chambers, "so that Jesus Christ can help Himself to my life at any moment for any purpose."

The goal of God has no extraneous motives, " . . . I seek not yours but you. . . ." Being abandoned completely to the Lord Jesus He has no end of his own to serve the goal of God. Also, it has no limits to our expendability: " . . . very gladly [rather] I will spend and be spent for you. . . ." In other words, in relation to your sphere of Christian testimony, your time, strength, interest, everything is absolutely at the disposal of others. "I will spend it all for you." Indeed, I will do it to such an extent that not only will I spend, but I will be spent as a candle which is lit and gives out light, but in order to give out the light it consumes itself in the interest of bringing light to others until there comes a moment when it splutters for the last time and is extinct. I will gladly spend and be spent for you like that.

Paul went so far as to say, writing to the church at Rome: " . . . I could wish myself accursed from Christ for my brethren . . ." (Romans 9: 3). He would rather go to hell than see them lost. Extravagant and fanatical language? Oh, no! The buffeting of life, the sentence of death upon himself over and over again, the affliction through which he had passed, all these things demonstrate that this man was passionate and governed by one tremendous, moving power within his heart and life which enabled him to face another Christian and say, in effect, "I am just here in order that Christ's interests in your life might be fulfilled. I have no other concern than that."

No limits to expendability, no extraneous motives, and no reward except, says Paul, " . . . the more abundantly I love you, the less I be loved." In other words, I do not expect anything in return; I do not care what you think about me too much, whether you like me or not. I will spend and be spent, though the more abundantly I love you, the less I am loved in return. I will deprive myself of anything if only I can get you through to God.

There was no question in Paul's mind concerning salary. He does not ask, what about social security? what about furlough? what about climate? What if I don't get married? What if I go through life and face old age alone, what shall I do then? After all, you have to think about these things! No, there were no reservations in Paul's mind. He had learned the word of his Lord, "He that would be the greatest among you, let him be the servant of all."

God's goal in this man's life was accomplished and achieved because he found that through all the buffetings he was being brought to a place where he was absolutely selfless, and he could say, "I am ready." I would say to any young people who are planning on offering to a missionary society, for the home ministry, or perhaps to serve in some capacity in your church, and who may say, "I am ready to come to you"—are you?

"Oh, yes," you say, "because I have been to university or Bible college and I have my degree. Of course I am ready!"

Are you? I am sure that all of these things will stand you in good stead and usefulness, but if you dare to go to the mission field or into the ministry and you have some other motive, some extraneous desire, if you put some limit upon your expendability, and you are expecting some reward, you are not ready. For it is in a life which has been made so utterly selfless as this that the Lord Jesus sees of the travail of His soul and is satisfied.

Today, when people think about missionary service, they ask what provision is made for retirement and furlough, what percentage will be set aside for travel, what percentage will be available for them when they come home. They want to be sure they have all the equipment and necessities. Such, however, is not God's goal for their lives.

Observe now God's grace in your heart. I wonder how Paul had become so passionate and selfless. We have to admit that we have failed here and must hang our heads. Why was Paul like this? It was because one little drop from an infinite ocean of love had entered his heart, one little spark from a fire that had its source in the very heart of God had kindled a flame within him, one echo of the voice of Jesus Christ was heard by him: that was all.

I am suggesting to you that these words would never have been uttered by Paul if they had not first of all been the Saviour's words, and He says to you, "I am ready to come to you: I am ready, because one day I stepped out of heaven to a manger and poverty. I am ready, because I lived a life that was utterly in obedience to My Heavenly Father with no rival claim at all. I am ready to come to you because I triumphed in every place where you failed. I am ready because I went through the garden of Gethsemane, because I endured the buffeting, the spitting, the shame. I am ready because they took Me up a green hill outside a city wall and nailed Me to a cross, where I paid the price to the limit. I am ready because they laid Me in a tomb, but the third day I arose from the dead and ascended into heaven, and today I am seated at the right hand of My Father in the place of all power and authority. Because of all these things I am ready to come to you, but I seek not yours, but you. I am not after your talents or your gifts, or your service primarily. I can do nothing with any of these things until first of all I have you."

The heart of God is only satisfied when we give our whole selves to Him just as we are, so that He might lavish Himself upon us. ". . . I seek . . . you." I wish that word *you* would grip the heart of someone with all sorts of emotional and moral problems, tempted by sin and evil, beset by psychological problems and every problem under the sun. You say you have given Christ your service, your gifts, your talents, but you have never given Him *you*. Perhaps you have been too ashamed to give Him yourself. The wonderful marvel of the grace of God to your heart is that Jesus wants to have *you*, with all your problems, your failures and defeats, with everything that He knows about only too well, and about which He can do literally nothing until He has *you*. He does not want a part of you, while the tyrant of self is left undisturbed deep down on the throne of your life. He wants all of you, so that you may say, ". . . I live, yet not I, but Christ liveth in me. . . ." That is God's goal for your life, and He will use a thousand experiences, buffetings, sadnesses, tragedies, disappointments, disillusionments, until there comes a moment when you answer His cry, "I seek not yours, but *you*"!

I am fearful for so many people who imagine they are serving the Lord when they have given Him their voice, or their talents or abilities, even their pocket books, but have never given themselves to Him. Not merely has the Lord no extraneous motives in relation to your life, but there is no limit to His expendability. He says, " . . . I will very gladly spend and be spent for you. . . ." Hear Him say that to you today: "I want you for My instrument, My tool, to get My will done on earth as it is in heaven. I want you in order that you may be used to establish My rule in the hearts of other people. I will place all My resources at your disposal in order that this may be accomplished. I will most gladly spend and be spent for you."

If only He can get you, then it will be no more a vain effort to flog an idle Christian into His service and get him moving. It will be to discover that in being possessed by Christ you are empowered by Him, and that emptiness in your life will be filled up with a great moving tide. It was that principle that enabled Paul to say, " . . . I also labour, striving according to his working, which worketh in me mightily" (Colossians 1: 29).

May the Word of God come to you like a sword from heaven as He says, "My child, I want not yours, but I want *you*. There is no limit to My expendability, and furthermore, I have no expectation of reward, though the more abundantly I love you, the less I be loved." No coldness of heart on our part, no lethargy, no indifference ever quenches the flame of love in the heart of Jesus Christ for His children. That is the grace of God, that He might be all that to you.

Finally, there is here the glory of God in your service. I doubt whether Paul could ever have said all that to the Corinthian church —or to anybody else for that matter. He could never have lived on this principle of expendability, he could never have satisfied the heart of God unless this was not merely the echo of what he had heard Jesus say to him, but his response in just those words to the Lord Jesus Himself.

Here is the heart of the whole matter. God's goal in your life is not only to get you living sacramentally with no extraneous motive, no limit to your availability, no expectation of reward (for He knows this is only possible when the Holy Spirit shows you this principle upon which Jesus is available for your life), but He waits for the day when He hears you say this very thing in answer to the grace of the Lord, "Lord Jesus, I am ready to come to you!"

Are you ready to come to Him today? Why? "Because, Lord Jesus, I seek not Yours, but You! It is not now the gift, but the Giver. It is not now the blessing, but the Blesser. It is not the joy, but it is You Yourself, Lord. I am not concerned about gifts, but I cannot live without You, and You have said to my heart, 'I do not want yours but I want you—and I am answering now.' Lord Jesus, I do not want Your gifts, I want You as a living, loving Saviour who will step into my life and keep me day by day, sheltering me from all the attacks of the enemy, and dealing with this strange, wretched me, of which I am so sick."

Perhaps for the first time there is no extraneous motive, for you are not looking at the Word or in the face of Christ today because of something you can get out of Him. You are looking not for blessing only, something that you can get from Jesus. Your heart is lonely, defeated, sad, beset with so many problems and difficulties, therefore you want only Jesus Himself.

Perhaps for the first time you have put no limits upon your expendability. You are willing to spend and be spent for Him, and you are not going to discuss terms any more with the Lord. For the first time you do not expect any reward for such devotion though " . . . the more abundantly I love, the less I be loved." You may lose many friends who will not understand, perhaps some of them very dear friends, but you will not put any reservations there. Has the Lord ever heard you say these things to Him?

This is the third time I am coming to you. In the mouth of two or three witnesses shall every word be established. I told you before, and foretell you, as if I were present, the second time; and being absent now I write to them which heretofore have sinned, and to all other, that, if I come again, I will not spare: Since ye seek a proof of Christ speaking in me, which to you-ward is not weak, but is mighty in you. For though he was crucified through weakness, yet he liveth by the power of God. For we also are weak in him, but we shall live with him by the power of God toward you. Examine yourselves, whether ye be in the faith; prove your own selves. Know ye not your own selves, how that Jesus Christ is in you, except ye be reprobates? But I trust that ye shall know that we are not reprobates? Now I pray to God that ye do no evil; not that we should appear approved, but that ye should do that which is honest, though we be as reprobates. For we can do nothing against the truth, but for the truth. For we are glad, when we are weak, and ye are strong: and this also we wish, even your perfection. Therefore I write these things being absent, lest being present I should use sharpness, according to the power which the Lord hath given me to edification, and not to destruction. Finally, brethren, farewell. Be perfect, be of good comfort, be of one mind, live in peace; and the God of love and peace shall be with you. Greet one another with an holy kiss. All the saints salute you. The grace of the Lord Jesus Christ, and the love of God, and the communion of the Holy Ghost, be with you all. Amen.

II CORINTHIANS 13: 1-14

23

THE PERIL OF SELF-DECEPTION

IN our studies of II Corinthians we have purposely made no attempt to analyze it. As a matter of fact, in a very real sense this letter more than any other of Paul's defies analysis, because it is simply the outpouring of a man's heart, and that runs away from analysis. It is like the breaking up of a fountain. Whereas I Corinthians was an objective and practical letter, this one has been subjective and personal. I Corinthians was a deliberate approach to a subject; II Corinthians is a passionate appeal.

Our concern in studying it has been to catch all that we can of the fire that burned in Paul's heart, and to learn his spiritual secret. It was in the midst of so much buffeting that he became a channel of blessing. As we come to the close of the letter, I remind you of some background facts against which Paul makes this final appeal.

In the first place, Corinth was a city in Greece which was a Roman colony with a very mixed population: Jews, Greeks, Romans, Asiatics, Phoenicians, to mention a few. A great expositor of Scripture, Farrar, has called it the "Vanity Fair" of the Roman Empire. It was famous for its wisdom and its wealth. It was also famous for its luxury and its license. In a very real sense, Corinth in the first century has its equivalent in the twentieth century in New York, Chicago, London, or Paris, where you have great centers of population, areas of people from different kinds of situations and backgrounds.

The church at Corinth, as you would read in Acts 18, was established by Paul, and it was composed mainly of the poorer and more unlearned people in Corinth (I Corinthians 1: 26-29). It was not by accident that God had done this. It was the purpose of God, and He had chosen such people in order that through them might be demonstrated a principle of life in the midst of all the philosophy and learning and wisdom of Corinth, that no flesh might glory in His presence. These were the people who had received Paul's two letters.

The first letter to the church at Corinth gives an indication of the condition and the character of the church, but Paul's second letter was a tremendous revelation of the life and character of Paul himself. The first letter exposed the wounds of sin, but the second letter tells us what it cost a man of God when he set about trying to heal the wounds. That is the distinction.

There is one outstanding thing that you cannot escape if you read this letter through carefully: it is the tremendous change in the tone between the first nine chapters and the last four chapters. In the first nine chapters Paul is writing with a wonderful sense of warmth, comfort, thanksgiving, and a sort of conciliatory attitude; but in the last four chapters, he is sad and severe again. Many reasons are suggested for this, but I think the exact one would be that in this church, as in most churches anywhere, there is a majority party and a minority party.

Titus had brought the message of the condition of the church that gave Paul much gladness: "Nevertheless God, that comforteth those that are cast down, comforted us by the coming of Titus; And not by his coming only, but by the consolation wherewith he was comforted in you, when he told us your earnest desire, your mourning, your fervent mind toward me; so that I rejoiced the more. For though I made you sorry with a letter, I do not repent, though I did repent: for I perceive that the same epistle hath made you sorry, though it were but for a season. Now I rejoice, not that ye were made sorry, but that ye sorrowed to repentance: . . ." (II Corinthians 7: 6-9). And so Paul was made glad because the majority of the church at Corinth had been chastened by his first letter, had responded to his message, had truly repented and turned to the Lord.

But there were some who had not, and they were showing it by attacking Paul's ministry. "For if he that cometh preacheth another Jesus, whom ye have not preached, or if ye receive another spirit, which ye have not received, or another gospel, which ye have not accepted, ye might well bear with him. For I suppose I was not a whit behind the very chiefest apostles" (II Corinthians 11: 4-5).

There was a minority group in the church, from which Paul had suffered severe buffeting, for they had never truly taken his message to their own hearts, and now they spent their time attacking him. It seems to me that the first nine chapters of this letter were written to the majority, and the last four were written to the minority who were accusing him.

Notice some of the things of which they were accusing him. They said that " . . . his bodily presence is weak, and his speech contemptible" (chapter 10: 10). "Though I be rude in speech, yet not in knowledge" (chapter 11: 6): they were accusing him of being rough and uncultured in his speech. They even accused him of being insane: "I say again, Let no man think me a fool; if otherwise, yet as a fool receive me, that I may boast myself a little" (chapter 11: 16). They are accusing him of dishonesty: "But be it so, I did not burden you: nevertheless, being crafty, I caught you with guile" (chapter 12: 16).

That is just a little of the buffeting this man of God had taken from the church at Corinth. He was accused of weakness, of roughness of speech, of insanity, of being contemptible in appearance, of being no apostle, and even of being dishonest.

Therefore we come now to consider his final appeal and vindication of his own ministry. His appeal was to those who would examine him, "Examine yourselves, whether ye be in the faith; prove your own selves." In verse 3 you see the context: " . . . ye seek a proof of Christ speaking in me . . . ," all right, examine yourselves whether you be in the faith. Consider his vindication of his own ministry: "For we also are weak in him, but we shall live with him by the power of God toward us" (v. 4).

I have taken time to say all that with a definite purpose, because I firmly believe that in this twentieth century counterpart of Corinth in which we live, we are in very serious danger of falling into the same trap and the same peril of self-deception which threatened disaster to the minority group in the church at Corinth. While we are very careful in criticizing and examining the viewpoint of others in theological and other matters, we very often fail to allow the searchlight of God's Word to probe our own hearts, and we are greatly in need of this same injunction, "Examine yourselves, whether ye be in the faith. . . ."

Furthermore, this objective criticism, which we direct anywhere except to our own heart, is apt to give us a completely false idea of the real standard of Christian discipleship by which Paul vindicated his own ministry. You want the evidence of reality and authority in me, Paul says in effect; very well, we are weak in Christ, but we shall live with Him in the power of God toward you. All thought that would avoid any possibility of self-deception is in this phrase: "Know ye not your own selves, how that Jesus Christ is in you, except ye be reprobates?"

That is the standard: Jesus Christ is in you; and the vindication of his own ministry was in taking them back to the cross, when he reminds the Corinthian Christians that Jesus, though crucified in weakness, was raised by the power of God. Paul opened his heart to show them that through all the buffetings of his life, he had been made utterly weak, until he came to the point where he had no confidence in the flesh, for no flesh shall glory in the presence of God. He had accepted that principle, and therefore found that he had been raised up in the power of God. " . . . Most gladly therefore will I rather glory in my infirmities, that the power of Christ may rest upon me" (chapter 12: 9).

We have this great appeal now for self-examination, in order that we might avoid the peril of self-deception and at the same time demonstrate the reality of our testimony. I realize that this is an unpopular subject, but I come to it with a deep conviction of its necessity, so I would elaborate upon the need for self-examination. In I Corinthians 11 Paul spoke about the Lord's table and preparing for the breaking of bread: "But let a man examine himself, and so let him eat of that bread, and drink of that cup. . . . For if we would judge ourselves, we should not be judged" (vv. 28, 31).

Therefore before breaking bread together, and also at other times, it is appropriate that we spend time in what the Book calls self-examination, because I am sure that a great number of professing Christians are living in self-deception, assuming that because externally things are more or less all right with them in their lives, then everything else can be taken for granted. They have a sound doctrinal basis of faith, their lives are lived more or less righteously, they are not conscious that anything is particularly wrong, but as Paul says here, if Christ is not in you, then there is nothing in you whereby you will be approved of God.

I am concerned not only about outward conduct but inward life. The question I ask my own heart in the presence of God is, Am I in the faith? Is Christ living in me? Is there any evidence of reality? How important that is!

A ship is very carefully examined before it is put out to sea, both before and after launching. After launching it goes through trials, and it has quite a period before it is entrusted with passengers and cargo. So Paul says, in effect, "Examine yourselves, but not only that, prove yourselves." That word *prove* is a stronger word still.

Some people's religion will stand a bit of examination, but when their religion comes into daily life, it fails to pass the test, it does not prove itself adequate. The objective test of matters of doctrine with which so many are satisfied these days is just inadequate. Now no one would give second place to me concerning the necessity for correctness of creed, for a sound, fundamental, Scriptural approach to all matters in life; but I would say that an objective test which merely submits myself to a statement of creed is not adequate, because I am not saved by a statement of creed. I am saved by a step of commitment of my life to Jesus Christ as Lord. Therefore it behooves me to examine myself.

I remind you that the Puritans recognized the need of this, and made provision for it. They believed in being much alone with God and surveying their lives in His presence with an unsparing scrutiny. I was reading of the members of the Holy Club in Oxford in John Wesley's day, who examined themselves every Sunday on the love of God and the simplicity of their faith; on Monday, they examined themselves on their love toward their fellowmen, and submitted themselves to twenty-seven questions; and so on throughout the week. Here are some of the questions, which I use in my own life, at least once a week, and often every day.

Am I consciously or unconsciously creating the impression that I am a better man than I really am? In other words, am I a hypocrite?

Am I honest in all my acts or words, or do I exaggerate?

Do I confidentially pass on to another what was told to me in confidence?

Can I be trusted?

Am I a slave to dress, friends, work or habits?

Am I self-conscious, self-pitying or self-justifying?

Did the Bible live to me today?

Do I give it time to speak to me every day?

Am I enjoying prayer?

When did I last speak to somebody else with the object of trying to win that person for Christ?

Am I making contacts with other people and using them for the Master's glory?

Do I pray about the money I spend?

Do I get to bed in time and get up in time?

Do I disobey God in anything?

Do I insist upon doing something about which my conscience is uneasy?

Am I defeated in any part of my life, jealous, impure, critical, irritable, touchy or distrustful?

How do I spend my spare time?

Am I proud?

Do I thank God that I am not as other people, especially as the Pharisees who despised the publican?

Is there anybody whom I fear, dislike, disown, criticize, hold a resentment toward or disregard? If so, what am I doing about it?

Do I grumble or complain constantly?

Is Christ real to me?

Do these questions find you out, and make you angry or resentful? They come straight to you from John Wesley and the Puritans of two hundred years ago. That kind of self examination has gone right out of our Christian living. I use these tests in my own heart because I find them necessary, and those who are most neglectful to use them are the people who are always the most quick to criticize others. That was the trouble at Corinth. They criticized Paul and failed to examine themselves.

The great question for us to settle today is, Am I in the faith? Is Christ in me? Have I come to Him as a sinner and pleaded for His mercy through the blood of His cross? Am I living by faith in Him? Am I receiving from His fullness grace upon grace? Does my life prove it? As I have said before, an unholy life is merely the evidence of an unchanged heart, and an unchanged heart is the evidence of an unsaved soul. What value is there in the kind of grace which makes us no different from what we were before? None at all.

It would be a good thing if you were to keep a copy of these questions and use them personally in your own life. I think you would find prayer would be an uncomfortable thing until your heart was made tender. Someone will say to me, "This is too morbid! Surely as a Christian I must never look into myself, but I must look up." True! The statement is made, "For every look within, take ten long looks at Christ."

Let me say a further word about the secret of self-examination, lest you get me wrong. This is given to us in Psalm 139: 23, 24, "Search me, O God, and know my heart: try me, and know my thoughts: And see if there be any wicked way in me. . . ." In other words, this self-examination is not something that I can do myself, but something which only God can do, and to attempt it without the Holy Spirit's guiding and enabling is indeed to lead to a morbid introspection and ultimately to psychological help in care and treatment. This is what happens to so many people, simply because of morbid introspection, but this is totally different.

In the kind of thing I am talking to you about a man is not looking for sin, he is looking for Jesus. He is not looking for evil—he does not have to look far for that for he knows that in the flesh dwelleth no good thing—but he is searching within his heart for evidences of indwelling Holy Spirit life. Ah, there are tokens within that Christ is in him by His Spirit as a living power, and because He is there, He is dealing with all these things.

To examine yourself, in fact, is to submit to the examination and scrutiny of Jesus Christ the Lord—and this is never to fix attention on sin but on Christ—and to ask Him to reveal that in you which grieves His Spirit; to ask Him to give you grace that it might be put away and cleansed in His precious blood. It is to search within your heart for the sense of His peace, His forgiveness, His cleansing, His presence. When these qualities are lacking and you cannot find them, you ask Him to point out where you have gone wrong, where the cloud has come between yourself and your Saviour, and to show the way to you so that fellowship might be restored.

It is self-examination that keeps the heart tender. It is self-examination which keeps the will submissive. It is self-examination which keeps the mind open to the leading of the Spirit of God. Spurgeon once said about another preacher, who was known for his freshness and life, his power and authority, "Do you know, that man lives so near the gate of heaven that he hears a great many things that we don't get to hear because we don't live near enough." May I say that is exactly what self-examination does. It takes the chill away from your soul, it takes the hardness away from your heart, it takes the shadows away from your life, it sets the prisoner free.

Have you submitted yourself in the presence of God to self-examination lately? That is how to come to the Lord's table; before you ever come into the house of God early in the morning, set your heart open before God and ask Him to search your heart. Have you done that recently? That is how revival breaks out in church. That is how it broke out in Ruanda, and how it has been maintained all through the years. There must be an openness in my dealings with Him and in my dealings with fellow-Christians; that is the secret of self-examination.

What is the standard of this self-examination? what is our goal in this? Paul goes right back to the cross to prove the reality of his apostleship. " . . . though he was crucified through weakness, yet he liveth by the power of God. For we also are weak in him, but we shall live with him by the power of God toward you" (v. 4). Here is the Apostle vindicating his own apostleship, testifying to the reality of his own witness and his own Christian life; here he is summing up all that it has meant to him to seek to heal the wounds. He goes back to Calvary. That is where you want to be.

Paul says concerning the Lord Jesus, " . . . He was crucified through weakness. . . ." Ah, yes indeed, and such was the extremity of His weakness that He died under it. He made no use of His divine strength at all. He gave Himself over to His enemies to be crucified and slain and His crucifixion was the greatest display of weakness that this world has ever witnessed. Yet He was raised again from the dead by the power of God. Here is the principle: in the absolute extremity of the weakness of our Saviour, power came to Him from another quarter altogether.

So Paul says the ultimate standard of reality is at Calvary, at the place of human weakness, of utter submission, the place where that is all met by the mighty power of God. That was the standard and reality of Paul's testimony. It seemed he had been overcome by his enemies, and had been powerless in their hands, yet in that weakness he too revealed the power of God, "For we also are weak in him, but we shall live with him by the power of God toward you." This ties up with the first chapter of his first letter, in which Paul reminds the Corinthian church that there were not many mighty and not many wise called. But you see, no flesh is to glory in His presence. This is the principle of the Christian life, the reality and evidence of it: "But of him are ye in Christ Jesus, who of God is made unto us wisdom, and righteousness, and sanctification, and redemption" (I Corinthians 1: 30).

Paul has told the story of buffeting to the Corinthian church, and to no one else. He did not tell it to Luke (if he had, Luke would have recorded it in the Acts of the Apostles), but he opened his heart to the people who challenged his authority at every point, to prove to them that in submission to all the buffeting he has demonstrated that the Spirit of God was in him, and because that was so, He had raised Paul up, and was working mightily through him. Just as in that human body Jesus became so weak and suffered and was buffeted to be raised by the power of God, so Paul in submission to all the buffeting has found exactly the same experience.

Examine yourselves, whether you be in the faith. Here is the ultimate standard, the plumbline for every one of us. How have you reacted in your own immediate circle of witness? What happens when you have been buffeted? Is the procedure and growth of your Christian life marked by a progressively increasing sense of weakness in yourself, so emptied of every trace of self-esteem and self-confidence that you find yourself being raised up by the power of God? Do you seek to be a blessing in your area? Do you seek to heal the wounds in some circle of Christian witness, on a mission field, in a Sunday School, in a church, somewhere in your immediate situation?

The Christian, if he is real, will always seek to heal the wounds, but as he does so he discovers that they are healed by the acceptance of the buffetings to such a point that he is brought right back to the cross where he is able at last to know that the words of Galatians 2: 20 are not a theory but are real: "I am crucified with Christ: nevertheless, I live; yet not I, but Christ liveth in me: and the life which I now live in the flesh I live by the faith of the Son of God, who loved me, and gave himself for me."

Examine yourselves. Prove yourselves. "Know ye not your own selves that Jesus Christ is in you, except ye be reprobate?" And if He is in you, then His strength is being perfected when you come to that place where, in yourself, you are utterly weak. That is the whole principle of I and II Corinthians. That is the reason why Paul wrote to demonstrate this great principle of Christian life, so that the church for all its history might know that it is "not by might, nor by power, but by my Spirit"; so the church may answer all the philosophy in any generation, all the wealth and all the wisdom, all the luxury and all the license. We may combat these things not on that level, but by apparently being knocked down to a point of weakness only to discover that we are raised up by the power of God to demonstrate His indwelling life. Is that your experience? May God help us to submit ourselves to self-examination in the power of His Spirit.